Behold My Glory

GREAT STORIES FROM THE BIBLE
AND THE MASTERPIECES THEY
HAVE INSPIRED

I. THE FALL OF MAN

*She took of the fruit thereof, and did eat, and gave also
unto her husband with her; and he did eat.* Genesis 3, 6.

Detail from 'Paradise' by Lukas Cranach the Elder
(1472–1553)

Photo Meyer

Behold My Glory

GREAT STORIES FROM THE BIBLE
AND THE MASTERPIECES THEY
HAVE INSPIRED

By William Purcell

HAWTHORN BOOKS, INC.

Publishers

NEW YORK

LIBRARY OF CONGRESS CATALOGUE CARD NUMBER 57-6367

Printed in Great Britain by Butler & Tanner Ltd. ,Frome and London

Author's Foreword

"FATHER, I will that they also, whom thou hast given me, be with me where I am; that they may behold my glory . . ." (John 17. 24).

In the great prayer in the seventeenth chapter of St John's Gospel Jesus asks that his disciples may truly see, that is, may look upon with adoration, the glory that is his. All truly inspired religious art in any age is a help to this end. It is not an end in itself; but it is a means whereby the imagination may be stimulated, and the emotions roused, to a fuller understanding of the splendor that is Christ.

The wonderful pictures in this book will stimulate in just that manner if they are viewed with such a purpose in mind.

The painters of them all drew their inspiration from the same source—the Book of Books. Each in his own manner, and in his own day and age, has labored to put on to canvas what that inspiration has brought to him, and has enriched the world by thus bringing beauty into the service of truth.

For there is truth in these pictures, as in all great art. What words, for instance, could ever hope to convey so revealingly the wondering astonishment of humanity at the birth of Christ, when "the Word became Flesh, and dwelt among us", as the expressions on the faces of the three shepherds in the Nativity of Hugo van der Goes? What could show more tenderly the relationship between the Boy Jesus and Joseph the Carpenter than the marvelous composition, with its subtle light and shade, of Georges de la Tour? And that skull, the emblem of death, combined with the one naked shoulder and pensive, heartsick expression in the picture of Mary Magdalene may well give the beholder a deeper understanding, not only of this woman in the Gospel story, but of the deep sadness of a life of sin.

There is, too, among the pictures of this book, a quite astonishing portrayal of the dead Christ, his torn body brought down from the Cross and displayed, curiously foreshortened, with grief-stricken faces looking upon him. There is no false sentiment here whatever; no stylized cloaking of reality. Therein lies its truth, and its value. For it emphasizes a fact without full realization of which the wonder of the Resurrection cannot be understood—that Christ really did die, and knew the bitterness of it, and the pain.

And so these pictures speak. Like the Bible itself, they will do so profoundly in proportion as they are given time to do so, and thoughtfully and reverently dwelt upon. They deserve it.

But also it is well to remember all the time that they have a factual background. The moon that shone down on the scene in the Garden of Gethsemane was the same moon we see. The water the woman of Samaria drew from the well was real water; the woman herself was real—real as the little bride at the wedding at Cana. Pontius Pilate truly was hot and worried on the morning of the Crucifixion; and the soldiers did play dice at the foot of the Cross.

In other words, these things happened. They are as much capable of being

5

reported and described as other events. Indeed, there is value in describing them in straightforward terms just because to do so helps to drive home the truth of it all.

Most of the stories and the majority of the pictures in this book are based upon incidents in the Gospels. In other words, the book is Christ-centred, which surely is as it should be. For the story of Christ as the Gospels give it us is, to use a phrase of Fulton Oursler's, "The greatest story in the world", and though some narratives from the Old Testament have an important place in these pages they are as background to the figure and to the actions of Christ Himself.

WILLIAM PURCELL.

The Contents

8   THE CONTENTS

The Color Plates

The endpapers are THE ADORATION OF THE MAGI by Peter Paul Rubens (1577–1640),
Royal Museum of Fine Arts Antwerp

The Color Plates

The endpapers are THE ADORATION OF THE MAGI by Peter Paul Rubens (1577–1640),
Royal Museum of Fine Arts Antwerp

Behold My Glory

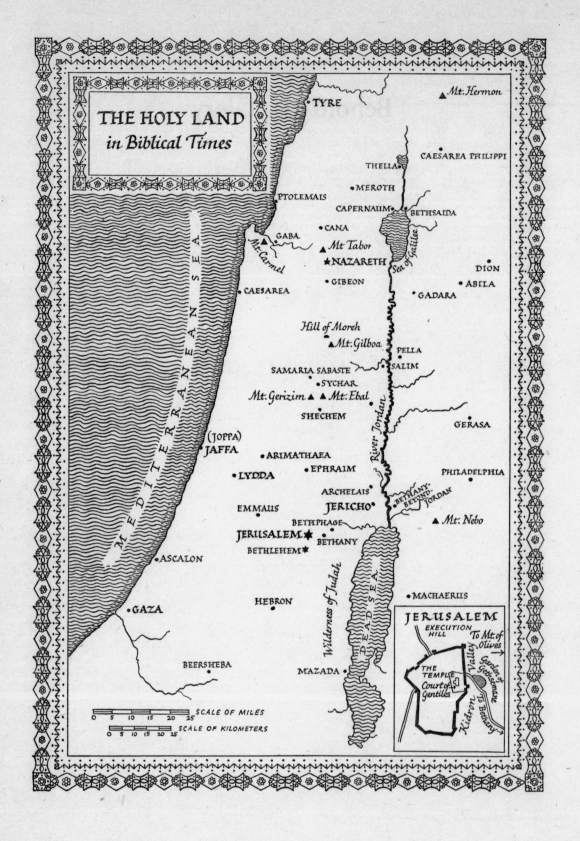

THE HOLY LAND
in Biblical Times

▲ Mt. Hermon

• TYRE

THELLA

CAESAREA PHILIPPI

• MEROTH

PTOLEMAIS

CAPERNAUM • • BETHSAIDA

• GABA • CANA

Mt. Carmel ▲ Mt Tabor
★ NAZARETH

Sea of Galilee

• CAESAREA • GIBEON

DION
• ABILA

• GADARA

Hill of Moreh
▲ Mt. Gilboa

PELLA •

SAMARIA SABASTE • SALIM
• SYCHAR

Mt. Gerizim ▲ ▲ Mt. Ebal

• SHECHEM

River Jordan

GERASA

(JOPPA)
JAFFA

• ARIMATHAEA

• LYDDA • EPHRAIM

PHILADELPHIA

ARCHELAIS •
EMMAUS • JERICHO • • BETHANY-
BEYOND-JORDAN

BETHPHAGE •
JERUSALEM ★ • BETHANY ▲ Mt. Nebo
BETHLEHEM ★

• ASCALON

Wilderness of Judah

• MACHAERUS

• HEBRON

JERUSALEM
EXECUTION
HILL
To Mt of
Olives

• GAZA

THE
TEMPLE
Court of
Gentiles

Kidron Valley

Garden of Gethsemane

To Bethany

• BEERSHEBA

MAZADA

DEAD SEA

MEDITERRANEAN SEA

SCALE OF MILES
0 5 10 15 20 25
SCALE OF KILOMETERS
0 5 10 15 20 25

II. THE EXPULSION FROM THE GARDEN OF EDEN

The Lord God sent him forth from the garden of Eden, to till the ground from whence he was taken. Genesis 3, 23.

Detail from 'Paradise' by Lukas Cranach (1472–1553)

Photo Meyer

Lost Paradise

Based on Cranach's

THE FALL OF MAN and THE EXPULSION FROM
THE GARDEN OF EDEN

LONG ago, when the world was young, two grown-up children lived in a garden. It was a wonderful place, the abode of perfect happiness. For Adam, and for Eve his wife, it was the ever joyful place of the here and now, where only the contentment of the sunny moment mattered. All their needs, for warmth, for food, for shelter, were met, out of the measureless resources of God. There was water to drink; there was fruit to eat; there were flowers to delight; nor was there any harshness in created things. Even the beasts of the field did not prey upon each other; the lion lay down with the lamb; the questing hawk did not stoop for prey. The very atmosphere of the garden, the name of which was Eden, breathed unutterable peace.

There was only one prohibition which God had placed upon Adam and Eve. It concerned a certain tree which stood in the midst of the place. All things which grew there were of great beauty, deep colored and tender to the touch. But the tree which grew in the center of it all was of quite singular loveliness: its leaves a deep, lacquered green, its golden fruit of a fabulous bloom, always ripe, always perfect. This fruit was the only thing in the garden which God had forbidden them to touch.

So always as the happy days passed in that timeless world the tree stood there inviolate, its globules of marvelous fruit pendant in the still, warm air. And though Adam and his wife, in their contented goings to and fro, often passed by, they never touched this fruit.

In those days the beasts of the field had the power of speech, and with one creature, the serpent, Eve delighted to converse, especially during the hours when Adam was absent. At such times the serpent would come rustling up to her through the grass, coil himself up at her feet, fix her with his brilliant eyes, and begin a fascinating conversation. He was most amusing; there was no other creature who could make the time pass so quickly or so delightfully.

One day, in the still time when the sun had just passed noon, Eve chanced to sit herself down at the foot of the forbidden tree. She was alone; but soon the usual rustle in the grass told her that the serpent once again was coming to join her. She saw his head appear, then the rainbow length of the rest of his body. He seemed to be very thoughtful that afternoon, not speaking for a while.

Then he laid his flat head on her knee and asked suddenly, in his low sibilant voice:

"Has God said, ye shall not eat of every tree in the garden?"

Gently, Eve told him:

"We may eat of the fruit of the trees of the garden: but of the fruit of the tree which is in the midst of the garden"—and here she nodded towards it—"God hath said, ye shall not eat of it, neither shall ye touch it, lest ye die."

The serpent lay with his eyes closed for quite a while. Then he said suddenly: "Ye shall not surely die."

Eve was startled and moved her knee a little, so that the serpent had to raise his head from it; but he continued to hold her with his eyes.

"God doth know that in the day ye eat thereof, then your eyes shall be opened," he said quickly, "and ye shall be as gods, knowing good and evil."

Eve did not reply to the serpent, but his words startled her very much. It was the novelty of them which went home: she had never thought of eating the fruit of the forbidden tree: she had never thought of doing anything beyond that which was permitted by God, the unutterably wise, the immeasurably kind. But now, when she came to look at the tree, there could be no doubt that the golden fruit did look exceedingly attractive, succulent and mysterious. Moreover, there was so much of it. Surely it could not matter if she were to take just one little bite out of one of those golden globes? It would be a thrill; it would be something to tell Adam about when he came home, and then perhaps he could take a bite as well.

Because there was no time in Eden, it was not possible to know how long the woman and the serpent stayed there, she with her long hair draping the loveliness of her naked form, the serpent with his flat, queerly-shaped head riding on the stalk of his body, staring at her without a movement in his jewel-like eyes. He did not speak again, and eventually slid off into the grass, leaving her there.

The sun declined over Eden; the birds sang in the trees, the streams chuckled in their courses. And Eve continued to think. It was a dangerous but exciting exercise, something which she had never done before. And, as she thought, the attraction of the forbidden fruit grew more compelling. It was so near; it would be so simple, and surely so harmless, to reach over and to pick one, and to bite it. After all, she thought at last, it would be good to be wise. So she walked over to the tree, closed her fingers around one of the fruits, which was warm to the touch, and gave a little tug. It parted quite easily from the branch and lay there, filling the palm of her hand. She raised it to her mouth and let her white teeth sink into its succulence.

Nothing happened. The only thing notable was the taste, which was extremely pleasant. She ate the whole of that fruit, and then another. After that, thrilling with the pleasure of it, she plucked two more for Adam to eat when he came home.

It was toward evening when he did so. Naked, like his wife, his body was of an equal perfection, muscled where hers was soft, and having a poise which came from the fact that God had made him chief over all other created things. And as in the Garden of Eden, in the days of the world's innocence, there was no disease, or pain or suffering, his physique was splendid.

He was serious at first when Eve told him what she had done. But the bright pleasure in her eyes, as she told her story and showed him the golden fruit, overcame his misgivings. So, in his turn and to please her, he also took one of the fruits and ate it.

This time quite a lot happened; not outwardly, but within themselves. The strong sun, now throwing his rays at an oblique angle because it was towards evening, still shone; the birds still sang, the stream still chuckled. But when Adam looked upon his wife he noticed for the first time that she was naked. And when Eve looked upon her husband she also noticed for the first time that he was naked. The discovery gave neither of them any pleasure. Instead it filled them both with a profound, sad embarrassment, as though that which had been thoughtlessly natural had become on the instant stained with a sense of wrong. For a moment Eve stood where she was, then gave a little cry. Twisting suddenly about, she ran off among the surrounding trees. Adam looked after her, frowning. Then he, too, turned himself about and sought the shelter of the woods. When they met again later each could see that the same impulse had moved both of them, for each had made a little apron of fig-leaves, so that they might cover their nakedness.

And now they grew fearful. It was the first time they had even known any unpleasant emotion, and it disturbed them deeply. For it was twilight now in the garden, and they knew that before long the Lord God would be paying them His customary evening visit. They did not know what they were going to say; they dared not think about what would happen when He discovered what they had done. So, like the children they were, they hid themselves among the foliage and, trembling, awaited His coming.

Soon they heard Him, that Voice in the wind among the trees calling them by name:

"Where art thou?"

Fearfully, Adam replied:

"I heard Thy voice in the garden, and I was afraid, because I was naked and I hid myself."

There was a long pause, then the Lord God asked:

"Who told thee that thou wast naked? Hast thou eaten of the tree whereof I commanded thee that thou shouldst not eat?"

They both stepped out before the Lord God then, ashamed, hanging their heads down. Adam said:

"The woman whom Thou gavest to be with me, she gave me of the tree and I did eat."

The Lord God turned to Eve:

"What is this that thou hast done?"

"The serpent beguiled me," she answered in a whisper, "and I did eat."

Now the serpent had drawn near to hear and the Lord God turned toward where his brilliant eyes were visible in the grass.

"Because thou hast done this," the Lord God said to the serpent, "thou are cursed above all cattle, and above every beast of the field; upon thy belly shalt thou go and dust shalt thou eat all the days of thy life: and I will put enmity between thee and the woman, and between thy seed and her seed; it shall bruise thy head and thou shalt bruise his heel."

The Voice had been terrible. It became a shade gentler as the Lord God, speaking to Eve, continued:

"I will greatly multiply thy sorrow and thy conception; in sorrow thou shalt bring forth children; thy desire shall be to thy husband and he shall rule over thee."

The Voice grew sterner again as the Lord God looked toward Adam:

"Because thou hast hearkened to the voice of thy wife and hast eaten of the tree, of which I commanded thee, saying, Thou shalt not eat of it: cursed is the ground for thy sake; in sorrow shalt thou eat of it all the days of thy life; thorns also and thistles shall it bring forth to thee; thou shalt eat the herb of the field; in the sweat of thy face shalt thou eat bread, till thou return unto the ground; for out of it wast thou taken; for dust thou art, and unto dust shalt thou return."

With a deep sigh, and as though speaking to Himself, the Lord God added:

"Behold, the man is become as one of us, to know good and evil."

Because Adam thenceforth knew good and evil, thereby transmitting to all the generations of mankind the measureless sorrows of humanity, it was not fitting that he should be permitted to stay any longer in the garden of innocence. So the Lord God drove out Adam and Eve, placing at the east of the Garden of Eden cherubim with a flaming sword, to guard for ever the tree of Life. And Adam took his wife by the hand and with her wandered out into the dark ways of the world.

III. THE SACRIFICE OF ISAAC

And Abraham stretched forth his hand, and took the knife to slay his son. And the angel of the Lord called unto him out of heaven . . . . . And he said, Lay not thine hand upon the lad. Genesis 22, 10–12.

By Caravaggio (1569–1609)

Photo Alinari

The Testing of Abraham

Based on Caravaggio's
THE SACRIFICE OF ISAAC

IT befell one day in the Plain of Mamre, in the hottest time when the sun just passed the noon meridian, when men of the desert such as Abraham were wont to sit in the shadow of their tent doorway until the heat lessened, that Abraham, looking into the shimmering haze of the level sands before him, saw three men approaching. Because they were strangers, and bedouin courtesy required that he should offer them the hospitality of his household, he bestirred himself to go out and meet them, offering them food and water. Moreover, these were lordly personages, so that he made special efforts for their reception, hurrying back to his tent to command Sarah his wife to make a cake of meal. After that he went to his herdsman to order that a calf should be slaughtered and dressed and offered, with butter and milk, for their delectation.

So the three strangers sat themselves down under a tree and addressed themselves to the meal, while Abraham saw to it that all their needs were met, as the host should.

While they were eating one of them said to him:

"Where is Sarah thy wife?"

Abraham was surprised at the question, since it admitted of only the obvious answer that she was where the women would naturally be, in the tent. When he told the stranger this, the man replied:

"Sarah thy wife shall have a son."

Now if Abraham was surprised by this sudden prophecy, Sarah was even more so, because she was well past child-bearing age. Also, being curious as to the identity of the strangers, she had been concealing herself behind the near-by tent door in order to hear what was spoken, and when she heard this statement that she would have a child, she allowed a little laugh to escape her.

Immediately the chief personage among the strangers, who was the Lord Himself, turned to Abraham and asked:

"Wherefore did Sarah laugh, saying, shall I of a surety bear a child which am old?" He added: "Is anything too hard for the Lord? At the time appointed I will return unto thee according to the time of life, and Sarah shall have a son."

It happened even as had been foretold, and in the fulness of time Sarah did indeed bear a son, a comely boy, and Abraham called him Isaac. He grew up a gracious lad, willing, obedient, and affectionate. Abraham loved him dearly, more than anything else in the world because Isaac was the son of his old age.

Now one day God came to Abraham with a terrible command.

"Take now thy son, thine only son Isaac whom thou lovest, and get thee into the land of Moriah; and offer him there for a burnt offering upon one of the mountains which I will tell thee of."

Abraham bowed his head low down upon the ground, both in obedience and to hide his grief. He knew only too well what this human sacrifice would require; first the building of a pyre of faggots, then the preparation of the sacrifice, beginning at the cutting of the throat. Then the setting fire to the sacrifice, so that the sweet savor of it should arise. But because he was a man of God he obeyed, though his heart was breaking.

Consequently, he took the boy, and two of his young men, and with them set off for the place appointed, first preparing the wood which they would require and packing it upon the ass which carried their equipment.

The journey was long, and though the boy, Isaac, rejoiced in it, ranging each day round the little party, in the sportive manner of a boy, trying out his sling against birds on the hillsides, Abraham for his part went his way bowed with a load of sorrow which he felt heavy upon him. On the third day of their journeying he looked up and saw the mountain of sacrifice.

Thereat he said to his young men:

"Abide ye here with the ass; and I and the lad will go yonder and worship and come again to you."

With that he untied the bundle of wood which they had been carrying upon the ass and gave it to Isaac to carry; in his own hand he took a knife. Thus burdened, both of them set off together.

For a long silent time they climbed up into the hills. At last Isaac spoke, asking his father where the lamb for the burnt offering could be, since they had already the wood and the means of kindling it. Without looking at the boy Abraham said:

"My son, God will provide Himself a lamb for a burnt offering."

At last, upon an eminence, in just such a place where sacrifices were wont to be made, Abraham prepared an altar of stones and on that the criss-crossed wood of a sacrificial pyre, the boy meanwhile standing by and looking upon all these doings with a lively curiosity. That completed, Abraham, knowing the moment had come and that obedience to God required this thing of him, with a quick, strong movement seized the boy, threw him down upon the rough altar, and raised his knife, averting his eyes from the terrified astonishment in those of the child beneath him. At that very moment, in the silence of the place, an angel of the Lord called out of heaven:

"Abraham, lay not thine hand upon the lad, neither do thou anything unto him: for now I know that thou fearest God, seeing thou hast not withheld thy son, thine only son, from Me."

Slowly, Abraham lowered the hand which had been holding the knife and relaxed his grip upon the boy. Only then did he open his eyes, and behold, as he did so, he saw a ram caught in a thicket by its horns. In that blessed moment he knew that all was well. For there, ready to his hand, was the sacrifice which God would accept in the stead of his son. So Abraham took the ram, and offered him up for a burnt offering.

A second time the angel of the Lord called upon Abraham, saying:

"By Myself have I sworn, saith the Lord, for because thou hast done this thing and hast not withheld thy son, thine only son, that in blessing I will bless thee, and in multiplying I will multiply thy seed as the stars of the heaven, and as the sand which is upon the sea shore; and thy seed shall possess the gate of his enemies; and in thy seed shall all the nations of the earth be blessed; because thou hast obeyed My voice."

Thus Abraham was tested by God and emerged triumphant. Therefore it was with Isaac his son, after all, that he was able to return to the young men waiting below with the ass. And they rose up and went together to Beersheba, and Abraham dwelt there.

It Happened at Midnight

Based on Luini's

THE DEATH OF THE FIRSTBORN

SOME 1,400 years before the time of Christ the people of Israel were dwelling in Egypt. The times were hard for them, for they were slaves. The days of Joseph and his brethren were over, and a new king had arisen in Egypt who feared the spread of this lusty, alien race within his borders. For the people of Israel multiplied exceedingly, in spite of the efforts of Pharaoh to check their growth. Therefore Pharaoh put them to forced labor, and the crack of the whip and the cries of the task-masters sounded over the bent backs of a subject people. They built for Pharaoh the great grain stores of Pithom and Raamses, and other mighty works. Yet still Pharaoh oppressed them, and the Israelites groaned under his tyranny.

Now a woman of the Hebrews one day gave birth to a son. And as she held him to her breast her heart sank because she knew that an order had gone out from the king that every male child of the Israelites should at birth be thrown into the Nile. This the mother could not do. Instead, she hid him for three months. When it became no longer possible to continue that life of concealment she made for her child a little ark of reeds, rendered it watertight by daubing the underside with slime and pitch, and, with the child inside, laid it among the bulrushes which swayed at the water's edge.

Now the baby had a sister. Filled with the desire to know what would become of her infant brother, this child hid herself in order to see what should transpire. Peeping between the tall reeds she soon saw something which filled her at once with fear and with hope. An Egyptian Princess, one of the daughters of Pharaoh, accompanied by her slaves and maids in waiting, was making her way down to the river to bathe.

The Princess, finding the ark among the bulrushes, stooped over it as the water dripped from her brown thighs. She exclaimed aloud, calling her maidens to her, as she saw the baby within and heard it cry. And because she was a woman the sight moved her heart and she said:

"This is one of the Hebrews' children."

All the girls were peering together at the baby when the voice of the child's sister spoke behind them:

"Shall I go and call to thee a nurse of the Hebrew women, that she may nurse the child for thee?"

So it was done, and the child was brought up by Pharaoh's daughter and she called his name Moses because she had drawn him out of the water. Neither she nor any of the people were to know that in so doing she had raised up a leader who was to liberate the people of Israel from their bondage.

Moses, he who had been the baby among the bulrushes, grew up, and as he did

20

so he became increasingly aware of the plight of his people. He saw the forced labor gangs, he heard their songs as they labored together in the heat; he heard the grunts and saw the sweat and the straining muscles as they heaved upon ropes and lifted great stones. Above all he heard the crack of the task-master's whip.

Now it so befell one day that the blood rose hot in Moses when he saw an Egyptian smiting one of his own people. It was just the one too many. He looked about; there was no one in sight; he killed the Egyptian and hid the body in the sand.

For two days he wondered whether the deed would be discovered. And then, by a chance remark made by two men of the Hebrews in whose quarrel he had intervened, he found that it had. For when he thought to separate the two men who were fighting together, one of them swung upon him, crying out in the passion of the moment:

"Who made thee a prince and a judge over us? Intendest thou to kill me as thou killedst the Egyptian?"

Therefore Moses, seeing his deed was known, fled from Egypt and dwelt in the land of Midian.

Now in that land there was a well to which the seven daughters of the priest of Midian were accustomed to go to draw water for their father's flock. Often they went fearfully, because the shepherds of the district would drive them off if they had the chance, rushing upon the girls with sticks and shouts, away from the precious water.

One day this happened, but Moses was near by and came to the rescue, scattering the shepherds in their turn.

Very grateful were the chattering girls as they returned to their father and told him the tale of how one whom they had supposed to be an Egyptian had protected them from the shepherds and how, with further courtesy, he had drawn the water for them and had watered the flock. The priest of Midian therefore asked:

"Where is he? Why is it that you have left the man? Call him, that he may eat bread."

That was how, for a space, Moses became of the household of the priest of Midian and took Zipporah, the daughter of the priest, for a wife.

Meanwhile, there was no respite for the people of Israel in bondage in Egypt, nor was there to be until God spoke to Moses as he tended the flock of Jethro his father-in-law in Midian by Horeb, the mountain of God. There, in that solitary place, the angel of the Lord appeared unto Moses in a flame of fire out of the midst of a bush. The sun was high in the heavens, and there was a ringing silence all around when Moses was drawn by the strange sight of a bush burning, but not being consumed. So he approached near to it until the voice of God called out of the midst of the bush:

"Moses, Moses."

"Here am I," Moses replied.

The voice continued:

"Draw not nigh hither; put off thy shoes from off thy feet, for the place whereon thou standest is holy ground. I am the God of thy fathers, the God of Abraham, the God of Isaac, and the God of Jacob."

And as Moses hid his face the voice proceeded:

"I have surely seen the affliction of My people which are in Egypt, and have heard their cry by reason of their task-masters; for I know their sorrows and I am come down to deliver them out of the hand of the Egyptians and to bring them up out of that land unto a good land and a large, unto a land flowing with milk and honey. . . . Now therefore, behold, the cry of the Children of Israel is come unto Me: and I have also seen the oppression wherewith the Egyptians oppressed them. Come now therefore and I will send thee unto Pharaoh, that thou mayest bring forth My people, the Children of Israel, out of Egypt."

And when Moses asked God for His name, in order that he may tell it to the Children of Israel, he received the mysterious reply:

"I AM THAT I AM. Thus shalt thou say unto the Children of Israel. I AM has sent me unto you."

At first Moses was hesitant to obey the command of the Lord, and therefore God gave him evidence of His miraculous powers. First He asked him:

"What is that in thine hand?"

It was the shepherd's staff which Moses carried. God said:

"Cast it on the ground."

Moses did so, whereupon it became instantly a serpent, wriggling in the sand. Then God said, as Moses ran away from it:

"Put forth thine hand and take it by the tail."

He did so, and once again the shepherd's staff was within his grasp.

Then the Lord said:

"Put thou thine hand into thy bosom."

So Moses tucked his hand into the folds of his shepherd's cloak and when he took it out again it was dead white with the skin disease which was called leprosy. Yet when, at God's command, he put his hand a second time within his clothes it was, when he drew it out again, restored to its normal state.

Yet still Moses was hesitant about obeying the command of God to go down into Egypt and deliver His people. This time he urged, as a reason for his reluctance, his lack of eloquence. Wherefore the Lord said that Aaron the Levite, brother of Moses, should go with him to be his mouthpiece.

So Moses returned to Jethro, his father-in-law, and asked his permission to do as the Lord commanded him. Then Moses took his wife and his sons, and the rod of God in his hand, and set off for Egypt.

On the way God spoke again to Moses, saying:

"When thou goest to return into Egypt, see that thou do all those wonders before Pharaoh, which I have put in thine hand: but I will harden his heart, that he shall not let the people go. And thou shalt say unto Pharaoh, thus saith the Lord, Israel is My Son, even My firstborn: and I say unto thee let My son go, that he may serve Me: and if thou refuse to let him go then behold, I will slay thy son, even thy firstborn."

After that God sent Aaron to meet Moses in the wilderness as he journeyed, and they met in the Mountain of God. And they went on together into Egypt.

So the two went before Pharaoh and told him that the Lord God of Israel commanded that he should let God's people go in order that they might hold a feast unto Him in the wilderness. But Pharaoh scorned that, saying:

"Who is the Lord, that I should obey His voice to let Israel go? I know not the Lord, neither will I let Israel go."

Moreover, he treated the people of Israel with greater rigor than ever before, giving orders to his task-masters that the Israelites were not henceforth to be provided with straw for the making of bricks, but were to find straw themselves. And although the officers of the Children of Israel, seeing that the plight of the people was desperate, went personally to Pharaoh with an appeal, he turned them away, crying:

"Ye are idle, ye are idle: therefore ye say let us go and do sacrifice to the Lord. Go therefore now and work; for there shall no straw be given you, yet shall ye deliver the tale of bricks."

Because of this Moses and Aaron were reproached by their own people, but the Lord strengthened Moses by saying to him:

"Thou shalt now see what I will do to Pharaoh; for with a strong hand shall he let them go, and with a strong hand shall he drive them out of his land. . . . And I will bring you out from under the burdens of the Egyptian and will rid you out of their bondage, and I will redeem you with a stretched out arm, and with great judgments, and I will take you to Me for a people, and I will be to you a God: and ye shall know that I am the Lord your God, which bringeth you out from under the burdens of the Egyptians."

But Pharaoh continued obdurate, even though Aaron, at the command of Moses, put down the rod before Pharaoh and his attendants so that it became a serpent. The magicians of Pharaoh equaled this by a similar magic with their own rods but Aaron's rod swallowed up theirs.

Thus God visited the Egyptians with a series of plagues, in which the order of nature was disrupted, so that the land knew a season of terror. First, God caused the Nile, the great river upon which the Egyptians depended for their life, to become polluted, swirling with flood water colored red, so that it looked like blood, with the red marl brought down from the Abyssinian mountains. And when the flood receded the river stank, so that no one could drink therefrom.

But still Pharaoh would not release the people of Israel. Next, God caused a multitude of frogs to come up out of the stagnant waters. Still Pharaoh would not relent. Therefore God sent a plague of gnats, and after that of flies. And after that He visited their cattle with a mortal sickness, and yet again after that He afflicted the Egyptians themselves with skin eruptions.

Even so the heart of Pharaoh remained hard, so that he continued to refuse freedom to the people of Israel. Wherefore when January came God sent storms of hail and destroyed the barley harvest, and following that the locusts descended upon the land, devouring every growing thing. And then dust storms, lasting days at a time, darkened the skies, so that for three days at a stretch a man could not see his neighbor. Only the people of Israel were able to have light in their dwellings.

Then God said to Moses:

"Yet one plague more will I bring upon Pharaoh, and upon Egypt; afterward he will let you go hence."

Then Moses said to Pharaoh:

"Thus saith the Lord, about midnight will I go out into the midst of Egypt: and all the firstborn in the land of Egypt shall die, from the firstborn of Pharaoh that sitteth upon his throne, even unto the firstborn of the maid servant that is behind the mill; and all the firstborn of cattle. And there shall be a great cry throughout all the land of Egypt, such as there has been none like it, nor shall be like it any more. But against any of the Children of Israel shall not a dog move his tongue, against a man or beast, that ye may know how that the Lord doth put a difference between the Egyptians and Israel."

Then God gave directions to the Israelites through Moses that each household should that night take a lamb, and slay it and eat it, every person with his loins girded, shoes on the feet and staff in hand, as though ready for their exodus. And He told them also that they were to take, each household, a bunch of hyssop and, dipping it in the blood of the lamb, should strike the lintel and the two side-posts of their dwellings. By that sign, the Lord, when he passed through the land of the Egyptians, would spare the Israelites.

Terribly then did the Lord pass as a Destroyer through the land at midnight, smiting all the firstborn in the land of Egypt, and there was not a house where there was not one dead, and a great cry rose up. And even while it was yet night Pharaoh sent for Moses and Aaron and said:

"Rise up, and get you forth from among my people, both ye and the Children of Israel; and go, serve the Lord, as ye have said."

So the Children of Israel, relieved from their bondage by the power of the Lord, journeyed from Raamses to Succoth, and ever afterward observed in the Passover the memory of their deliverance.

IV. THE DEATH OF THE FIRSTBORN

The Lord smote all the firstborn in the land of Egypt, from the firstborn of Pharaoh that sat on his throne unto the firstborn of the captive that was in the dungeon. Exodus 12, 29.

By Bernardino Luini (c.1480–1532)

Photo Roberto Hoesch

These Thy Gods

Based on Poussin's

THE ADORATION OF THE GOLDEN CALF

IN the Wilderness of Sinai it befell that the people of Israel on their journey camped before the Mountain of God. In their wanderings they had known danger, and hunger, and thirst, yet still they had held together, faithful to the God of Abraham, of Isaac and of Jacob, who had led them out of the land of Egypt.

But now, as they camped, the command of God came to Moses that he should, with Joshua his minister, go up into the mountain to commune with the Lord. He was gone a long time, and the people waiting below, at first missing him, came in time to relax their hold upon themselves. And whereas in adversity they had clung to their God, in this time of ease they began to lust after others, remembering especially the pagan gods of the Egyptians from whose land they had come.

Eventually, in the continued absence of Moses, they gathered themselves together about Aaron.

"Up, make us gods, which shall go before us," they cried; "for as for this Moses, the man that brought us out of the land of Egypt, we know not what has become of him."

So Aaron, weakening, told them to bring to him all the golden ornaments which they possessed in order that out of it he could make an image which they could worship.

The result was a golden calf, glittering, splendid, an idol which the people welcomed with shouts of joy;

"These be thy gods, O Israel, which brought thee up out of the land of Egypt."

And after that, seeing the people so joyful in their folly, Aaron built an altar in front of the golden calf and proclaimed the next day as a feast day. And on all the days which followed, from morning to nightfall, the Israelites gave themselves up to shameless licence, burning offerings before their idol, eating and drinking, and indulging, the men and the women, in all the shameful practices of a pagan orgy. Meanwhile, up on Mount Sinai, the Lord was speaking to Moses:

"Go, get thee down," He commanded; "for thy people, which thou broughtest up out of the land of Egypt, have corrupted themselves: they have turned aside quickly out of the way which I commanded them: they have made them a molten calf, and have worshipped it, and have sacrificed unto it, and said, These be thy gods O Israel."

Then in the heat of His wrath God said that He would destroy the Israelites who had done this thing. But Moses pleaded with Him until the Lord relented a little from His anger. And then Moses turned and went down from the mountain, carrying with him the two tablets of stone upon which God had written His Commandments.

As Moses and Joshua neared the foot of Mount Sinai they heard a confused roaring of many voices coming up to them from the camp.

"There is a noise of war in the camp," Joshua said.

But Moses thought otherwise.

"It is not the voice of them that shout for mastery," he said. "Neither is it the voice of them that cry for being overcome: but the noise of them that sing do I hear."

So they pressed on, and when they came into the camp they saw a shameful sight; the people dancing and rioting before their golden idol, all discipline, all morality, gone to the winds.

At the sight, Moses experienced a great anger, breaking the tables he carried by throwing them upon the ground. Then he rushed to the idol and overthrew it, smashing it to fragments, burning it and grinding it to powder. Only when this was done did he speak to Aaron, standing trembling before him.

"What did this people unto thee, that thou hast brought a great sin upon them?" Moses demanded.

Aaron said:

"Let not the anger of my lord wax hot: thou knowest the people, that they are set upon evil. For they said unto me, make us gods, which shall go before us: for as for this Moses, the man that brought us up out of the land of Egypt, we know not what has become of him. And I said unto them, whosoever has any gold let them break it off; so they gave it me: and I cast it into the fire, and there came out this calf."

Then Moses turned aside from Aaron and strode to the gate of the camp. There, in a great voice, he thundered:

"Whoso is on the Lord's side, let him come unto me."

The sons of Levi rallied to him. And when they were all gathered and armed Moses ordered them to go through the camp, slaying without mercy.

To the remnants on the following day Moses said:

"Ye have sinned a great sin: and now I will go up unto the Lord; peradventure I shall make atonement for your sins."

Then he turned, and climbed the mountain, and communed again with God.

"This people," he said, "have sinned a great sin, and have made them gods of gold. Yet now, if Thou wilt forgive them their sin—; and if not, blot me, I pray Thee, out of Thy book which Thou hast written."

To which God made answer:

"Now go, lead the people unto the place of which I have spoken unto thee: Mine angel shall go before thee: nevertheless the day when I visit, I will visit their sin upon them."

So Moses led the repentant people onward through the wilderness. And because of God's command, he took their ornaments away from them, and they did not wear them from that day onward.

V. THE ADORATION OF THE GOLDEN CALF

They have made them a molten calf, and have worshipped it, and have sacrificed thereunto, and said, These be thy gods, O Israel, which have brought thee up out of the land of Egypt. Exodus 32, 8.

By Nicolas Poussin (1593 or 1594–1665)

Photo Studio Fifty-One

Rod of Power

Based on Tintoretto's

THE WATER FROM THE ROCK

In the wild regions through which they were journeying, the people of Israel could find no water. And because thirst is the most terrible of torments, this which struck them in the wilderness broke the morale of the Israelites utterly.

In a place where the copper sun beat back from the parched sides of the hills, they gathered around Moses and Aaron his brother. Bitter words were spoken by men with cracked lips; but no words were more bitter than those in which they cried out against the misfortune which had prevented them dying before.

"Would God that we had died when our brethren died before the Lord!"

Then they demanded of Moses, "And why have ye brought the assembly of the Lord to this wilderness, that we should die there, we and our cattle? And wherefore have ye made us to come up out of Egypt, to bring us in unto this evil place? It is no place of food, or of figs, or of vines, or of pomegranates, neither is there any water to drink."

That was the terrible thing; no water to drink. No water to drink. The men panted for it; the children cried for it; the cattle blared for it. But there was no water to drink.

Therefore Moses and Aaron prostrated themselves before God.

And suddenly, as they lay there with their faces to the ground, they knew the Glory of the Lord was with them and, when they looked up, so it was.

God spoke.

"Take the rod," He commanded, "and assemble the congregation, thou and Aaron thy brother, and speak ye unto the rock before their eyes that it give forth its water; and thou shalt bring forth to them water out of the rock: so thou shalt give the congregation and their cattle drink."

Now it had happened some time before that God had chosen a way by which to put an end to the rebellious murmurings of the people of Israel against the leadership of Moses and Aaron. He had said to Moses that he was to command each of the tribes to be represented by the rod upon which their tribal name was to be inscribed. Rods, or staffs, were habitually carried by persons of importance, so that it was easy for the people to understand this command. But God had also told Moses that upon the rod of Aaron should be written the name of the House of Levi, because Aaron was a Levite. And God further commanded that these rods, thus gathered together, should be placed in the Tent of Meeting, which was the House of God. And He promised that He would indicate the man whom He should choose to be over the people by causing his rod to bud.

It was therefore done accordingly, and Moses laid up the rods before the Lord in the Tent of Testimony. Next day, when Moses had entered he found that it had happened even as the Lord had foretold, and that one rod, the rod of Aaron, had indeed put forth blooms. Then Moses had taken all the rods outside again and showed them to the people, and all had seen that the choice of God had fallen upon Aaron. And when everyone had returned to him his own rod the Lord commanded Moses to return that of Aaron to its place in the Sanctuary, so that it could be used always as mute evidence of His choice, and thus as a restraint upon any who should presume, by questioning the commands of Moses and Aaron, thereby to question the commands of God himself.

It was this rod therefore, this rod of Aaron's, which God now commanded Moses to bring out.

When Moses and Aaron had gathered the people together before the great rock which lay in the wilderness, Moses called out to the people:

"Hear now, ye rebels, shall we bring you forth water out of this rock?"

With those very words he lifted his hand holding the rod, and struck the rock twice with it. Immediately and dramatically water gushed out and the people ran forward, men and women and children, and cattle, and slaked their thirst in an agony of thankfulness.

But God was not pleased. He was not pleased because Moses and Aaron, by giving way to despair when first thirst had lain heavily upon the people, had doubted His ability to succor them. By so doing, they had called in question His promise to bring them safely out of the land of Egypt. In other words, they had brought pressure to bear upon God to accede to their requests. So God said to Moses and Aaron:

"Because ye believed not in Me, to sanctify Me in the eyes of the Children of Israel, therefore ye shall not bring this assembly into the land which I have given them. These are the waters of Meribah."

"Because," the Lord concluded, "the Children of Israel strove with the Lord, and He was sanctified in them."

State Visit

Based on Piero della Francesca's
SOLOMON RECEIVING THE QUEEN OF SHEBA

A THOUSAND years before Christ King Solomon reigned in a glory and a splendour that were not to be seen again. His people were as the sand of the sea: his kingdom was rich, prosperous, and peaceful. Every citizen dwelt in security. The king's wealth also was without parallel. He had forty thousand stalls and horses for his chariots, and twelve thousand horsemen. Provisions for one day alone in the royal household included thirty measures of fine flour and three score measures of meal; ten fat oxen and twenty oxen out of the pastures, and a hundred sheep, besides harts, and gazelles, and roebucks, and fatted fowls.

Wherever Solomon looked about him at the height of his career, he could see in Jerusalem evidences of his greatness. The Temple which he had built on the eastern hill, overlooking the Valley of the Kedron, was sixty cubits long and twenty broad, splendid beyond anything that had been seen in the land. Nearby rose his own palace rich in pillars of cedar wood and enclosed by a great court.

The great ones of the ancient world had traffic with King Solomon. Hiram King of Tyre sent his servants to work for him. The daughter of the Pharaoh of Egypt was within his household. He was reputed, too, to be wiser than all men, and his fame was in all the nations round about. He knew three thousand proverbs, and more than a thousand songs.

At the heart of all this wisdom and rich fortune lay the secret of a dream. For it so happened that, in the early days of his reign, King Solomon went to do sacrifice to God at the great High Place in Gibeon. There, when the sacrificing was done, Solomon one night dreamt God came to him and asked:

"What shall I give thee?"

Solomon had replied:

"Thou hast showed unto Thy servant David my father great kindness, according as he walked before Thee in truth and in righteousness, and in uprightness of heart with Thee; Thou hast kept for him this great kindness, that Thou hast given him a son to sit upon the throne as it is this day. And now, O Lord my God, Thou hast made Thy servant king instead of David my father: and I am but a little child; I know not how to go out or come in. And Thy servant is in the midst of Thy people which Thou hast chosen, a great people that cannot be numbered nor counted for multitude."

And then he had asked for the one thing needful; the great thing:

"Give Thy servant therefore an understanding heart to judge Thy people, that I may discern between good and evil; for who is able to judge this Thy great people?"

Pleased with this answer of Solomon's, God had said:

"Because thou hast asked this thing, and hast not asked for thyself long life; neither hast asked riches for thyself, nor hast asked the life of thine enemies; but hast asked for thyself understanding to discern judgment; behold, I have done according to thy word: Lo, I have given thee a wise and an understanding heart; so that there has been none like thee before thee, neither after thee shall any other arise like unto thee."

So Solomon was fortunate not only in the things of this world, but in the inner riches of wisdom and understanding, too. His like was not to be seen again, for after him were to come the divisions of the kingdom. But for the moment, suspended in history like a rare jewel, the kingdom of Solomon glittered upon the summit of fame and fortune. One incident romantically marked the glorious moment.

Far away, over the mountains, over the deserts, in southeastern Arabia there flourished a mysterious civilization. The Sabaeans who dwelt there were exporters of gold.

It was in keeping with the exotic character of this far land that it was ruled over by a woman, the Queen of Sheba, Queen of the South. And it was a sign of the distance to which the report of the magnificence of Solomon had carried that this queen resolved to travel to the court of Solomon to see its glories for herself.

She traveled in oriental luxury, the long lines of her camels making a colored convoy across the deserts. Her train was very great. The pack camels carried spices and gold and precious stones, and the bodyguard which surrounded the mysterious queen herself were dressed with a wild splendor such as few men had seen. She was a proud woman; yet not too proud to recognize and to use wisdom when she encountered it. And, because she recognized this kingly virtue in Solomon she unburdened her mind to him of all the thoughts and the cares which were in it, even down to her most intimate concerns. And Solomon, because he was so wise, was able to answer all her questions.

The wealth and the magnificence of the royal household impressed her profoundly. She, who was used to a splendour of her own, had yet never seen the like of its luxury and dignity.

When she parted from him, this queen who came from afar summed up for all time the glory that was Solomon's.

"It was a true report," she said, "that I heard in mine own land of thine acts and of thy wisdom. Howbeit I believed not the words until I came, and mine eyes had seen it: and, behold, the half was not told me: thy wisdom and prosperity exceedeth the fame which I heard. Happy are thy men, happy are these thy servants, which stand continually before thee, and that hear thy wisdom. Blessed be the Lord thy God, which delighted in thee, to set thee on the throne of Israel: because the Lord loved Israel for ever, therefore made He thee king, to do judgment and justice."

VI. THE WATER FROM THE ROCK

And Moses lifted up his hand, and with his rod he smote the rock twice: and the water came out abundantly, and the congregation drank. Numbers 20, 11.

By Tintoretto (1518–1594)

Photo Giacomelli

Victory through Defeat

Based on Rembrandt's

JEREMIAH LAMENTING THE DESTRUCTION OF JERUSALEM

THERE was a man long ago who drew victory from defeat, and who enriched the whole of mankind by the treasure of truth which he discovered under the stone of his own sufferings.

A native of Anathoth, near Jerusalem, he lived in a time of the breaking of the nations. For centuries the little kingdoms of Israel and Judah had existed precariously among the great powers of the world, occupying a place on the earth's surface which lay dangerously in the paths of marching armies. Egypt, Babylonia, and Assyria; each in turn stood like a dark cloud upon the horizon. And in the lifetime of Jeremiah, five hundred and more years before the time of Christ, one of these clouds broke in storm and overwhelmed Judah. Empires rise and fall, and that of Assyria fell before the Babylonians and the Egyptians. Nineveh fell in 606 to the Babylonians who were victorious at Carchemish in the following year. The land of Judah, caught up in these great events, ended its political existence and passed into the hands of the Babylonians. There was a revolt in 598 and, in the following year, the ultimate blow fell. Jerusalem, the sacred city, was captured by Nebuchadnezzar. Horror followed upon horror. The Babylonians deported, in two separate movements, the most able people in the population, sending them as slaves overland. The few remaining were placed under the governorship of a certain Gedaliah. But he was murdered, and many of those who had been left with him themselves fled to find political asylum in Egypt. So, in a few years, Judah ceased to exist and Jerusalem lay desolate.

Well was it written in the Lamentations of Jeremiah:

"How doth the city sit solitary, that was full of people! How is she become as a widow! She that was great among the nations, and a princess among the provinces. How is she become tributary!"

In the crucible of these terrible happenings, heated by the glow of burning passions, the character of Jeremiah was formed. Yet it was because he was a prophet, a man who lived under an inner compulsion to tell the truth which was in him, that his sufferings were of a very special kind. He had been called of God, and he had been told of God to utter God's truth. When he was a young man the experience had come to him. Of it, he wrote:

"Now the Word of the Lord came unto me, saying, before I formed thee in the belly I knew thee, and before thou camest forth out of the womb I sanctified thee; I have appointed thee a prophet unto the nations. Then said I, Ah, Lord God! Behold, I cannot speak: for I am a child. But the Lord said unto me, Say not, I am a child: for to whomsoever I shall send thee thou shalt go, and whatsoever I shall command thee thou shalt speak. Be not afraid because of them: for I am with thee to deliver thee, saith the Lord. Then the Lord put forth His hand, and touched my mouth; and the Lord said unto me, Behold, I have put My words in thy mouth: see, I have this day set thee over the nations and over the kingdoms, to pluck up and to break down, and to destroy and to overthrow; to build, and to plant."

From this prophetic mission Jeremiah never knew release. It drove him to say many unpopular things in the interests of truth as he saw it. It caused him to be the victim of violence at the hands of his own people, more than once.

As the anxious years passed, and the fortunes of war ebbed and flowed in the lands round about, so the hopes of those in Jerusalem fluctuated. There came a time, not long after the days in which Jeremiah had received his prophetic call, when the movement of reformation pressed men into believing that a stricter observance of outward forms of worship would turn the heart of God. But Jeremiah, while seeing much that was good in this, continued undauntedly to proclaim the truth, that it was in men's hearts that true reformation was necessary, rather than in these outward ways in which they worshiped.

This was a time when, standing boldly in the very gate of the Temple in Jerusalem to proclaim the word, he cried:

"Hear the word of the Lord, all ye of Judah, that enter in at these gates to worship the Lord. Thus saith the Lord of Hosts, the Lord God of Israel, mend your ways and your doings, and I will cause you to dwell in this place. Trust ye not in lying words, saying, the Temple of the Lord, the Temple of the Lord, the Temple of the Lord, are these. For if ye thoroughly amend your ways and your doings: if ye thoroughly execute judgment between a man and his neighbor, if ye oppress not the stranger, the fatherless and the widow, and shed not innocent blood in this place, neither walk after other gods to your own hurt: then will I cause you to dwell in this place, in the land that I gave to your fathers, from of old even for ever more. Behold, ye trust in lying words, that cannot profit. . . ."

For this, Jeremiah was placed in the stocks. Later, he was arrested under suspicion of being a traitor to the Babylonians. Beaten, thrown into prison, he continued to declare that it was a judgment of God upon the sins of the people that the city would fall. After this, placed in a pit and left to die, he was saved only by the intervention of an Ethiopian in the service of Zedekiah the king.

And then, in the fatal year of 586, Jerusalem fell, and though for a time Jeremiah was well treated by the conquerors, sorrow came to him again with the murder of Gedaliah, the Governor. It was as if there was to be no end of violence and suffering surrounding this man who, could he have chosen, would have been a man of peace. Truly for him the times were out of joint. Like many another man whose life has been filled with what appeared to be undeserved suffering, Jeremiah often wondered why it should be so.

"Woe is me, my mother," he once cried out, "for thou hast born me a man of strife and a man of contention to the whole earth!"

So, after years of frustration and defeat, after a lifetime with no silver lining to the dark cloud of his misfortunes, Jeremiah passed from the scene, fleeing to Egypt with other refugees, and suffering himself at the end a violent death. A mass of misfortunes lay like a stone upon his spirit, so ardent a spirit, so tender. Yet, though the tale of

VII. SOLOMON RECEIVING THE QUEEN OF SHEBA

And when the queen of Sheba heard of the fame of Solomon concerning the name of the Lord, she came to prove him with hard questions. I Kings, 10, 1.

By Piero della Francesca (1416 ?–1492)

Photo Alinari

the events of his time belongs to the distant past, the value of the truths which he discovered is eternal.

First, it came to him that God is not in one place only, not in any temple made with hands, but in the hearts of all who need Him and love Him. When the sad captives trailed over the deserts to Babylon their grief was immeasurable, because they supposed that they were leaving behind in desolate Jerusalem the God whom they had worshiped there. But Jeremiah, in immortal words, told them otherwise:

"For I know the thoughts that I think toward you, saith the Lord, thoughts of peace and not of evil, to give you hope in your latter end. And ye shall call upon Me, and ye shall go and pray unto Me and I will hearken unto you. And ye shall seek Me, and find Me, when ye shall search for Me with all your heart."

The words are ageless, because they speak, not only to a group of political exiles long ago, but to every person who, in the desolation of his heart, comes to think that, because the edifice of a life which he had known has by adversity been cast down, therefore God also has abandoned him. The truth is, says Jeremiah, that God is with us always and everywhere.

And then again he taught that people should look within themselves for the sins for which God punishes them, and should not blame the past, seeking to ascribe to the wrongdoings of their forebears the sufferings which afflict them in the present. The belief was strong in his own compatriots that the sorrows which had come upon them were God's judgment upon the sins of the past. But Jeremiah said:

"And it shall come to pass, that like as I have watched over them to pluck up and to break down and to overthrow and to destroy, and to afflict; so will I watch over them to build and to plant, saith the Lord."

God would forgive, he was saying, as well as punish. And also:

"In those days they shall say no more, The fathers have eaten sour grapes, and the children's teeth are set on edge. But everyone shall die for his own iniquity: every man that eateth the sour grapes, his teeth shall be set on edge."

And finally Jeremiah proclaimed a new covenant, or agreement, which God would make with His people. It would not be like the covenant which of old had been understood by the people of Israel as binding them to a peculiar degree to God, a covenant which depended in large measure on the observance of external ordinances and which, because of that, called for an obedience to an external law rather than to an inward change of heart. Therefore Jeremiah proclaimed:

"Behold, the day is come, saith the Lord, that I will make a new covenant with the House of Israel, and with the House of Judah: not according to the covenant that I made with their fathers in the day that I took them by the hand to bring them out of the land of Egypt: which My covenant they brake, although I was an husband unto them, saith the Lord. But this is the covenant that I will make with the House of Israel after those days, saith the Lord; I will put My Law in their inward parts, and in their heart will I write it; and I will be their God and they shall be My people; and they shall teach no more every man his neighbor, and every man his brother, saying, Know the Lord: for they shall all know Me, from the least of them unto the greatest of them, saith the Lord. For I will forgive their iniquity, and their sin will I remember no more."

To Mary—a Son

Based on van der Goes'

THE ADORATION OF THE SHEPHERDS

To a group of shepherds up on the lonely hills above Bethlehem it was a night like any other, dark, chilly, and rather anxious. Jackals, whose weird cries they heard often in the darkness, made it necessary to keep watch over the flock. Just before nightfall the shepherds had gathered the sheep into a stone enclosure surrounded by a low wall, and in this space the animals were now huddled together, their breath steaming into the night air. At the entrance of the fold one man sat huddled in his woolen burnous: around the circumference of the wall others of his comrades kept watch, vigilant against raiders, four-legged and two-legged, for it was not unusual for sheep stealers to try to make an entrance under cover of night.

They were simple men, these: not owners of the flock they guarded but hired servants. At long intervals they would cry out to each other, making sure that all were awake and reassuring themselves. This was their nightly duty; they were not to know that it was to be a night more holy, more sacred than any other by reason of something which was about to happen in the village of Bethlehem not far away.

A good deal had been happening there already. The place was unusually crowded. By a decision of the Roman authorities, seeping down from Augustus himself through Quirinius, Governor of Syria, and through him again to the public authorities of Judea, the order had gone out that a census was to be taken of all the population of the country. A periodical occurrence in all territories under Roman suzerainty, it was, in the case of the Jews, permitted to be taken under the auspices of the tribal system. This meant that the people scattered throughout the land gathered themselves into their places of origin and there were duly counted and docketed, the head of each household being required to make a return of all within his family in the place to which by origin it belonged.

Now there was a man up in the village of Nazareth in Galilee, three days' journey to the northward from Bethlehem, upon whom the census had fallen at an awkward moment. His wife was pregnant and nearing the end of her time. But he, whose name was Joseph, a carpenter by trade, was a native of Bethlehem, so that in accordance with the requirements of the tribal census, it had been necessary for him to make the journey south, accompanied by his very young wife in a condition which made it for both of them a very anxious time. She had made the journey on the back of an ass, he walking alongside, steadying her in the rough places with an arm about her waist. Tenderly, he had looked after her all along the way, but it had become increasingly clear to both of them as time went by that there was little chance of their being able to return home before the expected event took place. And on the third

34

day, when, toward the evening, the roofs of Bethlehem had at last come within sight, she had had to tell him that the pains were beginning.

The husband had frowned in anxiety. What he saw when they entered the village street made him more anxious than ever. At the best of times the khan, or inn, in such a small place as Bethlehem was not very comfortable. Such places rarely were, consisting, for the most part, of an enclosure for animals and of accommodation not much more refined for their owners.

Traders of many kinds put up at this inn; grain merchants, cloth merchants, captains of baggage caravans, drovers of pack mules and the like. The throng of these at sunset, as was customary, had turned into the little town. As Joseph with his wife neared the place he could hear the braying and the grunting of their many animals. But also to this customary crowd had been added the numbers of those who, like him, had come south for the census. Animals of these also overflowed the place and, as he tethered his own ass outside, leaving his exhausted wife to rest awhile, he saw that the situation looked grim as regards accommodation for the night.

The inn-keeper, hard-pressed, could only spread his hands apart and shrug his shoulders when Joseph asked him for a room. The simple fact was that there was none to be had. The guest room was full. There was no space to be had on the floor. The only possible alternative was for Mary and Joseph to seek out a corner of the lower half of the room among the animals themselves.

It was scarcely an inviting proposition, but Joseph knew in his heart that there was nothing else for it, and that his wife would accept the fact with her usual quiet stoicism. So he went out to her, tenderly pressing her hand as he explained. Then he helped her down from the back of the ass and together they made their way to the far end of the stable space in the lower half of the guest chamber, near the manger where ox and ass amicably munched. A musky smell rose from the beasts as they regarded the man and the woman with their large eyes.

The floor was of rock, and Joseph cleared a space upon it for the bed-mats upon which they were to sleep. That done, they prepared from their own saddle-bags a little cheese and bread for their evening meal. As they ate they could hear the uproar out in the courtyard of the inn still going on, shouts, arguments, the barking of dogs. As the hour grew later the people packed into the guest room and lay down on the floor to sleep. Quite early, for these were rough folk whose habit it was to work by daylight and sleep by night, they were all gone into the land of dreams.

Joseph tried to sleep too. But, at some hour when all the rest of the world was still, he felt Mary gently pressing his hand as he lay beside her. He awoke, and turned to her, knowing in his heart that her hour had come. He could hear the rhythmic cud-chewing of the oxen all around.

Some long time later, but before the first cocks had crowed, this placid sound of chewing was momentarily halted by the incursion of a new sound—the cry of a newly born child. Then the cud-chewing continued as before, peaceful, rhythmic and contented.

*　　　*　　　*　　　*

Meanwhile, out on the lonely hills an astonishing experience had befallen the shepherds. They never knew at what hour of the night it occurred, but it was certainly well on into the depths of it when a light suddenly shone around them, strong enough to show up the stone wall of the sheep enclosure and the woolly backs of the animals within. This was no ordinary light, but the Shechinah, a visible sign of the Glory of the Lord.

At this nerve-testing phenomenon the shepherds ran together, those around the wall joining their comrade who had stationed himself at the entrance to the fold. And while they huddled together there an angel appeared before them, the image of him seeming to quiver in the intensity of the light. The angel spoke:

"Be not afraid; for behold I bring you good tidings of great joy which shall be to all the people: for there is born to you this day in the City of David a Saviour, which is Christ the Lord. And this is the sign unto you; ye shall find the babe wrapped in swaddling clothes and lying in a manger."

At the last word which the angel uttered the vision suddenly expanded, revealing a multitude of the heavenly host, praising God.

"Glory to God in the Highest," it seemed to the shepherds that they sang. "And on earth peace among men in whom He is well pleased."

With the same instantaneous photo-flash with which it had come, the light vanished, and with it the angelic vision, leaving once again the blackness of the night and the wind on the hill.

The shepherds waited until they could see the loom of each other's faces. Then in a low voice, the elder, he who had been at the entrance of the fold, said to the others:

"Let us now go even unto Bethlehem, and see this thing that is come to pass, which the Lord hath made known unto us."

So, they made their way down to Bethlehem, poor souls from the uplands rudely dressed in the sheepskins of their calling. When they reached the inn they made their way straight to the stable in the lower part of the guest room. And behold, when they pressed in as far as the manger, they found Mary and Joseph and also, as the angel had foretold, a baby wrapped in swaddling clothes. The young mother smiled upon them as they gaped. And as they broke into many wondering exclamations, explaining to the folk around what they had seen and heard upon the hills, she kept silent, pondering, with wonder in her heart, upon the marvelous words which the Angel Gabriel had spoken to her nine months before:

"Fear not, Mary: for thou hast found favor with God. And behold, though shalt conceive in thy womb, and bring forth a son and shalt call his name Jesus. He shall be great, and shall be called the Son of the Most High: and the Lord God shall give unto him the throne of his father David: and he shall reign over the House of Jacob for ever; and of his Kingdom there shall be no end."

She had asked then:

"How shall this be, seeing I know not a man?"

The angel had answered:

"The Holy Ghost shall come upon thee, and the power of the Most High shall overshadow thee: therefore also that which is to be born shall be called holy, the Son of God."

Bowing her head she had made answer:

"Behold, the handmaid of the Lord; be it unto me according to thy word."

And so it had been to her according to that word. She looked down upon the tiny form stirring within the fold of her arms, and smiled upon him.

Men from Afar

Based on Sassetta's

THE JOURNEY OF THE MAGI

HAUGHTY, mysterious and reserved, the three men who arrived one night and put up at a caravanserai in Jerusalem felt no surprise at the stir their arrival caused. They had been a long, long time on their journey, traveling westward from Persia. The worn gear of their camels showed how long they had been on the road, and their own weather-beaten countenances, the eyes puckered through long exposure to sand-bearing winds, testified further to the fact. Moreover the further they moved to the westward, away from their own land, the more they caused curiosity. For they were manifestly strangers; strangers in dress, in manner, in speech.

But they were also in themselves odd, men who conducted themselves as those do who are apart in mind and spirit from everyday concerns. They could talk learnedly and obscurely among themselves by the hour, touching upon old prophecies and upon the connection therewith of the movements of heavenly bodies. Yet they had no small talk, brought no gossip to share around the courtyard fire in a caravanserai by night, and, concerning their own needs, food for their beasts and for themselves, they used few words, as though on the high plane upon which their thoughts dwelt, there was little room for such mundane concerns. Bearded and tall, they kept for the most part to themselves. When they were not conversing together they would sit, each with his chin sunk upon his breast, sunk in profound meditation.

For these reasons men had looked askance at them in the many trade-route inns which had from time to time received them. People speculated as to who they were, whence they came, whither they were going. But no one had received an answer. It was clear only that they were looking for something, and that that something lay ever before them. The feet of their camels measured out, day after day, the long desert miles. And now they were in Jerusalem. It was night; the beasts, with those of other travelers, were bedded down; and the company had eaten and was gathered around the fire of dry wood which cracked and snapped, sending off occasional bursts of sparks to be whirled upward toward the stars. This firelight shone strongly upon the faces of the mysterious strangers, so that many eyes sought them out.

Some had made guesses already among themselves. They were Persian astrologers, some said, who had traveled in those lands, probably magi, probably priests of the Zoroastrian religion, men learned in the arts whereby from the movements of the stars the destinies of men could be foretold. Because such wise men were regarded with respect and awe the company in the Jerusalem inn, feeling constrained in their presence, maintained a subdued silence. It was broken suddenly, without any preliminary, by one of the wise men himself.

Tilting his head back, his eyes upon the stars, and his forked beard jutted toward the fire, he enquired in a peculiar voice of no-one in particular:

"Where is he that is born King of the Jews?"

He put his question in the manner of one having no idea of the sensation it was likely to cause. Yet it passed like a wave round the fire. Not only the Jews had lived in expectation of the appearance of a Saviour, a Messiah; the whole eastern world for years past had thrilled with a similar emotion, looking for some nameless Great One who, by his advent, would bring a new age to pass. Yet nowhere was this expectation held with greater passion than among the Jews who saw in it, not only the fulfilment of many prophecies, but also the means whereby they would be released from the degradation of a subject people. The stranger with his forked beard could not have asked a more startling question. Yet nobody answered; the silence, because it was a silence of astonishment, remained unbroken. Sensing this, and perhaps feeling that some further explanation was necessary, the man added mildly:

"We saw his star in the east and are come to worship him."

That was enough to release a torrent of talk; questions, rumors, strange tales of what some of the speakers claimed they themselves had heard and seen. And while the talk thus rose and fell about the fire one man, who had been sitting there silently, arose and slipped out.

He was one of the agents of Herod the King, the cold and the crafty man, who had become Governor of Galilee in the year 47 B.C. and had assumed the title of King of Judea and ruled by consent of Rome. Inclining to his end, abhorred and feared, he was living his latter days in terror lest the witches' brew of hatred which bubbled all around him should overflow. More than anything else he feared supplanting by a new power which should arise. It was, consequently, the business of his many agents to keep him informed of any rumor going about among the people which should speak of such a thing. And here, with a vengeance, was such a rumor. The man who had been around the fire when the stranger had spoken hurried to his master to tell him.

Herod was deeply troubled. Consequently, as early as possible the following day, he gathered about him the Chief Priests and Scribes of the people, of whom, having repeated to them the tidings which his agent had brought, he asked how much there was likely to be in it. Where, for instance, was this King likely to be born?

"In Bethlehem of Judea," they told him, "for thus it is written by the Prophet"—they meant the prophet Micah—

> "And thou Bethlehem, land of Judah,
> Art in no wise least among the Princes of Judah:
> For out of thee shall come forth a Governor,
> Which shall be Shepherd of my people Israel."

It was enough for Herod. There and then he sent messengers to summon the strangers from their inn and to bring them before him.

Like all others who had encountered them he was extremely impressed. There was a curious mixture of authority and detachment about them which made him feel he was in the presence of something rare. This star, he asked them, what was it? When had it appeared? They told him; but he found it difficult to follow their astrological terminology. Consequently, withdrawing a little among his own advisers, he asked them to elucidate the matter. There was nothing of any precision which they could give him.

Herod stroked his beard. There was mystery here, and it made him most uneasy. Yet when he confronted again the strangers from the east his crafty face was creased into an ingratiating smile. If these men, he argued, could find this newly-born King of the Jews of whom they spoke, then it would indeed be a great convenience. It would enable him, Herod, to lay hands upon this upstart. So he sent them to Bethlehem saying:

"Go and search out carefully concerning the young child: and when ye have found him come and bring me word, that I also may come and worship him."

Gravely, the three salaamed before the king and withdrew.

Mounting again their travel-worn camels, they made their way whither they were directed. And there they came upon a great wonder. The star which had guided them for so long went before them in the east as they traveled till it came and stood over the place they were looking for, the place where the young child was. They recognized the star, and their hearts were filled with a mysterious joy. For there was the end of their road, the road which had started for them with the murmurs of old prophecies, with the poring over ancient documents, with obscure calculations of the conjunction of heavenly bodies.

Yet it was a simple scene they came upon. There was only a young Jewish girl with a baby in her lap and a grave man who was her husband standing behind her shoulder. For all that, the strangers, who knew so much and who humbled themselves before so little, knelt before the babe as he chuckled and played with his fingers. They knelt, bowing their heads until their foreheads touched the ground. Then, raising themselves a little, they offered the gifts which they had brought in their saddlebags for so many hundreds of miles. There was gold, and frankincense and myrrh—gold as a kingly gift representing the wealth of the world, frankincense betokening the worship of the world, and, strangely enough, myrrh, an Arabian gum, representing at one and the same time a gift that was fitting for a King and yet one that could be used for the embalming of the dead.

The journey was done: their mission was accomplished. They did not return to Herod, so that the schemes of the evil king came to naught. For that very night, as thankfully they rested, there came to them from God a dream, warning them against returning to Jerusalem. Wherefore, they departed into their own country another way.

The Home Life of Jesus

Based on de la Tour's

JOSEPH THE CARPENTER AND THE CHILD JESUS

THE little boy, cross-legged on the floor in the shade, continued to stare wide-eyed at his teacher. The man profoundly impressed him, had done ever since Jesus, for that was the little boy's name, had first been sent along to the village school in Nazareth. The teacher was the Hassan, a combination of clerk and verger, of the synagogue, who included among his duties that of teaching the boys. He had a deep, rumbling voice, and it was especially marvelous how it could keep on rumbling away hour after hour, although in the hottest part of the day he often grew sleepy. Ready to his hand, as he faced his boys, were the scrolls upon which the Law was written, and from these he would recite passages in his astonishing, indefatigable voice and then, looking sternly over the rim of it, while he held the scroll by its rollers on either side, he would command them to repeat the verses together.

In this way Jesus had already learnt by heart long passages. He could already repeat, and had delighted his parents by so doing, "Hear, O Israel: the Lord thy God is one Lord; and thou shalt love the Lord thy God with all thy heart and with all thy soul, and with all thy might. And these words, which I command thee this day, shall be upon thy heart; and thou shalt teach them diligently unto thy children and shalt talk of them when thou sittest in thy house, and when thou walkest by the way, and when thou liest down, and when thou risest up. And thou shalt bind them for a sign upon thine hand, and they shall be for frontlets between thine eyes. And thou shalt write them upon the doorposts of thy house, and upon thy gates."

All this, and much else, he had learnt at school, sitting cross-legged in the shade. It all meant a much sterner existence than he had known in the days of early childhood when, a little mite, he used to toddle after Mary, his mother, as she went about her household duties, or had wandered down to the carpenter's workshop of Joseph, to enjoy the wonderful pleasures of playing about with the tools and the shavings, all the long, careless days of infancy. Now he was on the way up toward young manhood, and it behoved him to learn, and to grow wise.

On the whole he enjoyed school. He even liked the Hassan. He could not feel the same for him as for Joseph, or of course for Mary his mother. But certainly he respected the teacher, respected his vast learning, his command of the scrolls, the authority which, for the boy, was reinforced by seeing the Hassan sitting up among the elders in the synagogue on the Sabbath. Yet best of all was the companionship of other boys; they were a merry lot, and it was good to be out and about with them when school was over. That was the moment he was waiting for now.

The rumbling voice ceased. The Hassan stood and began to gather up his scrolls. Late that day, Jesus knew, the same man would be sounding the trumpet which

40

VIII. JEREMIAH LAMENTING THE DESTRUCTION OF JERUSALEM

*How doth the city sit solitary, that was full of people!
how is she become as a widow! she that was great among
the nations, and princess among the provinces, how is she
become tributary!* Lamentations 1, 1.

By Rembrandt (1606–1669)

Photo Rijksmuseum

would at evening betoken the commencement of the Sabbath. It would happen just before sunset; but before that there would be time for fun.

The standing up of the Hassan, and his gathering up of his scrolls, was the sign that school was over. Gladly, even wildly, their long dammed-back energies released, the boys scattered, shouting, up the street. Jesus went with them. Out of the village, up the hillsides they went, Jesus running with them, his mouth open and a look of pure rapture on his brown, open face.

The hillside was wide and breezy. The boys as they played could perceive the flat roofs of Nazareth. And all around and below the panorama of the countryside lay outstretched. There were vineyards; there was a plowman moving behind his slow oxen. It was a fine place to grow up in, this quiet corner of the great world. The boy loved it. It was all he had ever known; it was all, at that stage of his life, which he wished to know.

Thinly from below toward the time of sunset the trumpet of the Hassan sounded, warning that soon the Sabbath would begin. At the summons the boys ceased their play and, quietly now, made their way down again to the village. As they went down they passed a line of sheep in single file following their shepherd to a fold among the hills.

Home, when he reached it, was a very humble place. Like the others in the village the house of Mary and Joseph was made of roughly dressed stone and had but one living room. In here the family ate and slept, amid a not unpleasant smell of camel-dung smoke, since there was no chimney and the only way out for the smoke was by the door. After nightfall light came from a clay lamp placed upon a stone shelf projecting from the wall. The furniture was sparse. In the same room was the family grain bin, set into the wall. To draw water it was necessary to go to the family well down the street, a journey which Mary often made, carrying her jar upon her head. The oven in which she cooked stood in a corner of the little courtyard outside.

His mother smiled at the boy as he entered, then turned to put the finishing touches to the meal. Joseph, Jesus saw, was already arrived home. He did not smile, because it was rarely his habit to do so. But he gave the boy a pleased nod of recognition, his eyes lighting as he did so. There was a profound affection between the two of them, an affection never breaking out into words, but deeply felt, for all that. Everyone, as Jesus well knew, greatly respected Joseph the carpenter for his skill, for his integrity, for his quiet, solid worth. But the boy loved him, liking to be near at hand as the other worked, thrilling with the privilege of it when Joseph allowed him to lend a hand in his workshop. And sometimes Jesus would look up and find the eyes of Joseph, very grave and kindly eyes, resting almost wonderingly upon him. He never quite understood that deep, considering look. Yet it thrilled and pleased him, and he would return it with a bright flash of his little white teeth.

When Joseph had asked a blessing upon the food, the family settled down to enjoy it. There was not a great deal of talk among them, for it was not the custom. But there was peace, and contentment, and, pervading everything, a deep sense of peace and security. It lapped the boy about like a warm tide. Later that night when he awoke for a space and lay listening to the breathing of his parents on the other side of the room, the lovely sensation of it filled his whole being with content. He sighed a little, stretching himself, then curling up again like a puppy, his head well down beneath the covering, and slept.

The next day, being the Sabbath, they all went to the synagogue. Here again was something familiar and dear to the boy. In some synagogues the women sat apart from the men; but here in Galilee the custom was less strict, so that Mary sat with her husband and the boy. It was a cool, dignified building, surrounded along its length by two rows of pillars between which the congregation sat on mats on the floor. Before them was the reading desk and beyond this, at the far end, a curtain shrouding the place where were kept the scrolls of the Law and the Prophets. The chief seats were set out in front for the elders and the Ruler of the Synagogue who thus occupied places of honor facing the people. Jesus looked upon these elders with great awe, recognizing among them the redoubtable Hassan who taught him during the week. There also was the Ruler of the Synagogue himself, to whom fell the duty of selecting the readers of the Scriptures.

The order of the service was as familiar to Jesus as the wind upon the hillside or the voice of his mother. It was of the very stuff and texture of his life. First there was the recitation of the Shema. Then the prayers, then the readings from the Law and the Prophets by those whom the Ruler of the Synagogue had called upon, seven readings in all. As each reader went up to take his turn he kissed the scroll as it was handed to him. And then often there would be an exposition of the readings, and after that the general exodus into the sunny street outside, and the long pause there for neighbourly talk among the elders while the boys scampered in and out among them.

But it was on a weekday, after school, that the happiest moments of the week came to Jesus. For then he would go down to the carpenter's shop, sometimes, if Joseph were working late, carrying with him a little food which Mary would have prepared, so that Joseph could make the most of all the hours of daylight without having to go home for his meal. The workship was a marvelous place, a very cave of wonders. Jesus would thrill even at the very smell; the smell of seasoned wood, of shavings and of oil. He thrilled at the sounds of the place; at the snoring of the saw, and the hiss of the plane, and the thumpings of hammer and mallet. Joseph was a highly skilled craftsman, hard-working and deliberate in everything that he did. The work was hard in itself, requiring, like all crafts, long hours of patient concentration.

Jesus liked it best when the bazaar was quiet and when the other craftsmen who toiled there, the shoemaker, the coppersmith and the rest of them, had gone home, and when, above all, there were no customers in the shop to hold Joseph's attention. For it was then that the carpenter would be able to give his whole attention to the boy, a thing which he delighted to do, teaching him with few words and much example, the mysteries of his trade. And sometimes, when the work in hand would be done, and they would both be tired, they would sit together in warm companionship upon the floor, not needing to talk much but feeling bound together by the comradeship of tasks shared. Then Joseph would rise, put on his sandals and, taking the boy by the hand, would lead him slowly homeward up the dark streets under the stars.

This, then, was some of the home life of Jesus; a simple life, a wholesome life. It was because of it, because especially of the loving care of Mary and Joseph, that a certain writer in after times called Luke was able to record of the childhood of Jesus that, "the Child grew and waxed strong in spirit, filled with wisdom, and the Grace of God was upon him."

IX. THE ADORATION OF THE SHEPHERDS

For unto you is born this day in the city of David a Saviour, which is Christ the Lord. Luke 2, 11.

By Hugo van der Goes (*died in* 1482)

Photo Alinari

Marvelous Boy

Based on Ribera's

CHRIST AMONG THE DOCTORS

THE boy watched from a little distance his father settle his mother comfortably on the back of the ass. She always rode like that, at ease and placid on the mats Joseph placed for her there. Then she was ready. The whole caravan was ready, brought, it seemed almost miraculously, into order after the usual exciting uproar of preparation. It had been like that when they had left their village, those few days ago which seemed already to the boy like an age. Then, as now, the big pack camels, laden with water-bags and impedimenta, had staggered to their feet, curling thick lips in infinite disdain of the world. And the dogs had barked and the donkeys brayed, and the dust risen, and the boys run in and out among the confusion, just as they were doing now.

One of them raced by in the white sunlight at that very moment calling a name. The boy standing warily back in the black shadow cast by the roof of a shelter built against the wall stiffened as he heard it. The name was his.

"Jesus!" yelled the lad out of the sun. He stopped, spun round, tried again: "Jesus!"

The boy in the shadow rubbed the bare instep of his right foot against the calf of his left leg. It soothed him. It was not easy to hold back when friends shouted an invitation to come out and have fun, especially some of the fun to be had out of running up and down the length of the caravan on the move, staring at strange households from other villages, listening, chattering, wondering together, then ranging off into fields alongside to try out a sling or start a flock of birds.

They would have all that fun again now on the way home, eighty miles to Jerusalem from Nazareth, down from the great city through the boulder-strewn Judean hills, where the streams ran one way to the Jordan and the other to the great sea. Then through the plain of Esdraelon, where the caravans, dozens, scores, hundreds of them, all returning from the keeping of the Passover, would begin to hive off, some to the north, to Damascus and beyond, some to homely villages in Galilee. And one at least, the one the boy knew he ought to be with, would go on until it came to a little place called Nazareth. And then the caravan itself would break up and its pilgrims become villagers again. And two would go to open up the carpenter's shop where they lived.

They would be sad. They would be wondering what on earth had become of him, their boy. Tears pricked his eyes as he thought of it. Yet it would be all right in the end. He would run all the way back if need be, a three days' journey at caravan speed, when he was ready. He would work for them, die for them, if need be. But, this much was certain—and the certainty burned in him as part of the fire the last

43

few days in Jerusalem had lit in his mind and heart—he had to stay here until some, at least, of his questions were answered. He knew where they were going to be answered, too, if at all. They would be answered in the Temple, where the most learned scholars in all Jewry sat among the colonnades and discoursed upon the Scriptures.

He peeped out to see if the calling of his name had been noticed by his parents. It hadn't, among all the other shouting that was going on. They would assume that he was among the other boys; they would not worry until later.

And now the full expanse of the enclosure where so many pilgrim caravans had rested during the Passover was on the move, a mass of color, noise and dust. In half an hour the place was deserted, so that he could look out over it and see only animal droppings and the remains of fires. They had gone. He felt suddenly lonely. He was on his own in the big city.

As he stepped out into the sun the hot sand stung his strong bare feet. He was strong all over, this boy. As his mother recalled many years later to a doctor called Luke, who wrote it down, "He waxed strong." He had jet black hair, swept back from the tall brow and hanging behind as far as his shoulders. He had a marked Semitic nose, full lips. His eyes were remarkable, ebony-black, needle-bright. He passed out into the streets of the city.

It was not yet a propitious hour for going to the Temple, since the learned Rabbis did not gather until somewhat later in the day, when the sun was up higher. Even so, the city was awake, and as he got among the narrow thronged streets the life of the place worked powerfully upon his acutely extended senses. He was, and knew himself to be, at an important point in life's journey, the point where a boy feels stirrings of the man within him. Twelve years old, an age in development perhaps equal to the late teens in a European or American boy of the modern world, he was even at that precocious for his age. All Jewish boys became at thirteen Sons of the Law, responsible thenceforth themselves for the keeping of its sacred ordinances. To mark the fact, their fathers would take them up to the Passover in Jerusalem itself, where they would for the first time see the ceremony; see the grave men go from the Court of the Women to make sacrifice in the Court of the Priests. They would see them emerge again with the sacred parts of the Passover lamb for their women to roast that evening and serve with wine and water and a blessing. All this happened to boys at thirteen, to lads who before had eaten the Passover only back at home. But Jesus had grown faster in understanding than most, and Joseph had taken him up to the Feast a year ahead of the customary age.

There were shouts now higher up the steep crooked street. The boy had to press himself back against a stall loaded high with dates and colored fruit to get out of the way of the procession coming through. It was headed by a supercilious Levantine wearing the chain of office of a House Steward, clearing a way with his staff. Then a litter, borne by slaves, flanked by a guard. Through the draperies of the litter the boy saw a languid Roman woman whose heavily kohled eyes passed over him as though he was a fly on the wall. All power here was Roman, outward power at least. The sun-catching helmets of troops upon the ramparts announced the fact. So did the trumpets of the garrison. But there was another power in the city as well, more ancient, more lasting, the power of an ancient faith and race, and the majesty of their God.

That faith and that race were his too. The boy kindled at the thought, remembering all that his father had told him and the Rabbi in Nazareth taught him of the great past of Israel, of how God had chosen them to be His people, of their heroes and mighty deeds; of Moses and Abraham, Saul and David, of Solomon who had made glorious this very place. And he remembered, too, the mysterious teaching of how one would come who was greater than all these, the Messiah of Israel.

The thought stirred in his brain like a little animal beneath leaves. It was always stirring there, as if trying to get out and tell him something.

The crowd now was filling the alley again, muttering. Some of the fruit which had been spilled from the stall behind into the road by the crush lay about. The boy helped pick it up, and the man who kept the stall threw him an orange with a shout and a grin. Jesus wandered on, thoughtfully peeling the fruit.

There was certainly excitement in the air, even though the Feast was over. Jerusalem was still packed with more than a million pilgrims, Jews from every country in the known world, Gaul, Spain, North Africa; from every part of the enormous empire of Rome they had come. Here were new horizons, stimulating for the boy, with their glimpses of a great world far beyond the little confines of Galilee which were all he had hitherto known. And here were Jews of a kind utterly different from the peaceful peasantry he had been born among. Sharp-featured, cosmopolitan people these, merchants, traders, a thousand different crafts and backgrounds.

The boy wandered on, drinking it all in. It was afternoon when he entered the Temple. The place was enormous, one of the wonders of the ancient world. A vast outer Court ran clear around it. On its southern side a seven-hundred-foot-long architectural masterpiece had a cedarwood roof supported by marble pillars, greater than the greatest trees. Crowds moving over the marble floor were made insect-like by the proportion of the surroundings. Yet this was but the outer fringe of this splendid House of God. Beyond, through further Courts, lay the core of it all, the Holy of Holies on the sacred rock. Even from afar miles distant from the city as seen from pilgrims ascending to it, and singing, probably, the song of ascents, "I will lift up mine eyes unto the hills, from whence cometh my help", the Temple dominated. Here within, it was overpowering.

As the boy entered the Court of the Gentiles through its archway the din of the place struck him like a blow. Animal noises rang high over all; the blaring of cattle, bleating of lambs, the strange, gurgling, cooing of thousands of doves. For here was where animals were bought for sacrifice, to be taken in further as offering in the Court of the Priests. And here was where the money-changers worked, doing big business at this peak Passover season. One on the right of the gateway especially caught the boy's eye. The man's table was piled high with stacks of coins which he fingered often, as by a nervous tic, the while looking around left to right, and back again, sharp as a bird. And then as a client approached a smile creased the man's face and he bowed, hands clasped before him.

The boy felt his high ideals injured for the first time since he had entered the Holy City. What did that man or his like care that he was upon sacred ground? What did it mean to him that devout Jews often from the other end of the world counted it the privilege of a lifetime to come here at all?

There was an anger born in the boy Jesus that day. And there was to be another time, far in the unimaginable future, when in that very place, at that very Passover season, he was to upset the tables of those same men, sending the coins bowling all over the tessellated floor, and crying out in a man's big voice, "My Father's House is a House of Prayer; but you have made it a den of thieves."

But that was not yet: he was a boy. He was a boy of twelve with questions in his head. So he passed straight on through the Court of the Gentiles until he came to a marble screen, through one of the openings in which he went on, climbing steps to do so, into an inner part of the place. Here was a Stone of Forbidding, a notice carved in Greek warning off all but Jews from passing that spot. And on the marble terrace at the head of the steps was what he had come to find. The Masters in the Law were gathered.

Already there was an appreciable crowd around: a thoughtful crowd. Here was no place for the simple. The privilege of hearing exposition of the Scriptures by the most highly trained theological minds of the ancient world was one which in the nature of things appealed largely to the intelligent. But there were many such among the Jews, a religious people whose Scriptures were their culture.

So now many were gathered about the Rabbis, some leaning against pillars, some seated on the floor, all listening keenly. For the first time the boy felt a certain shyness as he drew softly near. And, being shy, he stood awhile silent, while the whole scene impressed itself for ever on his memory. This Court was in parts open to a sky of brilliant blue so that the white of the pillars and the red and gold and brown of garments were picked out dramatically in the strong light. Further on, a noble sight, up a perspective of marble steps lay the central buildings of the Temple. It was quiet, too; the din of the Court of the Gentiles was here fallen to a murmur. Of the turbulence of the city without there was not a sound. Within the group ahead of him the boy heard an old, old voice reading, pausing to speak, then reading again. He recognized the words. They were from the Book of the prophet Isaias.

Those on the outer fringes of the crowd stirred with curiosity as the lad, very gently, made a way between them. One whispered to a neighbor, both smiled. It was rare to see a child in such a gathering. But now his persistence had brought him to the front, so that he could see the venerable figures of the learned men themselves.

They were incredibly old. He felt he had never seen such seamed faces, such white and silken beards, nor, for that matter, such splendor of academic attire. But age and wisdom were the distinguishing marks of them all. Age especially so. The hands of the reader, as he clutched the rollers of his scroll, were like claws. His rheumy eyes, down-dragged and red beneath like an old bloodhound's, peered closely at the Hebrew letters. The old voice read on:

"He was despised and rejected of men; a man of sorrows and acquainted with grief, and as one from whom men hide their faces, he was despised and we esteemed him not. Surely he has borne our griefs and carried our sorrows, yet we did esteem him stricken, smitten of God, and afflicted. But he was wounded for our transgressions; he was bruised for our iniquities, the chastisement of our peace was upon him, and with his stripes we are healed."

He paused. The boy drew a very deep breath. This was it. This was what he had stayed in Jerusalem for. What did it mean, this prophecy veiled in splendid words?

X. THE JOURNEY OF THE MAGI

There came wise men from the east to Jerusalem, Saying,
Where is he that is born King of the Jews? for we have
seen his star in the east, and are come to worship him.
Matthew 2, 1–2.

By Sassetta (c.1400–1450)

Photo Metropolitan Museum

And then it seemed that he could no longer be silent. He spoke; the ancient turned his bloodhound eyes to the direction of the young voice, the crowd moved closer. . . .

*   *   *   *

Not until the evening of that day did Mary and Joseph discover that Jesus was missing. It was nightfall by then and the whole caravan was encamped, each family at its own tent. The children, sleepy from the day's journey, stared owlishly into the fires, the men murmured in talk while the women prepared the meal. But at no fire could Joseph find the boy, although he went round all his kinsfolk and acquaintances. Everywhere it was a shaken head. Not even the lads who were closest friends of Jesus had seen him.

Joseph searched through the whole camp until he was at the edge of it, under the stars, looking out into the darkness beyond. He was very seriously concerned. Out back there was bad country. The Samaritans, for instance, way toward Mount Gerizim, were none too friendly. There were robbers, too, bad characters who haunted the gullies in the hill country watching for stray pilgrims. If the lad had fallen somewhere, maybe lamed himself . . . Joseph muttered, pulling his beard. He should have kept an eye on the boy. And yet, it was puzzling. The lad was a good boy; lively, it was true, but dutiful and obedient beyond the common run. It was not like him to stray off.

Joseph turned. There was no point now in pretence. Mary would have to know. He went back with long strides through the camp, where the dogs barked, until he was by their own fire. Mary looked at him across it. He could only stretch his hands apart, palms upward, in a gesture of emptiness.

"Not a sign of him," he said. "I've been everywhere, asked everybody."

He added peremptorily, as she began to speak, "There's nothing we can do about it tonight; nothing. Let us eat. Tomorrow, we'll turn back."

But the morrow brought no trace of him, nor, incredibly, the morrow's morrow either, though the pair hunted far and wide, re-tracing the wide slow zigzags the way they had come. Samaritan villages, bleak valleys in the hills—they tried them all. There was only the city left. It was the morning of the third day when, wearily, they addressed themselves to the long climb once more. It was afternoon when they entered the Temple, brought there by one last hope. In grim silence, Joseph tethered the ass before turning to join his wife in the Court of the Gentiles. The place was still packed and noisy. Mary looked at him as he went to her. "No," was all she said, "not here." Her sweet face was already marked with the worry of the last three days. From his own greater height Joseph looked carefully round. Then he too shook his head. A small remnant of hope died within them. There was no Jesus, no sturdy boy's figure to be seen, anywhere at all.

Yet there was a further place to look, at least, though unlikely enough, in all conscience. Mary followed as he strode in up the steps past the Stone of Forbidding, into the wide marble spaces beyond. Then they stopped. Over in the left-hand corner among pillars was a crowd, the backs of the crowd were all turned. No-one took any notice as the two came up behind them. Mary, a small woman, could see nothing; but there was certainly something she had heard—a boy's voice, speaking with amazing eloquence and ease. She turned to her husband.

He silenced her with a gesture. Not even the fact that it was the voice of their own child could pardon the utter impropriety of a woman speaking in such a company. There were great Rabbis in there. The men around, moreover, were all grave and reverend elders of a kind in whose company the village carpenter felt himself abashed. Irresolute, intimidated, he stared over the shoulders before him.

Yes, there was Jesus. He stood in the very midst of the doctors, among the scrolls and the cushions and the old, old men. One of them was now interrupting, gesturing at a parchment while the boy listened courteously, humble yet at ease, both at the same time. And then he continued his former speech. Joseph felt he had never in his life seen so astonishing a thing. There were the greatest masters of the Law in the world. And they were listening, yes, listening, to a mere boy.

Joseph started as Mary broke suddenly from him, pushing through the crowd ahead. He saw her emerge from the front ranks, press right among the doctors, to throw herself on her knees by the boy. Her arms went round him.

"Oh, Jesus," she cried, "at last. Why have you done this to us? Your father and I have looked everywhere for you."

There was a complete silence, created by more than the fact that a woman had broken in upon the company. Joseph sensed also an intense curiosity in those around. He watched closely as the boy turned to look down upon his kneeling mother. The lad's face was a study, like that of one coming down with difficulty from a rarefied state of being to the level of every day. It was beautiful too, as a prophet's is who comprehends the unutterable. At the sight, Joseph felt the anger that had been in him, the anger with the cause that follows a quick relaxing of tension, flow out of him like sawdust, leaving him puzzled and, for some reason, ever so slightly afraid. Truly, this was a strange lad.

The silence held as Mary led the boy through the crowd that parted for them. "Come," she said quickly and joyously to her husband. He followed slowly, in a daze, until a hand was laid upon his arm. It was one of the men who had detached himself from the crowd. "The lad is yours?" he asked. Joseph bowed, saying nothing. The clothes and manner of the questioner bespoke a distinguished person, so that the carpenter felt overcome. "Then well you may be proud," the other said. "Not in all my years have I seen the like. A marvellous boy, that. These two days has he held the Masters in converse upon the Scriptures, and never have they bettered him. Nay, they have learnt from him. I say again, friend, a marvelous boy. Guard him well, go in peace."

"Go in peace," Joseph echoed.

Mary and Jesus were waiting for him by the ass in the outer Court. There was a constraint upon them all. But Mary, when settled upon the animal's back, asked again, "Why did you do it, Jesus? Just tell us why."

The boy thought, staring at the ground, tracing a pattern in the dust with his toe. Then he lifted his face with the relieved smile of one who suddenly knew what the utterly reasonable answer was.

"You should not have worried," he said; "you see, I *must* be in my Father's House."

So they started off again for Nazareth, the man leading the ass by the head rope, the boy contentedly by his side. Behind, Mary watched them both, thinking and remembering many things.

XI. JOSEPH THE CARPENTER AND THE CHILD JESUS

Is not this the carpenter's son? is not his mother called Mary? Matthew 13, 55.

By Georges de la Tour (1593-1652)

Photo Vizzavona

Desert Battle

Based on Tintoretto's
TEMPTED OF THE DEVIL

THE solitary figure of a man was the only thing moving in a landscape desolate as some part of a dead planet. For some while he had been following a goat track; but this had now petered out. All around were only the grey slopes of naked hills. Where the ground was flat in this part of the Judean desert rocks of brown stone lay littered about. For thirty miles north to south and for fifteen miles west to east there was nothing at all.

Yet the view from the high places of this wilderness was thrilling. The place lay westward into the mountains from Jericho. Away to the northeastward beyond Samaria could be seen the peak of Mount Hermon. To the westward lay Jerusalem. Southward the desolation extended until it reached the point where the land fell away to the still waters of the Dead Sea. Eastward, far away beyond the River Jordan, the ribbon of which could be seen winding along its valley, lay the expanses of Arabia.

The solitary figure was Jesus, and he was climbing toward the Jebel Qarantal, or Mountain of the Forty Days, where he was to go through a period of testing more severe than can be understood by ordinary mortals. There, in the silence he was to wrestle to the ultimate with the power of evil itself. Yet he went there voluntarily at the crucial period of his life. As Moses had spent forty days upon the mountain communing with God, and as Elijah had fasted for the same period before reaching Horeb, so the Son of Man was also to endure.

It was not many days since the baptism of Jesus by John at Bethabara. There, as Jesus had come up out of the water, the Spirit of God had descended upon him as a Dove and a Voice had spoken out of the heavens saying:

"This is My beloved Son, in whom I am well pleased."

He knew now his identity, and he knew now his task. He was indeed and in truth the Son of God. Those intimations of his Divinity which had starred his childhood and youth and manhood had been brought to certainty at the moment of baptism. Now he knew that his task was to bring all men unto him, teaching them the Gospel of the Kingdom. He was God's chosen, and as such thenceforward he would have to act. This was the finally revealed truth; he was the Messiah, he was the one of whom he had heard learned doctors in the Temple reading from the Scriptures when he had stayed that time among them as a lad, taken up to Jerusalem by his parents for the Feast of the Passover.

Such was the overwhelming knowledge which accompanied Jesus into the wilderness. He needed to meditate, to pray, to wrestle with powers not of this world before he could be certain within himself of the true way ahead. To him, as to all mystics, silence and withdrawal were necessary in order that he could come face to face with those realities which lie always deep beneath the surface of life.

For forty days he fasted, bringing the body, by iron discipline, into subjection, refining his sensibilities to the point where, struggling free from the enfolding flesh, his soul could commune with the Infinite. About him all the time was the ringing silence; with him all the time were the pains of hunger. And as he passed through this time of testing his physical state—being wholly man, he was subject to the same physical limitations as the rest of humanity—brought with it sharp emotional changes. From a mood of exaltation, he moved as time passed, from the heights to the depths, sinking, as the body grew weaker, into ever-lengthening periods of self-doubt. The end of the time of trial therefore found him pitifully exposed to the assaults of Satan. It was then that the temptations began.

First Satan attacked Jesus at the point of physical weakness—his hunger. Still all around, as throughout the forty days previously, the brown stones like nightmare loaves of bread lay mockingly upon the desert floor. Now came the whispering voice:

"If thou art the Son of God, command that these stones become bread."

It was a subtle thing to say to a man suffering the cravings of starvation. But Jesus knew that it would be treachery to his divine destiny if, by any exercise of the supernatural powers which he now knew to be his, he were to satisfy a physical need in a way not open to ordinary humanity. In this, as in other ways, he had to be tested, and he had to triumph. Had not his own people gone hungry in the desert when, in ancient times, Moses had led them through the wilderness? This was in his mind as he made answer to Satan in words taken from the Book of Deuteronomy:

"Man shall not live by bread alone, but by every word that proceedeth out of the mouth of God."

He was saying that he would suffer as his people had suffered; that he trusted in God. He who had preserved Israel in the wilderness would also preserve him.

Westward over the hills, as Jesus struggled in the wilderness with his ghostly adversary, lay Jerusalem. In that holy city, the centre of the Jewish world, Jesus knew that his mission would have to begin. In the Temple crowning the city he knew he would have, somehow, to capture the attention of the devout crowds who swarmed to the place.

Now on the south of that same Temple was the Royal Porch, and above it were still higher turrets, the whole overlooking a deep precipice plunging down into the valley of the Kidron. From the summit of the Royal Porch, the place where Roman soldiery were accustomed to take station during the greater feasts in order that they could overlook the throngs below, people moving at the foot appeared small as insects. It was a traditional belief that when the Messiah, long expected of Israel, were to appear, it would be upon that very place, the pinnacle of the Temple.

Now to Jesus in the wilderness the whispering voice of Satan came again, transporting him in imagination there.

"If thou art the Son of God," hissed the voice, repeating the mocking phrase with which he had begun his first temptation, "cast thyself down."

For he had set Jesus upon the topmost turret of the Royal Porch, and was saying, "Go on; cast thyself down." It would be safe; the fall would be arrested by the miraculous powers which guarded the Son of God.

And here Satan quoted Scripture for his purpose. The words came from the ninety-first psalm:

"He shall give his angels charge over thee,
  To keep thee in all thy ways.
  They shall bear thee up in their hands, lest thou dash thy foot against a stone."

Yet to this also Jesus had the answer. It was true that the temptation was one of terrible power. How difficult, how painstaking, how strewn with sufferings was the path of patient teaching which he knew it was his duty to follow in comparison with the sensational use of supernatural powers! Even so, the one way was as surely wrong as the other was as certainly right, and undeviatingly he chose the right. In his answer to the first temptation he had declared his utter trust in God. It had been part of the subtlety of Satan to base the appeal of the second temptation upon that very fact. If God, he was suggesting, were strong enough to save Jesus from starvation in the wilderness, would he not also be strong to save him by stretching forth the right hand of his power if the Messiah were to cast himself from the topmost pinnacle of the Temple? Let him test God by doing that very thing.

Jesus replied, quoting once again the Book of Deuteronomy, where Moses gives to the people the Commandments of God:

"Thou shalt not tempt the Lord thy God."

He meant that it was wrong to put God to test. By doing so a lack of trust was implied. Those who are sure of God do not need to test him. Again his thoughts were with the sufferings of his people in their trek through the wilderness when, being without water, they had questioned the ability of God to help them. "Is the Lord among us, or not?" they had cried before God had told Moses to strike upon the rock from which water sprang out.

So Satan was defeated in the first and in the second of the temptations. The third which followed was the most searching of all.

At the eastern edge of the wilderness, where the stark mountains ended at the plunge into the rift of the Jordan valley, was a point from which it seemed possible to survey all the kingdoms of the world.

To the west, beyond the setting sun, over the crinkled mountains of Judea, lay the cities of the plain, beyond them the great Sea, and beyond the great Sea, Rome, and beyond Rome the territories of the Empire stretching away to the very limits of the known world. To the north, far beyond the little lands of Samaria and Galilee, lay Antioch and Damascus and many another city half as old as time. Eastward, across the deserts, were Babylon and Assyria, the great rivers Tigris and Euphrates, and beyond all these yet again, Persia. Thus, shrouded in the distances visible from that solitary high point at the edge of the wilderness of Judea, it seemed that all the empires of the world could be comprehended: Greece and Rome, Egypt, Babylon, Assyria, and distant Persia, all of them teeming with humanity, with human souls ready to be caught in the great net of God.

As, one day toward the end of his period of trial in the wilderness, Jesus meditated in this high and lonely place, the devil came to him a third time and whispered:

"All these things will I give thee, if thou wilt fall down and worship me."

He was showing to Jesus from that high mountain all the kingdoms of the world and the glory of them. And he was offering to Jesus dominion over the world in exchange for his soul. The world was Satan's by right of ancient possession. This, as Jesus well knew, was attested by ancient teaching. Satan, when he offered the world, was speaking of that of which he had the right to dispose if he so wished.

The profound attraction of the offer was that he was laying before Jesus the opportunity of using the ways of the world to win the world. Those empires and cities below there had all known their conquerors, their leaders and captains of men; their dictators, their tyrants, their kings, their emperors, to whom men for a little while had given honor. All had ruled by the power and might of their own right arms; all had known their hour of triumph before going down to dusty death. The rulers of the world governed by the methods of the world. It behoved Jesus, on the other hand, whose kingdom was not of this world, but which was one of love and not of power, to triumph by different means.

Nonetheless it was a great temptation. His own people, the Jews, longed for the coming of the Messiah who would lead them to victory over their oppressors. They looked to see in such a deliverer a power greater, more sensational, more dramatic, than anything possessed even by Rome itself. By far the most direct solution to the problem facing Jesus—the problem of how to gain the ear of his own people in order that, beginning with them, he might preach the Gospel of the Kingdom—was to appear before them as a great national liberator, a leader who would focus upon himself all the loyalties of nationalistic enthusiasm. Indeed, he was to find, throughout his ministry, how often men would expect him to be that very thing. They would turn from him in bitter disappointment when they found that he was not. Thus in rejecting this third temptation to give him dominion over the powers of this world, he was letting himself follow to the bitter end the way of self-subjection leading inevitably to the Cross.

He answered without hesitation:

"Get thee hence, Satan; for it is written"—and here he drew again upon the Book of Deuteronomy—" 'Thou shalt worship the Lord thy God, and Him only shalt thou serve.' "

It was a final answer. It was the answer with which Jesus put aside the temptation of building an empire of this world. After that, knowing himself to be defeated, Satan withdrew from Jesus for a time, leaving Jesus, this solitary inner struggle in the desert over, to go down again into the world of men.

The Man who left Everything

Based on Vivarini's

SAINT MATTHEW

ON a morning of strong sunlight a man called Matthew, or Levi, emerged from the doorway of his house in Capernaum and set off for his place of business. The narrow street smelt of fish, a smell which the heat of day would bring out increasingly. Fish heads and offal lay here and there in the roadway, and the flies were already getting busy on them. Matthew walked hurriedly, with short steps, and a little bent forward. His shadow, blackly bobbing along the wall of the buildings on the side of the street, accompanied him as he went. The shadow, that of a portly little man, was, like so much else associated with this individual, faintly ridiculous.

There were at least three reasons why Matthew felt this was not one of his best mornings. First, he was going to work. The day lay before him: another day of sitting at the receipt of custom by the lakeside and collecting dues from those who crossed over the frontier at that point. Second, he was not feeling too well. As he progressed into middle life, and put on weight, and ate and drank too much, this often happened. Third, he felt himself out of touch with events which, having taken place recently in the vicinity, had stirred everyone. Matthew knew he was out of touch because his despised trade of publican made of him one whom his fellow Jews did not take into their confidence.

But he had heard of the doings in the district in recent days of Jesus of Nazareth.

There had been, for instance, the case of the leper up in Galilee, a man marked with the scrofulous skin disease which, common throughout the country, went under the general name of leprosy. This man, it was reported, had gone up to Jesus and, kneeling down before him, had said: "If though wilt, thou canst make me clean." The man from Nazareth had but stretched forth his hand, touched him, and said: "I will; be thou made clean." Many, it appeared, had been witnesses of the fact that immediately the hideous eruptions of the man's skin had cleared away. The erstwhile leper had himself spread the news, talking excitedly about what had happened to him. The stir had been so great that Jesus found it impossible to avoid the crowds which henceforth had been awaiting him in every populated place. As a consequence, he and the men with him had tended to spend much of their time out in the open country.

And then, too, there had been the astonishing miracle of the centurion's servant. As Matthew made his way through Capernaum that morning he soon came in sight of a certain imposing building with the erection of which this same centurion had had much to do. It was the synagogue, built of white limestone, and the pride of Capernaum. Matthew, as a Jew himself, knew about this Roman, and of the high regard in which he was held by the best elements in the town. An old soldier, he had, very unusually for his kind, made himself friendly and helpful to the local people. It was he who had helped build the synagogue, and it was this fact which had led directly to the miracle which Jesus of Nazareth had worked upon the soldier's servant.

The servant had been very ill indeed. And hearing of this, and knowing the man was dear to his employer, the elders of the Jews had gone to Jesus and had made a request to him that he should save him. Jesus had listened to their tale, heard their praise of the centurion, and had gone with them toward the house of the Roman.

Now it appeared that Jesus, with the elders, had been met on their journey by certain friends of the centurion who had brought with them a message from him. It had been in these words: "Lord, trouble not thyself, for I am not worthy that thou shouldst come under my roof: Wherefore neither thought I myself worthy to come unto thee: but say the word, and my servant shall be helped. For I also am a man set under authority, having under myself soldiers; and I say to this one, Go, and he goeth; and to another, Come, and he cometh; and to my servant, Do this, and he doeth it."

When Jesus heard this he had turned to those with him and had said: "I say unto you I have not found so great faith, no, not in Israel." Soon afterward, when the friends of the centurion had returned to the house, they had found the servant fully recovered.

Nor was this all. Among the many other stories of the doings of this wonder-working Rabbi which Matthew had heard had been the strange case of the mother-in-law of Simon. She had been sick of a fever. After leaving the synagogue in Capernaum Jesus had gone with James and John to the house of Simon and Andrew. On the way they had told him of the woman's illness, thus explaining in advance why she would not be able to help with hospitality. There had been a big gathering in the house that evening, so that many had been witnesses of what had happened.

In the telling, it sounded quite simple; Jesus had merely gone to her, taken her by the hand, and raised her up. The extraordinary thing was that the fever had promptly left her and she had been able to rise and help with the service of the meal. Yet Simon's wife's mother had been, like the centurion's servant, really ill. Those present had seen for themselves beyond a doubt how she had lain shaking and sweating in acute distress. And these same people had been witnesses of her total recovery.

Then again—and this had probably caused more talk than anything else—there had been the awesome incident in the synagogue itself just before this healing of Simon's wife's mother. When it had come to the turn of Jesus to be called upon, according to custom, by the Ruler of the Synagogue, to read and then expound a portion of Scripture he, standing upon the dais before all the congregation, had spoken—just as it was said he had done in his own local synagogue at Nazareth— with such authority that all those present had been amazed.

To listen to him, people said, was not a bit like hearing one of the Scribes, whose detailed exposition of which was more often marked by pedantry than passion. It was as though a new, invigorating understanding were blowing like the wind of the Spirit through the musty pages of old things, making them wholly new.

Among the congregation of the synagogue at Capernaum had been a man upon whom this had worked with peculiar force. He was a distorted kind of individual, said to be possessed of an unclean spirit. Suddenly, appalling everyone present, he had shouted out: "What have we to do with thee, thou Jesus of Nazareth? Art thou come to destroy us?"

Those round him had tried to restrain the man. But with many jerkings of his body, he had raved on: "I know thee who thou art, the Holy One of God!"

Jesus had rebuked him, saying: "Hold thy peace and come out of him." That very thing had immediately happened. The unclean spirit, tearing him and crying with a loud voice, came out of him. But the incident had been enough to break up the gathering. Pouring out into the roadway the people, excitedly talking among themselves, had said things like: "What is this? A new teaching! With authority he commandeth even the unclean spirits and they obey him!"

All these things and others Matthew was pondering as he made his way to his place of work that morning. Capernaum was a frontier town, the meeting place of trade routes from Hauran on the east and Phoenicia on the west. Caravans coming down the highway from Damascus and making for the Mediterranean ports also converged on the place. Hot, busy and commercial, it was an important centre for the collection of customs dues. Among the minor officials who collected these taxes were the publicans. They were hated and despised. And Matthew, as he was constantly and daily made aware, was one of them.

A very particular kind of odium attached to the whole class of publicans, going much deeper than the general unpopularity of the tax-gatherer the world over. The hatred—and it is not too strong a word—stemmed from the fact that the publican served the interests of foreign masters, collecting moneys for Rome as well as for Rome's creatures, the Tetrarchs. Against the power of Rome, of whose world-spanning Empire their land formed only an insignificant part, the Jews opposed an unrelenting pride of race and religion, considering themselves, not without cause, to be the intellectual and spiritual superiors of their temporal masters.

It followed therefore that anyone who served the enemy, in however humble a capacity, stood necessarily condemned as base. And though it was true that the publicans on the whole operated only on a minor scale, yet it was certainly true that their general standard of honesty was not high. Not all the taxes they collected reached the purses of their masters. Some went to swell their own. And the size of the house which Matthew was able to maintain in Capernaum was testimony to the fact that his purse was no exception.

But the publican was despised for quite other reasons. Because his work took him into daily contact with the heathen, that is to say, with many not of his own race, he was, in terms of the Law, in a state of defilement, soiled by his professional contacts beyond hope of redemption. He was an untouchable, and treated accordingly.

Nor was it only the Pharisees and the Scribes who regarded him thus: the common people also looked down upon him, seeing in him the ignoble exactor of taxes which they considered unjust. So, although there was a living, and quite a good one, to be had out of being a publican, there was not much of a happy life to be gained thereby. The publican was generally driven for his society to the less desirable members of the community; the vulgar, the doubtful, and the shady.

It was not a long walk for Matthew that morning from his house to his place of business by the busy lakeside. At the top of a flight of stone steps leading up from the water to the wharf was a table under an awning. As he sat behind this table he was conveniently placed to intercept fisher-folk coming up from their boats moored below with their catches. Often at busy times there would be a guard nearby to back up by a show of force the due collection of money.

Everyone in that close-knit community knew Matthew the publican, regarding him with a mixture of contempt and amusement. It had long been known that, unusually for a publican, he was sensitive to sarcastic remarks about his work. "There you are," the bronzed fishermen would say, throwing down the amount due onto his table, "so much for them"—nodding to the sentry—"and so much for you." And quite often they would see him wince, muttering something into his black beard and hunching himself a little further forward as if in self-defence.

Matthew was not a happy man. He had always been a publican; but often as the years passed there had stirred within him aspirations after higher and better things. The iron weight of habit kept him where he was; yet it was often as though the spirit within him fluttered its wings against the bars of circumstance. To be something different, something nobler, to discover in life, before it was too late, a nobler destiny; above all, to find inner peace, had been the essence of the unformed thoughts which had for long moved within him. He did not know, that morning, that a destiny beyond imagination splendid was on its way toward him.

It came in the form of the single mast of a fishing boat approaching across the Lake. He saw its curved sail hauled down near the jetty, and then all but the tip of the mast was hidden from him as the craft drew in to the wall. A crowd began to gather at the head of the steps, as though the new arrival were noteworthy. Matthew would have liked to go forward with the rest and peer over into the boat to see what was going on. But he knew he would not be welcomed. Besides, there was the money on his table to keep an eye on. So he stayed where he was, looking upon the backs of the crowd. Soon the people began to give way, forming an opening through which the newcomers could reach the wharf.

Matthew recognized the first ones easily. They were Galilean fishermen, James and John, Simon and Andrew; he had seen them many a time. But behind them, last to ascend the steps, was a tall, dark, youngish-looking man. As he stepped forward into the crowd he smiled upon them, and a murmur of admiration and curiosity went up. Matthew knew then who it was: the marvelous Rabbi of whom so many things were being said.

The publican looked upon him with curiosity. He was certainly a striking-looking person, a man of kingly grace. For some curious reason which he could not for the life of him fathom, Matthew hoped that this man would not notice him, the publican, sitting there behind his piles of money.

But Jesus did notice him. It happened in a flash; the other Galileans who had come out of the boat had drawn a little ahead and, as Jesus turned to follow them, his eye was caught by the little man behind the table. With three strides he was before it and had stopped and was looking down. The eyes of the two of them met over the money; met and looked into each other for a long, long time. Then Jesus spoke, two simple words:

"Follow me."

It was as simple as that. But Matthew knew in a moment of truth that here, in

XII. CHRIST AMONG THE DOCTORS

And it came to pass, that after three days they found him in the temple, sitting in the midst of the doctors, both hearing them, and asking them questions. And all that heard him were astonished at his understanding and answers. Luke 2, 46-47.

By Ribera (1589-1652)

Photo Meyer

some strange way, was the answer to all his inner longings. Here, inexplicably offered, was the opportunity of a new life. What would be meant by following this man, where it would take him to, and what he would have to become, he did not know. He knew only that the years of self-dissatisfaction were over; the past was dead; the future was living.

Without at all knowing why, but filled with the urge to obey, he stood up suddenly and went round to the other side of the table, and stood face to face with the man who had so thrillingly summoned him. The other overtopped him by a good foot. As the people around stared, and as some began to laugh, Jesus laid his hand upon the shoulder of Matthew and gently urged him forward. Together they went on, leaving behind for ever the table with its money and its staring, nonplussed sentry.

That evening, in the house of Matthew the publican, there was a supper held the like of which the place had never seen before. So great was the excitement that people stood in the very doorway to watch. For Jesus, to the mingled joy and trepidation of the publican, had said that he, with his friends, would sup there.

Matthew had been anxious as to how his usual associates would behave themselves. But he need not have worried; Jesus put them all at their ease. The wine flowed and the meal was enjoyed in the utmost good fellowship. It was a marvelous evening; the first of Matthew's new life. Only one thing marred it.

Certain of the Scribes and Pharisees, anxious to know about this Man from Nazareth had come down into Galilee to see for themselves. They were appalled to know that he had invited himself to the house of a publican. They could scarcely believe it. They came to see for themselves, pushing through the crowd at the door. The talk died away as these impressive men came to the front.

Ignoring the rest of the company, and looking directly at Jesus, one of the Pharisees asked:

"Why do ye eat and drink with the publicans and sinners?"

Calmly, Jesus answered:

"They that are whole have no need of a physician, but they that are sick. I am not come to call the righteous but sinners to repentance."

Still they pressed the matter.

"The disciples of John fast often," another of them said, "and make supplication; likewise also the disciples of the Pharisees; but thine eat and drink."

"Can ye make the sons of the bridechamber fast, while the bridegroom is with them?" Jesus said. Briefly he added, while all the company listened quietly: "But the days will come, when the bridegroom shall be taken away from them, then will they fast in those days."

There was a man sitting near him, one of the rather shabby friends of Matthew, who chanced to be wearing a much patched cloak. Touching this cloak, Jesus said:

"No man rendeth a piece from a new garment and putteth it upon an old garment; else he will rend the new, and also the piece from the new will not agree with the old."

Then, pressing home his point with another illustration, he gestured toward a wine skin lying in a corner of the room, "And no man putteth new wine into old wine skins; else the new wine will burst the skins, and itself will be spilled, and the skins will perish. But new wine must be put into fresh wine skins."

B.M.G.—H

Matthew understood that part of what the Master was saying, at least. The novel doctrine which Jesus taught replaced obedience to the Law with obedience to the Law of Love. It was something in itself so new that no old and traditional forms could hold it. It demanded a new start in every respect. To attempt to include the new Gospel within the framework of the old Mosaic Law would be as hopeless an undertaking as patching the worn-out garment with new material, or as the pouring in of new wine into old containers.

Yet there was, too, a personal interpretation which, that evening, came home much more closely to Matthew. For he understood, because he had that morning upon the quayside experienced it himself, that to follow Jesus in obedience meant dropping everything in one's own old life, its predilections, its habits, its prejudices, its likes and dislikes. It meant starting gloriously all over again. He understood, because he had done that very thing himself.

XIII. TEMPTED OF THE DEVIL

And when the tempter came to him, he said, If thou be the Son of God, command that these stones be made bread. But he answered and said, It is written, Man shall not live by bread alone, but by every word that proceedeth out of the mouth of God. Matthew 4, 3-4.

By Tintoretto (1518-1594)

Photo Giacomelli

Water into Wine

Based on David's

THE MARRIAGE IN CANA

THE bride sat demure and silent, as it was fitting she should. She had been carried to her husband's house in a chair and had exchanged the traditional promises with her husband beneath the bridal veil. That accomplished, the festivities had begun, destined to last several days in accordance with Jewish custom. As she looked shyly about the room she saw with pleasure that things had got off to a good start; the wine was flowing, the men-folk, reclining about the table each on an elbow, were settling down to enjoy themselves.

It was a big wedding, this one in Cana of Galilee, for the bride's and bridegroom's parents were well-off folk, prosperous enough to be able to afford a Governor of the Feast, or Master of Ceremonies. It was also a big company, so numerous that as many as six water-pots, containing two or three firkins apiece, had been necessary at the doorway to provide water for the ceremonial purifying of the guests. The water-pots now stood empty, their contents having been used before the wedding feast began.

The place, Cana, was 1,600 feet up in the hills some six miles from Nazareth. The guests were for the most part local, friends of the bride's parents and her husband's. With a glance round the table she was able to recognize several. There was Philip, for instance, from Bethsaida, down below by the Lake of Galilee. There was his friend Nathanael, who belonged to Cana itself. There was also the imposing-looking man who had come with them, Jesus from Nazareth, the son of the carpenter there. The bride did not know him; but she did know Mary, his mother, who, in company with the other women-folk, was helping with the service of the meal.

The deep voices of the men filled the cheerful room. The bride, so newly emerged from girlhood, enjoyed noticing how the men's teeth flashed between the full lips surrounded by the dark beards as, throwing back their heads, they laughed out loud at some sally. What she did not know, and was never to know, was that this wedding feast of hers up there in the Galilean hills, was destined to become the most famous wedding feast in history because of something which happened there.

It was several hours later when it came to pass. The Galilean wine, fermented from grapes grown in the vineyards round about, had flowed freely, according to custom. But now, among the women-folk helping with the service in the background, there had arisen a domestic crisis. The wine had run out. The women, while doing their best to conceal the catastrophe out of loyalty to the bride and bridegroom's people, were troubled to think whatever they would do when the Governor of the Feast should clap his hands together and cry out for more wine.

But Mary, the mother of Jesus, had an idea. She had grown used, as the years had passed, to seeking the advice of this immensely capable son of hers. It was with her as with her husband Joseph, who had developed the same habit of turning to Jesus even in the little matters pertaining to his carpenter's work. Mary, for her part, never hesitated to go to him on small details of domestic management.

It was therefore natural for Mary to take this particular concern to her son. She went to him where he was reclining among the guests and, stooping down, whispered in his ear: "They have no wine."

All around them the loud merry talk rose and fell. Jesus looked up at his mother. Then he said:

"Woman, what have I to do with thee? Mine hour is not yet come."

The words neither surprised nor disconcerted the mother of Jesus. Abrupt to modern ears, to her they came perfectly naturally. That he addressed her as "Woman"—he was to do the same thing later on from the Cross itself—betokened no disrespect whatever. On the contrary, it was an honourable title, hallowed by ancient usage. Similarly, "What have I to do with thee?" rather implied, "What is a little thing like that to you and me?" or "Why bother me with this?", as though she well knew that so comparatively small a matter lay easily within his compass to put right.

At any rate, as a mother, she knew her son. A smile of understanding passed between them. Quietly withdrawing, she said to the servants as she passed from the room: "Whatsoever he sayeth unto you, do it."

A little longer Jesus stayed where he was, then, rising from his place, and in his turn going to the door, he said to the servants:

"Fill the water-pots with water."

They stared at him for a moment; but there was authority in his look. Going to where the six empty stone water-pots stood at the entry of the house, they filled them to the brim, watched meanwhile by Jesus. That done, they looked at him again as though to wait further orders. He said only:

"Draw out now, and bear to the Ruler of the Feast."

The Master of Ceremonies had been about to call for wine. He was all the more glad to see the servants entering with what he took to be a fresh supply. When they had set a vessel of it before him he, as good manners required, tasted it before nodding his agreement that it should be passed round. The servants, who but a moment or so before had poured in water, now saw, when the Governor of the Feast tilted the vessel to pour a little into his own cup, that the familiar red Galilean vintage flowed out. *The water had become wine.*

The Governor of the Feast sipped, then let a smile of surprise cross over his face. This was really good. It was better than the wine they had been having. Jovially, from where he was at the foot of the table he called up the length of it towards the bridegroom sitting at the head with his silent bride beside him.

"Every man setteth on first the good wine," he called out, "and when men have drunk freely then that which is worse; thou has kept the good wine until now."

He was referring to the common usage among these homely folk of serving the best first and, when sensibilities had been somewhat lessened, of following it with a cheaper wine.

Neither he nor the bridegroom nor anyone else among the guests around the table except Philip and Nathanael knew the origin of this new vintage which he had just tasted. But the servants knew, because they had seen the command of Jesus carried out. And Philip and Nathanael, the Lord's disciples, knew because they had been on either side of him when Mary his mother had come forward and whispered, "They have no wine."

For them the miracle had a special meaning: it was a startling manifestation of the Lord's power underlining the authority with which he had called them to his service two days before.

The writer of the Gospel of St John, who tells the story of the Marriage at Cana in his second chapter, has, immediately before it, his account of how Jesus had called Andrew, and Simon Peter. On the day after that he had encountered Philip and called him, also. Philip in his turn had spoken of Jesus to his friend Nathanael, saying unto him, "We have found him of whom Moses and the Law and the Prophets did write, Jesus of Nazareth, the son of Joseph."

Nathanael at first had been sceptical; but Philip had persuaded him to go and see this Jesus for himself. And, as Jesus had seen Nathanael approaching, he had said to those about him, "Behold an Israelite indeed in whom is no guile." Nathanael, overhearing this, had asked: "Whence knowest thou me?" To which the answer of Jesus had been: "Before Philip called thee, when thou wast under the fig tree, I saw thee."

He meant that he had known of the inner thoughts of Nathanael in all those moments of meditation and self-communion during which the thoughtful Nathanael, sitting apart in silence under the shade of the tree, had mused of God and man. The mysterious words implied that he who thus told Nathanael that he had seen him under the fig tree, was the very God of whom Nathanael had been thinking. The disciple-to-be had joyfully recognized this when he had answered: "Rabbi, thou art the Son of God; thou art the King of Israel." To which Jesus had made reply: "Because I said unto thee, I saw thee beneath the fig tree, believest thou? Thou shalt see greater things than these. Verily, verily, I say unto you, ye shall see the heavens opened, and the angels of God ascending and descending upon the Son of Man."

And now here was this miracle at Cana. To Philip and Nathanael it was full of significance. They remembered how it was written in the Scriptures, in the Second Book of the Kings, that the prophet Elisha had filled with oil the vessels in the house of the widow and how she had been enabled to settle her debts by selling the oil. Yet here was one greater than any prophet performing a miracle strangely reminiscent of this ancient one.

And besides, had not Moses turned the water into blood at the commencement of his work? These things thought Philip and Nathanael, understanding through them something of the power and authority of He who had called them.

Yet there was more meaning still in the miracle even than that which Philip and Nathanael at the time perceived. As the water originally in the water-pots had been used for the ceremonial purification according to the ancient Law, and as this had been replaced by a new wine, so the old Law of Judaism was to be replaced by the new wine of the Gospel of Jesus Christ. Here, in fact, was a symbolical miracle which, because of its vast importance, the writer of the Gospel of St John placed at the very outset of his work.

"This beginning of his sign did Jesus in Cana of Galilee," says the same writer, "and manifested his glory; and his disciples believed on him."

He fell among Thieves

Based on Bassano's

THE GOOD SAMARITAN

THERE was a stretch of road between Jerusalem and Jericho where bad things happened too often. It was the easiest thing in the world for a man to get his throat cut along that solitary way. Even in appearance the route was dramatic and daunting. For most of its thirty-odd miles it wound precipitately downhill, dropping more than 3,000 feet, from Jerusalem on the heights to Jericho, 800 feet below sea level. Stony all the way, it corkscrewed among naked hills and great boulders, each one of them, in the mind of anyone who traveled alone, posing the question as to whether there were someone behind it, waiting. The mid-part of the way, especially, was the favorite lurking ground of robbers who made a speciality of quick, ruthless attacks upon passers-by. They could pounce from behind a rock, fell a man with a cudgel blow on the head, or drag him from his ass with a knife in his back; rob him, strip him and be off up the ravine among the hills long before anything could be done about it.

The best thing to do, therefore, on the way between Jerusalem and Jericho was either to travel in company or to travel fast. There was an ancient inn, or caravanserai, some way along, and most travelers when they reached it were more than glad to see the place, and all were even gladder when the next stage of the journey was done.

Yet this savage road careering down the contours between sinister hills was the setting of one of the great parables of God's love which Jesus told. It happened in this way.

One day, when he was around Jerusalem, a lawyer put to him a question.

"Master," he asked, "what shall I do to inherit eternal life?"

It was a leading question because inherent in it was a greater—which is the greatest commandment? Many theologians among the Jews had debated this. If all the Mosaic Law was of equal importance and binding force, could it be said that any one part of it was of more importance than the rest?

The man who put this question to Jesus was himself a Teacher of the Law, an expert in such matters. Well aware of this, Jesus answered him in his own vein.

"What is written in the Law? How readest thou?" he asked in his turn.

The Teacher of the Law responded immediately, as Jesus had known he would, with a quotation from the Law itself:

"Thou shalt love the Lord thy God with all thy heart, with all thy soul, and with all thy strength, and with all thy mind; and thy neighbor as thyself."

"Thou hast answered right," Jesus said gravely. "This do, and thou shalt live."

But there was yet a further question to be faced. In the Book of Leviticus in the nineteenth chapter, it was laid down that, "Thou shalt not hate thy brother in thy

XIV. SAINT MATTHEW

And as Jesus passed forth from thence, he saw a man, named Matthew, sitting at the receipt of custom: and he saith unto him, Follow me. And he arose, and followed him. Matthew 9, 9.

By Alvise Vivarini (c.1446-1505)

Photo Giacomelli

heart: thou shalt surely rebuke thy neighbor, and not bear sin because of him. Thou shalt not take vengeance, nor bear any grudge against the children of thy people, but thou shalt love thy neighbor as thyself."

The Teacher of the Law, therefore, came to the heart of the matter when he went on to ask:

"And who is my neighbor?"

He knew the answer as it was given in the Law, because there the word "neighbor" meant "fellow-citizen", in other words, any other Jew. It did not mean anyone of any other race.

Jesus looked upon his questioner thoughtfully for a moment, then leant forward in a way which, to the watching and listening disciples, was characteristic of him when he was about to tell a story.

"A certain man," he began, "was going down from Jerusalem to Jericho——"

The road with which they were all familiar came immediately to their minds. They saw the naked hills, they heard the chatter of the stream which ran at the foot of the gorges, and they felt in retrospect the fear which they had all known as travelers along the way. So they were not surprised when Jesus went on:

"He fell among robbers which both stripped him and beat him, and departed, leaving him half dead."

This was a grimly familiar picture. In their mind's eye the listeners saw the traveler, a tiny figure dwarfed in scale against the backcloth of mountain. The ass he was riding picked her way delicately among the stones on the steep incline, rump in the air, forelegs splayed as she steadied herself against the downward pull. The scrabbling sound of her feet on the loose surface came loud against the silence.

They saw in imagination the swirl of the dirty robes, the lithe muscular figures which sprang from behind the boulder. They saw the brown arms pulling the traveler from the back of his animal; they saw the hands go over his mouth; they heard the grunt as the cudgel cracked on the skull. And then they saw him sprawled in the dirt, breathing hard through his mouth, while the robbers busied themselves about him, ransacking his saddle-bag, emptying his wallet before throwing it contemptuously down the hillside, then stripping the man himself down to his loin cloth.

Jesus continued:

"And by chance a certain priest was going down that way——"

Here was a thoroughly familiar mental image for the listeners, too. The priest would be one, most likely, from the staff of the Temple in Jerusalem who, having business in Jericho, would have to risk the road. They saw him riding, like the first traveler, on an ass which, as always, looked absurdly small in comparison with the bulky figure on her back.

This animal picked her way carefully also, but even so her rider urged her on now and then by jabs of his sandaled heels. Steep and difficult as the way might be, he was as anxious as any other traveler to press on to the safety of the inn beyond.

He pulled his ass abruptly to a halt, the bit sawing her mouth, as he spied, some distance further down the road, a saddled ass with empty stirrups standing patient by the wayside. The priest knew what that meant. Muttering within his beard he looked up; looking behind and before; there was not a soul to be seen. He touched his own animal with his heels again and moved cautiously forward.

The solitary animal standing by the roadside turned her head to look mildly upon them as the priest on his own ass drew near. He noticed the rifled saddle-bags. And then he saw something else.

There were two naked feet, soles toward him, protruding from behind a house-sized rock on his right. The rest of the body lay in the black shadow on the further side.

Two fears surged to the surface of the priest's mind. The first was the fear of defilement. If that which lay there were a corpse, he as a priest would be in danger of ceremonial uncleanness if he approached nearer or touched it in any way. The second fear was a purely human one lest that which had happened to the man lying yonder should also happen to him. So, without any further examination of the situation, he jerked the head of his ass away, dug his heels into her sides, and clattered downhill and away as fast as he could make it. Silence descended once more upon the valley and the road.

Jesus went on, speaking of this action of the priest's, "He passed by on the other side."

The Master went on with the story:

"And in like manner a Levite also, when he came to the place and saw him, passed by on the other side."

Once again, in their mind's eye, the listeners saw the scene enacted; the mounted figure coming down the corkscrewing road from above, the startled noticing of the abandoned ass, the sight of the body, betrayed by its protruding feet, and then the scared hurrying away. They noted especially that the two travelers who thus passed by on the other side were both of the priestly caste.

"But a certain Samaritan," Jesus continued, "as he journeyed came where he was: and when he saw him he was moved with compassion, and came to him and bound up his wounds, pouring on them oil and wine."

A sigh of amazement passed over the company. The Samaritans were the traditional enemies of the Jews, for deep and ancient reasons. It was therefore amazing that the Lord should thus bring a Samaritan into his story, and even more so that he should present him as showing compassion where the priest and the Levite had failed to do so.

Nonetheless, there it was, and they saw in imagination this third traveler coming down the road. When he came abreast of the tragic scene by the boulder, he immediately dismounted and, with no thought of his own safety, went round the rock and knelt down by the prostrate figure.

It could be seen at a glance that the man was in a bad way. There was clotted blood at the back of his head, as the Samaritan saw when he moved him a little. At the disturbance the flies which had settled on the wound rose, buzzing. If the robbers had not for purposes of concealment dragged him into the shade it was, as the Samaritan well knew, most likely that by this time he would have died.

He hurried round the rock back into the road again to rummage in his saddle-bags for the oil and the wine which he carried there. This also the listeners to Jesus knew well, since oil and wine were the customary remedies used in the dressing of wounds. Returning to the victim on the other side of the rock, he poured on the fluids. The man opened his eyes. At first there was terror in them. But as they took in the kindly countenance looking down, they cleared.

XV. THE MARRIAGE IN CANA

And the third day there was a marriage in Cana of Galilee; and the mother of Jesus was there: And both Jesus was called, and his disciples, to the marriage. John 2, 1-2.

By Gerard David (1460 ?-1523)

Photo Vizzavona

It was not long before the man was strong enough to be assisted out into the roadway. But here a difficulty arose. The man's own ass, which for so long had stood patiently waiting, had now, with the unpredictability of its kind, strayed far down the hillside. The Samaritan could see at a glance that, encumbered as he was with the man he had assisted, the animal was well beyond his reach. So he set the sagging figure on his own beast and, walking beside him, and supporting him round the waist with one arm, conducted him along the rocky road. Several miles further on, at a turning in the gorge, they came to the inn.

Scarcely a single one of those listening to Jesus, as he told his story, had not personally passed by that caravanserai. It was thus easy for them in imagination to conjure up for themselves a memory of the arched entry into its courtyard, and of the dusty, open space therein, with a well in the middle and the guest rooms round about. They saw the Samaritan enter in under the arch and call for assistance. They saw the people of the inn come forward, with expressions of concern and indignation.

They saw all this, as Jesus, continuing with his story, said:

"He set him on his own beast and brought him to an inn and took care of him."

Anxiously, tenderly, all night the Samaritan stayed by the side of the man whom he had succored, listening to his mutterings in his sleep. He was still awake when dawn came. It was the morrow, and it behoved him, the Samaritan, to be on his way.

But the wounded man was not yet in a state to be moved. So the Samaritan summoned the keeper of the inn, paid him in advance enough for several nights' lodging.

"And on the morrow," Jesus said, "he took out two pence and gave them to the host, and said, 'Take care of him; and whatsoever thou spendest more, I, when I come back again, will repay thee!'"

Now Jesus, ending his story, looked at the Teacher of the Law and put to him the final, penetrating query:

"Which of these three, thinkest thou, proved neighbor unto him that fell among the robbers?"

The lawyer replied, because he could do no other:

"He that showed mercy upon him."

Quietly Jesus said:

"Go, and do thou likewise."

Episode at the Well

Based on de Flandres'

CHRIST AND THE WOMAN OF SAMARIA

AROUND noon on a hot day a woman came out of the village of Sychar, and made her way toward the well some half a mile away. Round her waist was coiled a long rope and on her head she balanced a water-pot, steadying it with one hand against the side of the vessel as she walked. There were few people about; the country shimmered in the heat, streams ran low in their courses. Naked mountains rose on either hand. A Roman road ran beneath them, east to west, crossing that which went south to north from Jerusalem up into Galilee.

The woman was halfway between the village and the well when she saw approaching a group of men. Her eyes, bold and not at all shy, hardened as the group came close enough to be identified. Unmistakably, they were Jews; she could see it in their looks and she could recognize it in their speech. What they were doing there, in that hostile country of the Samaritans, she could not imagine. Jews did not often pass that way. There was no welcome for them if they did. For the Samaritans loathed the Jews, and the feeling was returned with interest. So the Samaritan woman, for such she was, turned her eyes carefully away as the group passed, and they, in their turn, fell silent.

But as they drew away from her, she fell to wondering again. What could they be doing there? The feud between her people and the Jews was old, very old indeed, reaching far back into the history of the two peoples.

Centuries and centuries ago, after the death of King Solomon, the country of the Jews had been divided into two kingdoms, Judah and Israel. Profound differences arose between the two, the northern kingdom, in the eyes of the south, adopting idolatrous ways. Thereafter, as the storms of history broke upon northern and southern kingdoms, the differences widened rather than grew less. And when, after the Exile, the remnants of Judah returned to gather up the fragments of their national and spiritual life, they kept themselves rigidly separate from the Samaritans, in whom they saw all the evils of continuing false belief. On their side, the Samaritans had no love for the Jews. The sanctuary of the Most High, which they had built on Mount Gerizim—which to them was as sacred as Jerusalem to the Jews—typified the unhealed and unhealable division between the two peoples.

To the woman of Samaria going out to the well that afternoon the dry facts of history meant little. But the living facts of her own day meant much. The Jews were enemies; their presence in Samaria was as unusual as it was unwelcome.

There were trees about the well to which she was going. It was a famous well, and very old, having been dug by Jacob seventeen hundred years ago for the watering of his flock. He in his turn had given it and the surrounding land to Joseph, whose tomb stood adjacent.

It startled the woman of Samaria to see the figure of a man sitting under the trees. He was reclining in the attitude of one who, being very weary, had lain thankfully down to rest. He was a youngish man, and he seemed to watch her as she drew nearer.

At the brink of the well, without any word, for it would have been unseemly in her to speak first, she moved the jar from her head and began to unwind the rope from about her waist, the rope which she had brought for the purpose of lowering down the vessel into the dark depths of the shaft. Then the man spoke:

"Give me to drink."

The woman swept him with her eyes, noting his dress, which was simple, and his manner, which seemed benign and somehow authoritative, both at the same time. Without answering for the moment she lowered her jar on the end of the rope down the well. When she heard the splash of its contact with the water far below, and the tug on the rope as the vessel began to fill, she turned herself about, still holding with both hands on to the rope over the parapet, and asked:

"How is it that thou, being a Jew, askest drink of me, which am a Samaritan woman?"

His reply was most strange.

"If thou knewest the Gift of God, and who it is that saith to thee, give me to drink, thou wouldst have asked of him, and he would have given thee living water."

The woman felt a stir of unease. It was after such a manner that the Prophets and holy men spoke.

Yet, being a plain factually-minded kind of person, she sought round first for some commonplace explanation of what he had said. He had talked of water, but she could see no receptacle for it in his possession, nor any sign that he was concerned with procuring one. So she asked:

"Sir, thou hast nothing to draw with, and the well is deep; from whence then hast thou that living water?"

Beginning now to draw up the rope, she continued, not without a touch of irony:

"Art thou greater than our father Jacob which gave us the well and drank thereof himself and his sons and his cattle?"

"Everyone that drinketh of this water shall thirst again," came the mysterious answer. "But whosoever drinketh of the water that I shall give him shall never thirst; but the water that I shall give him shall become in him a well of water springing up to eternal life."

This was as impressive as it was puzzling. The sense of being in the presence of something quite incalculable stirred again in the woman of Samaria. Though she knew that the very fact of talking with a strange man in a deserted place, especially with a Jew, was utterly against custom, she felt somehow compelled to go on.

The muscles of her strong, brown, housewife's arms tensed. Hand over hand, she drew up the jar on the end of its rope, brought it up brimming, and steadied it upon the parapet. Then, brushing back a lock of hair which the exertion had caused to fall forward on to her forehead, she said, half jocularly, half uneasily:

"Sir, give me this water that I thirst not, neither come all the way hither to draw."

As if he had guessed her thought about the irregularity of thus speaking with a strange man in the absence of any men-folk of her own, he said:

"Go, call thy husband, and come hither."

The woman found herself held by the singular intensity of his scrutiny. It was as though he was looking through her, seeing in some extraordinary manner her secret thoughts. In the apparently innocuous remark about her husband, he had touched her to the quick, for the fact was that she was living with a man, but was not married.

Generally, it was a matter she would have kept secret; but now, she felt oddly compelled to let out the truth.

"I have no husband."

She rubbed her wet hands on the sides of her dress to dry them, betraying in the movement the nervous agitation which was gripping her. It was not exactly fear, for this stranger did not inspire fear: rather it was an odd and unfamiliar embarrassment, an emotion which, such had been the life she had led for a long time, was something she had scarce experienced since girlhood.

The stranger's gaze never wavered at all.

"Thou saidst well," he said evenly, " 'I have no husband', for thou hast had five husbands; and he whom thou now hast is not thy husband; this hast thou said truly."

It was true. Yet how could he possibly have known? The woman recognized immediately the only explanation.

"Sir, I perceive that thou art a prophet."

Then, remembering that she was a Samaritan and he a Jew, and feeling within herself the ancient difference that was between them, she went on, now that the talk had moved on to religious ground:

"Our fathers worshiped in this mountain and ye say that in Jerusalem is the place where men ought to worship."

The stranger moved over to the parapet of the well beside her and leant forward to look reflectively down into the depths.

"Ye worship that which ye know not," he murmured. "We worship that which we know: for salvation is from the Jews."

He looked up, across the mouth of the well and into the distance beyond where, outside the chain of trees, the sun beat down upon the parched earth.

"But the hour cometh, and now is, when the true worshippers shall worship the Father in spirit and in truth: for such doth the Father seek to be His worshipers. God is a Spirit; and they that worship Him must worship Him in spirit and in truth."

Because she was so awed, the woman searched among her own simple religious knowledge for something which would match the gravity of his tone. So she said, rather hesitantly:

"I know that Messiah cometh (which is called Christ): when he is come he will declare unto us all things."

With grave, deliberate movement the stranger turned to her. First he straightened from where he had been leaning on the parapet of the well, then turned to face her, then spread out his hands a little on either side of him, palms upwards. The pattern of light and shadow which the sun made striking through the trees overhead dappled his head and shoulders. He spoke.

"I that speak unto thee am he."

They stood looking at each other for an appreciable time; she wide-eyed, with the fingers of one hand to her mouth; he still in the same strangely appealing attitude, half submissive, half kingly. In the long pause the woman of Samaria could hear the grasshoppers creaking and chirping in the fields around.

And then, superimposing itself upon the warm noonday hush, came the sound of voices. It broke the spell. The woman lowered her hand from her mouth and looked out into the sunlight. The stranger beside her relaxed his attitude. Up the road from Sychar was approaching, the woman saw, the same group of Jews whom she had encountered going in the opposite direction.

They were the disciples of Jesus, and they were on the second day of a journey which was taking them northward from Jerusalem into Galilee. It was from Galilee that Jesus had, earlier in the same year, gone to the Holy City for the Passover Feast. There, by his teaching, as well as by the spreading tidings of his mighty works, he had incited the hostility of the priests. There, on a memorable night, he had interviewed in secret Nicodemus, a member of the Sanhedrin itself, and had spoken to him of how a man may be born again. Subsequently, when Jesus with his followers had been preaching the Gospel of the Kingdom of God round the villages of Judea, had come the news of the arrest of John the Baptist. Thereupon, turning north, in order to preach the good news in Galilee where John would no longer be able to do so, the Master had chosen to take the hill road which led through the country of the Samaritans. The alternative—and the more usual route—would have been to take the Jordan valley route. That, however, at such a time of the year as this, would have been stiflingly hot. So there they were, in the unfriendly neighbourhood of the Samaritans, into whose village of Sychar they had been going in order to buy food when the woman had met them on her way to the well. They had all gone in a bunch, leaving the Master to rest, because the reassurance of numbers was worth having in so unfriendly a place. Not without difficulty they had managed to buy a little bread and fruit and were now bringing it back to share it with the Master apart from the folk of the surly village they had just left behind.

The woman watching their approach saw astonishment upon their faces as they realized that the stranger to whom she had been talking had been in conversation with her. Yet, as she was quick to notice, none of them dared to utter the questions which were obviously on their lips. No one demanded of this stranger who was so clearly their Master, "Why speakest thou with her?"

Without a word she left her water-pot where it was, still standing on the parapet of the well, and hurried back through the heat into the village, not pausing until she came to the headman's house. There, sundry of the men-folk of the village were gathered in the heat of the day.

Without ceremony, for she was highly excited, the woman burst in upon them.

"Come!" she cried, "see a man which told me all things that ever I did."

The wild thought that had been in her mind ever since Jesus had made his declaration now came from her lips:

"Can this be the Christ?"

The men scrambled up and followed her out into the heat toward the well among the trees.

Meanwhile in that place, the disciples, having prepared the food they had brought, were now offering a portion to the Master.

"Rabbi, eat," one of them was saying, holding out a loaf of bread with a few dates.

But Jesus did not take the food. Instead he spoke to the company gathered there in the shade;

"I have meat to eat that ye know not."

The disciples were astonished. Surely no-one could have brought him some food while they had been away on their errand to the village.

"Hath any man brought him aught to eat?" they asked among themselves.

"My meat is to do the will of Him that sent me, and to accomplish His work," Jesus continued.

Thinking of the Samaritan woman, and all the other peoples of the world who had yet to hear his Gospel, he continued:

"There are yet four months and then cometh the harvest. See not ye this?"

He gestured out toward the cornfields.

"Lift up your eyes and look on the fields that they are white already unto harvest. He that reapeth receiveth wages and gathereth fruit unto life eternal."

This he said thinking of the harvest of human souls which was to be brought to the knowledge of salvation through the preaching of his word. He continued: "He that soweth and he that reapeth may rejoice together. For here is a saying true, one soweth and another reapeth."

He looked slowly round upon all the listening faces.

"I sent you to reap that whereon ye have not labored: others have labored and ye are entered into their labor."

He broke off at the sound of a press of people coming toward the well. It was a crowd of the villagers themselves led by the woman, walking before them and gesticulating as she came. The men who were with her looked curiously upon Jesus as she pointed him out to them.

"He told me all things that ever I did," she kept repeating.

Jesus received them with every courtesy. Then slowly, as he talked with them, the disciples behind him tensely listening, there took place something which had not been seen between Jews and Samaritans since any could remember. The two groups mingled together in common wonderment at the Master whose words came to them with a wisdom and grace which was compelling.

They sat there by the well until, toward evening, the headman of the village came to Jesus with the urgent invitation that he should, with his friends, stay in their village awhile and teach them further. So Jesus abode with them there two days. And when at last he came to depart the villagers turned to the woman and said:

"Now we believe, not because of thy speaking: for we have heard for ourselves and know that this is indeed the Saviour of the world."

Woman of the Town

Based on de la Tour's

MARY MAGDALENE

SIMON the Pharisee, a most respected citizen of Capernaum, stood in the court-yard of his house contemplating the evening. This, the time before the arrival of guests for the supper which he was giving, was an agreeable pause in the business of the day. He did not, however, permit himself any relaxation in the enjoyment of it. His dress, a plain white robe, like his face, was severe. During the day he often wore on his temples the phylacteries, small boxes containing verses of the Law. These were customarily worn by Jews at times of prayer. But by some Pharisees they were worn habitually as a sign of their greater piety.

The Pharisees were an ancient sect, puritanical, plain-living, high-thinking. They were by no means wholly bad; in some ways they were wholly admirable. But they could be called narrow-minded in their extreme aversion to any pagan influence and in their contempt for any whose way of life differed from their own. In Israel they were a minority; but they were a formidable and influential minority. And though their devotion to the faith of their fathers as they interpreted it was praiseworthy, their lack of charity toward the world at large was one of their less attractive characteristics.

Not all the Pharisees by any means were wealthy. Some, indeed, were quite humble folk. But Simon was comfortably off; he had a largish house, and he had servants. One of these now crossed the courtyard to him to announce that the arrange-ments for the supper were complete, and to ask him to be good enough to inspect them.

Now when Simon surveyed the room in which the supper was to be held he ob-served that all was in order, except that no arrangements had been made for the host—Simon himself—to wash the feet of his chief guest, nor to anoint his head with oil, as was customary. The omission did not surprise Simon. He had given orders that the usual rites should, on this occasion, be omitted.

The chief guest of the evening was to be Jesus of Nazareth. Simon had invited him largely out of curiosity, and he intended to give certain other Pharisees, Doctors of the Law and Scribes who shared his own profound interest in all religious matters, the opportunity of meeting the man who was held by common report to possess rare spiritual powers. Even so, Simon was not prepared to grant to him the full courtesies that were generally due to a chief guest. After all, the man was not a Pharisee; in origins he was nothing more than a simple Galilean. So, although Simon felt it would be proper as well as interesting to offer the man reasonable hospitality, he did feel that a certain formality of approach, as became a Pharisee dealing with a lesser mortal, would not be amiss.

He turned at the sound of voices at the entrance to the courtyard and, looking over, saw that his guests had begun to arrive. He went over and began to greet them sever-ally, grave and reverend men such as himself. The last to arrive was Jesus, and he came alone. By that time the rest of the company was assembled. It was an all-male gathering, since it was the rule that women were not admitted to so serious a conclave. The men, therefore, reclining on the low couch surrounding the central table, having removed their footwear at the door, addressed themselves to the business of the evening.

It was a restrained, formal occasion, one for which Simon, sitting in dignity at the head of the table, made a fitting host. Throughout, he continued to watch Jesus closely, feeding his curiosity about the man, noting the grace and skill with which he dealt with the many questions put to him—noting particularly the many ways in which he seemed so curiously unconventional. It was this fact especially which con-demned Jesus in the eyes of the Pharisee. So tolerant, so broad-minded a person, one so obviously uninterested in the minutiae of the Law, could scarcely be one of the elect. Behind the invitation which Simon had issued to Jesus to attend the supper there had lain the uneasy thought that the man from Nazareth might be a Rabbi of exceptional power. The uneasiness began to leave him as the evening progressed. He experienced a certain pleasure in the feeling that, after all, the man might not be anything other than an ordinary Galilean. An incident which befell some half-hour after the beginning of the supper at first strengthened him in this conclusion.

The supper had attracted a good deal of local attention. So, since the entrance to Simon's house through the courtyard was open to the public street, many had come in to press about the doorway. The men about the table looked up as a disturbance appeared to break out in the rear of the crowd at the door. There was a scuffling, followed by a parting of the crowd, then an irruption into the room itself of an appari-tion so startling that Simon, who had been in the act of putting some food into his mouth, paused with the morsel at his lips. There was a woman there.

That was irregular enough in itself. But a far more disturbing feature of the matter —so disturbing that he could not for once think of any action suitable to the occasion —was her identity. She was the local prostitute, a woman of the town. Her long black hair hanging down as far as her waist was symbolic of the looseness of her life.[1]

There were such women, tragic in the steepness of their fall and in the degradation of their lives, in Jewish society in the ancient world as in any other. Theirs was the oldest of all professions. Nothing more fantastic or extraordinary could be imagined

---

[1] The question of the identity of this "woman who was a sinner" presents a considerable problem. It is one of the unsolved mysteries of the Gospels. Only St Luke has this account of the anointing in the house of Simon the Pharisee, most likely at Capernaum, during the Galilean ministry of Our Lord. Matthew XXVI, 6–13, Mark XIV, 3–9, and John XII, 1–8, describe a closely similar incident in the house of Simon the leper at Bethany, near Jerusalem, during the last days of Our Lord's life. It is possible that the two versions relate to the same happening, in which case this "woman who was a sinner" would be Mary of Bethany, the sister of Martha and of Lazarus. The extreme improbability of the devout woman who sat at the feet of Jesus while her sister prepared the meal being the same as the loose woman of Capernaum may surely be taken as enough to invalidate this proposition. Who, then, was the woman in the house of Simon the Pharisee? That she was Mary Magdalene ancient tradition has persistently maintained, the same woman from whom, St Luke tells us, seven devils were driven out. By him, Mary Magdalene is listed among those women who, having thus experi-enced the healing power of Christ, elected thenceforth to follow him. It was certainly Mary Magdalene who, on the Resurrection morning, heard the risen and glorified Lord calling her by name. What, therefore, is more likely than that this woman of the town, recognizing the true nature of Jesus in the house of Simon the Pharisee, should, her life decisively changed by that encounter, have thus been among those who followed him to the end?

XVI. THE GOOD SAMARITAN AND THE MAN THAT FELL AMONG THIEVES

A certain Samaritan, as he journeyed, came where he was: and when he saw him, he had compassion on him, And went to him, and bound up his wounds. Luke 10, 33-34.

By Jacopo Bassano (1510 ?-1592)

Photo Studio Fifty-One

than that such a one should stand under the roof of a man of such conspicuously austere life as Simon the Pharisee. What is more, everyone present knew it. Why the harlot had thus forced her way in no one could imagine. She was disheveled and upset; her large, dark eyes stared wildly around the room. All had fallen silent, the men around the table, the crowd at the door. Everyone was waiting to see what she would do next.

The woman's eyes eventually came to rest upon Jesus.

She carried in her hand a small vessel such as was commonly used for carrying aromatic ointment used in anointing. The mouth of this container was sealed. She placed it on the floor beside her as, having with a quick movement gone to where Jesus lay, she knelt at his feet.

Still no one spoke. Quite unexpectedly, after one quick glance into the face of Jesus, she burst into a passion of tears. As she bowed her head forward her tears fell upon his feet. With the long tresses of her hair she wiped the tears away. After that she broke the neck of the vessel she had brought. With the sweet-smelling ointment which came therefrom, she anointed the feet of Jesus. Then she remained kneeling.

As the strange scene had progressed Simon had been thinking hard, although no trace of his thoughts had appeared on his calm face. He had been thinking that, if this Jesus were truly the prophet which popular rumor claimed him to be, then he would have been gifted with sufficient insight to recognize the woman who had thus intruded upon them for the kind of person she was. He would have recoiled from her touch as from defilement. "This man," he told himself, "if he were a prophet, would have perceived who and what manner of woman this is which toucheth him, that she is a sinner."

Now, for the first time since the woman had entered the room, Jesus spoke, turning himself a little on his elbow in order to look the host straight in the face.

"Simon," he said, "I have somewhat to say unto thee."

Rather startled with the suddenness of it, Simon replied:

"Master, say on."

Raising his voice a little so that all the company could hear, Jesus said: "A certain lender had two debtors: the one owed five hundred pence and the other fifty. When they had not the wherewith to pay, he forgave them both. Which of them therefore will love him most?"

Never a man to be hurried into an incautious reply, and having by that time gathered himself, Simon replied: "He, I suppose, to whom he forgave the most."

"Thou hast rightly judged," Jesus told him.

He turned to the kneeling woman at his feet, whose long, dark hair spread on the ground at either side of her lowered head.

"Seest thou this woman?" he asked Simon. Then he went on to add words which showed clearly that he had observed the lack of courtesy with which he had been received into the Pharisee's house.

"I entered into thine house, thou gavest me no water for my feet; but she hath wetted my feet with her tears and wiped them with her hair. Thou gavest me no kiss" —he meant the ceremonial kiss of peace and welcome—"but she, since the time I came in, hath not ceased to kiss my feet. My head with oil thou didst not anoint; but she hath anointed my feet with ointment."

B.M.G.—K

Speaking with compelling authority, he added:

"Her sins, which are many, are forgiven; for she loved much; but to whom little is forgiven, the same loveth little."

He continued to look straight into the old, watchful eyes of the Pharisee until they dropped before the penetrating gaze. Only then did he turn to the woman and say: "Thy sins are forgiven. Thy faith hath saved thee; go in peace."

Slowly, very slowly, she raised her head until the black tresses were clear of the ground. Then she rose, made another deep obeisance, and, without any further word or any glance at the rest of the company, withdrew from the room, the throng at the door making way for her as she passed through.

Instantly babel broke out.

"Who is this," they asked in astonishment among themselves, looking at Jesus, "that even forgiveth sins?"

But Simon the Pharisee knew, as he sat gazing at the table before him. He felt he had learned a great lesson—and that he had learned it from a wonderful person.

XVII. CHRIST AND THE WOMAN OF SAMARIA

Jesus answered and said unto her, Whosoever drinketh of this water shall thirst again: But whosoever drinketh of the water that I shall give him shall never thirst. John 4, 13-14.

By Juan de Flandres (fl.1496-1506)

Photo Vizzavona

Mountain Miracle

Based on Fra Angelico's
THE TRANSFIGURATION

PEACEFUL as the scene was, quiet and still though the day, Peter knew in his heart that something was about to happen; something of momentous import, something strange. It was afternoon, and the disciples were resting by one of the streams running among the foothills below Mount Hermon, the 2,800 foot peak standing to the northeastward of Galilee a little beyond the city of Caesarea Philippi.

One or two of the men were drowsing; others lay with their wrists dangling in the cool, chuckling run of the water. But Peter, sitting with James and John on the lush grass of the stream side, kept a watchful eye on Jesus. The Master was a little apart, apparently very deep in thought, just as he had been for the past few days. It was awe and reverence, above all it was love, which kept Peter the fisherman constantly wondering what it was which so occupied the Master's mind.

Somehow, but in a manner past his understanding, he sensed that it was connected with what had happened near Caesarea Philippi six days before. The emotional disturbance arising from that still surged to and fro in Peter himself.

They had come northward out of Galilee away from Capernaum and Bethsaida and, crossing the Bridge of the Daughters of Jacob, had passed out of the territory of Herod Antipas into that of Philip, his half-brother. Thence they had continued north, climbing steadily in the opposite direction to the flow of the Jordan making its way to the Lake of Galilee southward. And then, in a quiet spot near one of the villages where Jesus had been teaching, it had happened.

Jesus had been praying alone, as was his frequent custom. Quite suddenly, he had risen to his feet and come over to them.

"Who do the multitude say that I am?" he had asked abruptly, as one who had finally made up his mind to a course of action. They had been all rather taken aback. There had been plenty of multitudes lately, for the fame of the teaching of Jesus had spread far and wide. Who, then, did these people, speculating upon the matter among themselves, say Jesus was? Some of the disciples, searching their memories, said, "John the Baptist." Some others—for they had all heard different things—said, "Elijah." Yet others asserted that the crowds were saying that in Jesus one of the old prophets was risen again.

He had listened to them closely. Then had come the direct, crucial question:

"But who say ye that I am?"

The truth had come to Simon Peter in a blinding moment of insight, and he had cried aloud:

"Thou art the Christ, the Son of the living God!"

The face of Jesus had lit up.

"Blessed art thou, Simon Bar-Jonah," he had said, "for flesh and blood hath not revealed it unto thee, but my Father which is in heaven. And I also say unto thee that thou art Peter, and upon this rock I will build my Church; and the gates of Hades shall not prevail against it. I will give unto thee the keys of the Kingdom of Heaven; and whatsoever thou shalt bind on earth shall be bound in heaven: and whatsoever thou shalt loose on earth shall be loosed in heaven."

Afterward he had told all of them that they were not to reveal the fact that he was the Christ to anyone: for it was clear that he desired to do that in his own good time. The strange and, indeed, the disturbing sequel had come a little later, when Jesus had been telling them that the Son of Man would have to suffer many things and to be rejected by the elders and the chief priests and the scribes, and be killed, and that after three days he would rise again. This had been too much for Peter, so that he had begun to expostulate. But Jesus had most sternly rebuked him:

"Get thee behind me, Satan," he had said, "for thou mindest not the things of God, but the things of man."

Turning to the disciples he had added:

"If any man would come after me, let him deny himself, and take up his cross and follow me. For whosoever would save his life shall lose it; and whosoever shall lose his life for my sake and the Gospel's shall save it. For what does it profit a man to gain the whole world, and forfeit his life? For what shall a man give in exchange for his life? For whosoever shall be ashamed of me and of my words in this adulterous and sinful generation, the Son of Man also shall be ashamed of him, when he cometh in the glory of his Father with the holy angels."

It was the deep emotional reaction from this incident which still moved Peter and which made him sense that there was yet further revelation to come. So he watched the Master while the others relaxed. And as he watched he saw Jesus rise to his feet, look over toward the three of them, Peter and James and John, and with a well-known sign, command them to follow him.

Peter rose hurriedly, beckoning the other two to do the same, for they were the trio whom the Lord often called apart with him when he had a special purpose in his mind. It did not occur to any of them to question what that purpose was; the Lord beckoned, and they followed.

He led them steeply up the slopes of Mount Hermon itself, keeping well ahead as they climbed together up towards the clouds. The view on either side expanded vastly as the altitude increased.[1] They could see, after several hours' hard climbing, from the desert to the sea, from the east to the west. There was, too, about the place near the summit where Jesus eventually paused, that ringing silence characteristic of the high places of the hills. There was also a heaviness about the atmosphere; not a breath of wind stirred, and every now and then a bee droned by.

There was a ringing in Peter's head too; but whence it came he knew not. Nor could he account for the drowsiness which he could feel fast overcoming him. When he looked at John and James it was clear that they were similarly affected. With one

[1] Mount Tabor, situated in the middle of the Plain of Galilee, has been traditionally regarded as the Mount of the Transfiguration. But Tabor is only some 600 feet high, and it is known that a Roman fortress stood on the summit, a fact which later archaeological research has made plain. Furthermore, Mount Hermon is close to Caesarea Philippi, where Jesus was shortly before the event took place. It seems clear, therefore, that Hermon was the scene of the Transfiguration.

accord they sank down upon the dry, aromatic grass clothing the mountain slope, reclining sideways, each on an elbow, so that looking further up the steep incline toward the summit, they could clearly see the figure of Jesus outlined against a sky of the deepest, most perfect blue, interspersed here and there by high-sailing, pure white, fair-weather clouds.

Peter never knew how long afterward it was when he noticed a change in the appearance of the Master. Perhaps he had slept. Neither he nor John nor James, often as they discussed the mystery secretly in later times among themselves, was able to say with exactitude what had happened. Not that it mattered; the marvel of the sight which Peter suddenly beheld when, dazed and heavy, he looked up the mountain slope, was enough. He looked; he stared; his bearded jaw fell a little in token of the amazement which gripped him. Then hurriedly and silently he shook the other two.

Now they all saw it. The fashion of the countenance of the Master was altered, and the robe he was wearing had become white and dazzling. There was light all about him, most intense about the head and shoulders, seeming to come from no external source but to burst out, as it were, from within. To Peter, who, fisherman as he was, had the devout Jew's knowledge of the Scriptures, it was startlingly reminiscent of the Glory which shone from the face of Moses after he had been in communion with God on Mount Sinai.

Immediately it seemed to Peter—and, by the quick intake of breath he heard beside him, it was evident that John and James had seen the same thing—that there were the figures of two men with the Lord, one on either side of him, similarly glorified and shining with the same mysterious light. They were Moses and Elijah. Watching, petrified, the disciples clearly heard their voices speaking with the Lord about things which were to come to pass in Jerusalem when Jesus, as he had foretold to his disciples at Caesarea Philippi, would die and rise again.

Groping in his thunderstruck mind for a meaning for this astounding vision Peter came to the knowledge that, as always, the answer was to be found in the Scriptures. Moses and Elijah represented the Law and the Prophets; and was it not recorded in the Second Book of the Kings that Elijah had been taken up into heaven? And was it not commonly believed that the same was true of Moses? Most significant of all, each had in his time held communion with God and the rabbis taught that each would reappear before the Coming of the Messiah. Peter, kneeling by now on the grass, felt his fingers tighten upon the earth. This, then, was the sequel to the self-revelation of the Master at Caesarea Philippi. Peter had said then that Jesus was the Christ, the Son of God, and here, now, was this miracle upon the mountain supernaturally to underline the truth of it.

Peter sprang to his feet and moved forward, scarcely knowing what he did or said. He cried out:

"Master, it is good for us to be here: and let us make three tabernacles; one for thee and one for Moses and one for Elijah."

Even as he spoke a cloud came looming over the mountain, rising unexpectedly and terrifyingly from over the summit behind the Lord. The shadow of it raced down the mountain-side and engulfed him. The three disciples crouched low upon the ground, their faces pressed upon the grass. They recognized that cloud. It was no ordinary one. It was the Shechinah itself, the very Glory of God, such as that in which the Lord moved when, in the wilderness, he went before his people by day in a pillar of cloud.

Now a voice was speaking out of the cloud, ringing, echoing, unforgettable.

"This is My Son, My Chosen: Hear ye him."

For a long time they remained crouching upon the ground. Peter was the first fearfully to raise his head. When he looked up the slope he saw Jesus only.

None of them spoke. Soon afterwards Jesus led them back again down the mountain, pausing only once to warn them that they were to tell no man of what they had seen.

XVIII. MARY MAGDALENE

Mary called Magdalene, out of whom went seven devils.
Luke 8, 2.

By Georges de la Tour (1593-1652)

Photo Vizzavona

The One Thing Needful

Based on Vermeer's

CHRIST IN THE HOUSE OF MARTHA AND MARY

DURING the closing months of the year 29 there was a little household in the village of Bethany which often received a distinguished guest—one indeed so distinguished that no home since has ever entertained his like. Yet there was nothing at all outstanding about the house, or about the people who lived there. The building itself, stone-built and flat-roofed, was much the same as any of the others in the village street. Its door looked out on the dusty way, standing in which it was possible to look, in the clear air, over toward distant mountains and downward toward where the road from Jerusalem dipped down into the gorge which led toward Jericho. For Bethany stood high upon a shoulder of the Mount of Olives. It was also very quiet, although Jerusalem was not more than an hour's walk away. It was thus possible to be in and about the city during the day and yet to find in Bethany a blessed peace and privacy when evening came. This may well have been the reason why Jesus—for it was he who was the distinguished guest—chose to stay in this humble home in Bethany.

Two sisters, Martha and Mary, kept house there, and their brother was that Lazarus whom Jesus raised from the dead.

One evening these two sisters were awaiting the coming of the Master. The doorway onto the street stood open and, in the doorway, her head leaning pensively against the frame of it and hands clasped behind her back, for all the world like a little girl, was Mary, the younger of the two. The wind stirred her headdress; but her eyes, clear and placid as a nun's, never stirred from the end of the street toward which she was looking. There was expectancy in every detail of her poise; even her lips were slightly parted, and now and again a half smile, as of pleased anticipation, moved across her features. Behind her, from within the house, came the chinking of utensils and the sound of busy feet moving to and fro. Martha was laying the table and preparing the meal, a task which, in that servantless household—for they were poor folk—had need to be done by the women themselves. Once Martha came to the door, a bowl in one hand and a cloth in the other.

The difference between the two women could be seen at a glance. It was not so much that Martha was somewhat the sturdier and the bigger of the two, but that her whole attitude, her manner of movement, the very set of her features, spoke of practical activity. Martha, indeed, was a woman to whom industry was the greatest of the virtues. To be up and doing from morning till night, to have a task on hand and to see it through conscientiously to the last detail, was the ideal she constantly set before herself.

She swirled the bowl round in her hand, and then pitched the water that was in it out into the dust of the street. Mary, still leaning against the door frame, moved her eyes once to watch the liquid settle into the dust.

Martha, now vigorously wiping the inside of the bowl with the cloth, allowed herself one brief glance up the street. But it was only a very brief glance: she was busy; there was much to do. She hurried into the house again. Soon the sound of her movements about the table drifted out once more into the quiet evening. Mary stayed where she was, moving only slightly as she transferred the weight from one sandaled foot onto the other.

Inside, Martha continued to be busy about the preparations for a monumental meal. All the meals that Martha prepared were monumental. She was that kind of woman. The table was already set to perfection, the round cakes of bread neatly stacked, the figs and dates set ready, the bowl and ewer for the guest to wash his feet efficiently in position, with an immaculate towel, in a corner on the right of the door. Yet there always seemed something else to do. That cushion, now, where he would recline for the meal, struck her as perhaps not quite what it should be. She was always trying to find time to make a new cover for it; but somehow time never seemed to be available. She picked up the cushion and carried it to the door to scrutinize it in the evening light.

The movement took her for the second time to her sister's side. With work-creased fingers Martha carefully picked out a fragment of the cushion's stuffing, flicking it off to the ground. She was about to say something when Mary beside her suddenly stood upright.

Martha allowed herself to stay only long enough to see, over the rise of the street, breasting the winding way which came up from Jericho, a group of men. Then she hurried in; there was the lamp to light. Being thrifty she always left it till the last moment in order to save the oil. But Mary remained where she was. Now she held her hands clasped before her as a tall, broad, bearded man detached himself with courtesies from the group which had been accompanying him and came down toward the doorway of the house. He greeted her with gentle gravity in a deep voice, before stooping to pass within. Mary followed. When he had made himself ready, and settled down beside the table, she sat herself at his feet in the time-honored attitude of a disciple before a teacher.

Meanwhile, Martha was hurrying anxiously to and fro. This, the feeding of so honored a guest, was her busiest time. Little beads of perspiration formed on her upper lip as she bent over the fire where fish was broiling. She darted little glances towards her sister. The Master was talking now, evenly and calmly, and Mary, never stirring, sat rapt.

And then it all came to a head with a mishap to the fish, which overset and fell on to the coals.

Perhaps it was the irritation of this which led Martha to her next action. She loved her sister dearly. Yet there were times, like this, when things went wrong, when she wished very much that Mary would be a little more practical, would see that there were things to be done. It was not in any way that Mary was indolent. She was the most helpful of sisters; but when Jesus was with them Mary seemed to give all her time just to listening to him. So Martha indignantly straightened herself and marched over to the table, leaning over it to break in upon their conversation:

XIX. THE TRANSFIGURATION

Jesus taketh with him Peter, and James, and John, and leadeth them up into an high mountain apart by themselves: and he was transfigured before them. And his raiment became shining, exceeding white as snow; so as no fuller on earth can white them. Mark 9, 2–3.

By Fra Angelico (1387–1455)

Photo Alinari

"Lord, dost thou not care that my sister did leave me to serve alone? Bid her therefore that she help me."

The Master turned half round to look at her. His gaze, full of kindly understanding, seemed to reach her innermost soul. He smiled.

"Martha, Martha," he said, "thou art anxious and troubled about many things: but one thing is needful, for Mary hath chosen the good part, which shall not be taken away from her."

It was said with the utmost sympathy and kindliness. Yet the words, with their undercurrent of profound meaning, sank deep into Martha. It seemed to her all at once as if the things which had been occupying her to the exclusion of all else were in fact of comparatively small import. The great thing was to be with Jesus while it was possible to be so, while his earthly presence was vouchsafed. It was not that to eat and to sleep and to live were not important; rather was it that these should always take second place to the necessity of quiet contemplation and worship; as Mary was doing as she sat at the feet of the Lord, in reverence and love, hearkening to his words. That was the one thing needful. Martha understood then that to be busy was not everything; but to worship the Lord was all.

What neither of the sisters could know was that an event had taken place that very afternoon which gave particular point to these words of Jesus. For this was the day, as St Luke suggests—since in his Gospel the two stories follow on—that the Master had met with the lawyer upon the road between Jerusalem and Jericho and, in reply to his questions as to who is a man's neighbor, had told him the story of the Good Samaritan.

Now the Good Samaritan, by his merciful conduct toward the man in need, had demonstrated what must always be one side of the coin of true religion—a concern for doing practical works of mercy. That is one aspect of Christianity in action. But there was another side to the coin, and that other side was now being made plain by Mary's giving priority to quiet contemplation. The two things go together, and the first without the second can only be the ordinary doing of good without the deep love of God which should and must, if it is to last, inspire it.

That is why the two stories—that of the Good Samaritan followed immediately by this of Martha and Mary—make a complete picture of the twofold nature of the Christian life in which love of one's neighbor is always accompanied by, and energized by, the love of God.

Jesus was not condemning Martha, that kindly, busy, hospitable, practical woman. But he was defending Mary against her sisterly indignation by making it clear that Mary, seeing with the inner eye of spiritual perception what was really necessary, was making plain the great truth that lies for ever at the heart of true religion.

For true religion in any age and place needs to be contemplative and reflective as well as abundant in good works. And contemplation and reflection are to be found best at the feet of Christ, where Mary sat that evening.

How a Grave gave up its Dead

Based on Froment's

THE RAISING OF LAZARUS

It was a winter's day and the place was Bethabara, a village by a ford on the eastern bank of the River Jordan, deep down in the gorge of the river some ten or twelve miles south of the Sea of Galilee. Westward the brown hills towered up. The heights there now were cloud capped, the clouds immobile in the quietness of the day. Jerusalem to the south was two days' journey off, so that the little group gathered about Jesus in a house in Bethabara felt safe by that much distance from the mortal hatreds which were gathering there about him, born of the fears and suspicions which his growing fame had nurtured in the hearts of the priests. But here in Bethabara, a place for Jesus himself full of sacred memories of his own baptism there by John, there was for a little while peace; peace in which to fortify his own spirit in seclusion; peace in which to go on with the all-important teaching of his followers against the time when he would be no longer there in the flesh himself.

And then there came suddenly a knocking on the door. It was immensely startling, at so quiet an hour, in so secluded a place. The disciples looked at each other with fear in their eyes; but the voice of Jesus continued calmly until he had reached the end of what he had been saying. Then, with a sign to one of the twelve, he bade him go and see who was there. As the rest of them tensely waited, they heard the door open a little, a muttered colloquy and the sound of the door opened further. A moment later their companion ushered a stranger into the room.

All looked at him at first keenly, then with quick relief. He was a villager from Bethany, way toward the south, a friendly fellow who they had met before. But now it was clear he had come far and fast. He carried the staff of one who makes a lone journey, and his feet and legs and the lower hems of his garments were still wet with his crossing of the river by the ford at the foot of the village. He made a deep obeisance to Jesus, and a general greeting to them all. After that, as became a man of few words and direct manner, he said at once to Jesus:

"Master, I have come from Mary and Martha. They sent me to say that their brother Lazarus, he whom you love so much, is seriously ill."

He seated himself then, adding as he did so, "A hard trip I've had of it too; took me two days along the trackways; still I said I would come, and here I am."

But now the disciples were all looking at Jesus, knowing that the news would touch him deeply. The little household from which the news came was especially dear to him. It was not only Lazarus that he loved, but the sisters also. They were three people upon whom he had gladly expended the treasures of his love and friendship, and who had richly responded. The danger, therefore, of the news lay in the fact that the Master, thus summoned to the aid of his friends, would, if he answered the call, be returning to an extremely dangerous area. Bethany was not much more than a couple of miles from Jerusalem itself. And it was only recently that the Temple authorities there had gone to the horrible length of attempting to have him stoned to death.

The memory of that fearful occurrence was vividly alive in them all. It had happened at the Feast of the Dedication when, one day, Jesus had been walking in the Temple in Solomon's Porch. That something darkly premeditated was afoot had been clear when the hostile crowd had gathered around him.

"Tell us," one of them had begun, a sharp-featured priest obviously chosen to start things off, "tell us plainly if thou art the Christ. How long doth thou hold us in suspense?"

And Jesus had told him curtly in reply:

"I told you, and ye believe not: the works that I do in my Father's 'name, these bear witness of me. But ye believe not, because ye are not of my sheep."

That had been the signal. Shrieking that Jesus blasphemed because, being a man, he made himself out to be God, the ringleader of the crowd had stooped to pick up a sizeable rock from the roadway. By means of such missiles, lethal when in many hands, not a few in that place had come to a brutal end, shielding themselves at first from the shower of stones and then, knocked unconscious, or dazed by a hit on the head, fallen to the ground, there to be pounded into pulp. It had seemed miraculous that the Master had escaped. Indeed it was miraculous, the way he had blended himself away into the press of onlookers.

Even before that happening at the Feast of the Dedication there had been gathering against him the hostility of the priests. In summer at the Feast of Pentecost when he had healed a man at the pool of Bethesda they had hated him for what they had seen as a desecration of the Sabbath. At the Feast of the Tabernacles he had healed a young man of his blindness, and drawn further fame upon himself. For all these reasons it had become perilous for Jesus to be in the vicinity of Jerusalem. And now here was this messenger from Bethany asking, by the implication of the news he bore, that Jesus should return to that very place.

It was therefore with infinite relief that they heard his calm reply:

"This sickness is not unto death. But for the glory of God, that the Son of God may be glorified thereby."

They did not know fully what he meant; but at least they knew that he was not venturing south into the jaws of danger. And so they relaxed in the little house in Bethabara and addressed themselves once more to the Master's teaching. The messenger returned to Bethany that evening.

Yet two days later Jesus abruptly announced that he was going there, after all. He made the announcement after the evening meal, when he had been sitting apart awhile, silent and thoughtful. Then he said only, "Let us go into Judea again."

Immediately all protested. "Rabbi," one of them stammered, "the Jews were but now seeking to stone thee; and goest thou thither again?" In reply Jesus gave them a proverb. "Are there not twelve hours in the day?" he said, meaning that, so long as a man's time, as ordained by God, had not arrived, he cannot perish until that hour comes. And then he added the sentence which thoroughly puzzled his followers.

"Our friend Lazarus is fallen asleep," he said. "But I go that I may awake him out of sleep." They were simple men, these followers of the Master, and not for the first time took his words with a literalness that was a sign of their simplicity. "In that case," one of them said, while the others nodded in agreement, "if he is just sleeping, then he will recover."

At that the Master's manner altered. Turning full upon them he said, "Lazarus is dead. And I am glad for your sakes that I was not there, to the intent ye may believe; nevertheless let us go unto him."

They could see then that his mind was made up, set upon some mysterious point beyond their understanding. It was plain also, that he meant to walk back into danger. They were deeply disturbed. But Thomas, a brave follower at all times, called out over the rising argument, "Very well then; let's all go together, that we may die with him."

They set off the next day, along the trackways by the western bank of Jordan, traveling southward and climbing steadily above the floor of the river gorge. When they arrived at Bethany they were told that Lazarus had been already four days in his tomb. So it was right then; Lazarus was indeed dead.

The household, when they reached it, was plunged into the full depth of oriental mourning, full of relatives and friends of Martha and Mary who had come over from Jerusalem. As they neared the place the keenings and wailings of women came from the house over which lay the shadow of death. Some of the men who sat without, seeing the approach of Jesus with the twelve along the dusty road, went into the house to report their coming. The result was dramatic. A tall woman, distraught with grief, but yet bearing herself with the strong self-possession characteristic of Martha, emerged from the house and came down the road toward them.

Jesus paused to await her coming. When she stood before him he listened with obvious emotion to her grief-strained voice.

"Jesus, Lord," she breathed, "if thou hadst been here, my brother would not have died." As if at a suddenly conceived wild hope she added, "Even now I know that, whatsoever thou shalt ask of God, God will give thee."

Still standing where he was in the shadow of the road Jesus said to her, "Thy brother shall rise again."

But the momentary wild hope had subsided in Martha, so that she understood him only at the level of everyday events, and supposed him to be speaking of the life to come. Neither she, nor any of those within earshot, could for a moment guess at the tremendous event which was about to take place. So all Martha said was:

"I know that he shall rise again in the Resurrection at the last day."

Then came from Jesus the immortal words; that echoing phrase which has brought comfort to countless generations of Christians down the ages: "I am the Resurrection and the Life; he that believeth on me, though he die, yet shall he live: and whosoever liveth and believeth on me shall never die."

Then he looked keenly at Martha, so keenly that her eyes fell before his.

"Believest thou this?"

She was very much shaken. In a low voice, almost a whisper, she replied:

"Yes, Lord: I have believed thou art the Christ, the Son of God, even he that cometh into the world."

Then she turned about abruptly and hurried back into the house.

Now Martha well knew that Jesus was in mortal peril every moment he spent there in Bethany. So that in the shuttered, sweat-smelling room of mourning, packed close with relatives of the deceased, she whispered privately to her sister, "The Master is here: he wishes to see you."

Mary, always the more emotional of the two, and already overstrained by days of grief, leapt up with a cry. Disordered as she was, she ran, her long hair about her face, out into the sunlight and down the road. To the mourners it seemed the act of a mad woman. Supposing her to be about to run to the tomb of her brother, they streamed after her lest she do herself some violence.

It was this that brought them into sight of Jesus with his group of friends down the road. From that moment the presence of the Master in Bethany was known and his peril all the more increased.

Yet Mary had no thought for that; she was beyond it. Sobbing and crying, she fell down in the dust before Jesus, moaning in her turn what her sister had said before; that if he had been there her brother would not have died.

It seemed to the disciples that the Master himself was unusually agitated. He groaned, his sunburned face working with grief. "Where have you laid him?" he asked.

It was a rock tomb to which they led him, in the gaunt burial place of the village, ruinous and cyprus-hung. For here few were buried in the ground whence the jackals by night would have dug them up. Instead, the dead were lodged in crevices in the hillside, containing usually a ledge to hold the body wrapped in its grave clothes. The entrance was then sealed by having a stone rolled before it. One such, rough hewn and big as a circular mill stone, lay now across the entrance of the silent tomb. To this, with Mary pulling at his sleeve in the extremity of her grief, Jesus was now led.

Still the strong emotion held Jesus in its grip. And as the unaccustomed tears of a strong man ran down his face those around exclaimed among themselves how great his love for the dead Lazarus must have been. Yet some among them sneered, for he was now in the vicinity of his enemies and some were among the mourners from Jerusalem.

"If this man," they muttered among themselves, "according to the popular tale, cured a man of blindness, how is it that he couldn't prevent his friend from dying?"

When they were close upon the great stone Jesus said something which electrified them all, friend and enemy alike.

"Take away the stone."

It was Martha, the practical-minded, who rushed forward then.

"Master! Lord! He has been dead four days!"

She was voicing what they were all with horror thinking; the body in that climate, four days after death, would be well advanced in decomposition. It would be dreadful to uncover the tomb.

But now there was overwhelming command in every gesture and tone of the Master's. Appalled as they all were, they had to obey. He repeated again, in an even stronger voice, "Take away the stone!" Turning to Martha he added, "Said I not unto thee, that, if thou believest, thou shouldst see the glory of God?"

Many of those round about had fallen back by now, But four of the boldest, impelled by the authority of his command, put their shoulders against the stone. First it resisted, then gave a little, then, at a final heave, rolled forward. A semi-circular, pitch-black entry was revealed. The place had become so tensely quiet now, that every word of what Jesus said next came clearly to the terrified listeners. It appeared to be a prayer, for he stood with head thrown back and hands outstretched looking up towards the heavens. "Father, I thank Thee that Thou heardest me. And I know that Thou hearest me always: but because of the multitude which standeth around I said it, that they may believe that Thou didst send me."

His voice altered abruptly, changing to a loud startling shout: "Lazarus, come forth!"

All eyes were fixed now upon the black entrance of the tomb. Suddenly, the shriek of a woman in the terrified crowd behind Jesus spoke of what they had all seen. It was petrifying; almost, until one grasped the marvel of it, horrifying.

There was something moving in the darkness.

There was something moving which gradually resolved itself into the tottering figure of a man, wrapped around in the white linen cerements of the dead; hands bound, head swathed, with a cloth to hold up the jaw as in a sling, knotted at the top. This astounding figure moved weakly, like a wasp or a bee feeling a way into the sunlight after the hibernation of winter. It reached the daylight at the entrance of the tomb, stood a moment leaning weakly against the side of the entrance, then tottered fully into the open. The crowd gave way before it. But Martha, though her face was pale as ivory, caught the figure in her arms.

The power which had seemed to hold Jesus in its grip, departed from him. It was in a normal voice, that he said, "Loose him, and let him go."

Thus did Jesus raise Lazarus from the dead. Thus did the Lord of Life show himself to be the overlord of death also. All this took place in Bethany in Judea. And before the day was out the High Priest in Jerusalem had heard the news, and feared this wonder-worker the more.

The Beginning of the End

Based on

THE ENTRY INTO JERUSALEM

ascribed to Fra Angelico

FOR days past Salome, a middle-aged woman with an anxious, busy mind, had been planning what to do. The difficulty lay in finding the moment and the courage to do it.

And now time was running short. Already the road led even more steeply down-hill. Already the hills towered up more steeply on either side, brown scrub and rock reaching up to a deep blue sky of early spring in the clarity of which, seen now and then, buzzards swooped and floated in the uprising currents of warm air. In front, lower down, beyond the tortuosities of this road lay the ford over the Jordan. Behind lay Peraea, the country to the southeast of Jordan across which the last stages of the journey of Jesus and his little company had been leading them. In that country they had been journeying for days past. Before that, ever since the early months of the year, they had been afoot in the lands east of Jordan, coming down in a wide sweep through the country of Decapolis, with its Greek cities of Pella, Dion, Gerasa and Philadelphia. It had been a long, incident-packed journey that the company had made, since they had set off from the little town of Ephraim, on the west of Jordan, to strike across the river. Now they were approaching the territory of the bitterly hostile Herod Antipas, in whose lonely stronghold of Machaerus John the Baptist had been murdered. The way now led also toward Jerusalem itself, where Annas, Caiphas, and all the dread power of the Sanhedrin lay in wait for Jesus.

But that was not at all how the prospects appeared to Salome. The fact of being caught up in great events beyond their understanding does not prevent little people from going on being little people even in the midst of them. And in this Salome was no exception. Puzzled she certainly was by some of the things Jesus had been saying. Several times already he had used mysterious, indeed, incomprehensible words to describe what lay ahead. "Behold," he had said not so long before, "we go up to Jerusalem; and the Son of Man shall be delivered unto the chief priests and scribes; and they shall condemn him to death, and shall deliver him unto the Gentiles to mock, and to scourge, and to crucify: and the third day he shall be raised up."

But for her, and for the rest of them too, it seemed inconceivable that this journey could end in anything other than the most tremendous triumph for the Master, he whose tall, long-striding figure was now way out ahead of them down the road. And Salome's anxiety—the desire that had kept her awake under the stars the night before—was for her two sons. She was the mother of James and John, and it was her wish that they should have honored places in that kingdom which was to come, which Jesus would assuredly rule, and before the throne of which all Israel would do homage.

But time was pressing. Only a little further on this comparative solitude in which they moved now would give place, once the ford over the Jordan were crossed and Jericho were reached, to the mad excitement of pilgrim crowds. There would be little chance then, or afterward, for a quiet word with the Master.

And yet she felt a certain trepidation. It had become his custom of late to walk apart and ahead as though an immense preoccupation lay upon his soul. He was ahead now. And she, because she had discreetly manœuvred herself into that position, was the next in line. She gave a quick glance behind her; some ten paces back walked her two sons. And behind them, in a compact group, came the other disciples talking among themselves. They were out of earshot, but she could catch the high excited volume of their talk. For they too were animated, speculating on the destiny that lay ahead.

She looked forward again. She could see only the back of Jesus. Not for the first time that morning she pondered within herself as to what exactly would be the best way of getting a private word with him. To run up and tug his sleeve? To call after him? Both were unthinkable. The only thing to do was to wait until some pause in the journey presented to her the opportunity. And so she walked on, bent forward a little, breathing hard, her mind wandering over the happenings of the last few days.

There had been that rare experience of seeing the Master angry. It had happened in the last upland town they had been in, where he had been teaching and healing according to his wont. Of course there had been women and children among the crowd around him; there always were. And these same women, wanting maybe a blessing from the Master upon their little ones, had brought their children to him. Of course they had been noisy. What crowd of children is not? And of course some of the mothers may have been pretty demanding and intrusive about it all. Yet it was not to be wondered at that they had sought the Master's blessing, so compelling, so magnetic was his whole presence. It was always so. But the disciples—and perhaps it was a symptom of their tenseness at that time—had hustled the women. And then Jesus had rounded on them. Even at his look—a look at the memory of which Salome thrilled as she thought about it—the disciples had stood crestfallen. Still she remembered his words, and the indignation that spoke in them.

"Allow the little children to come to me," he had said. "Do not forbid them: for of such is the Kingdom of Heaven." And there and then he had gathered them about him, and laid his hand severally upon the small heads one by one and looked softly into the faces turned wonderingly up at him. And without another word he had walked on and the disciples shamefacedly had followed him.

But even then they had not been done with that place, for there had followed immediately the odd incident of the young man who had wanted to know, as he had put it, what he should do to inherit eternal life. Maybe he had been among the crowd watching when Jesus had blessed the children. Certainly, something about the Master had worked powerfully upon his emotions, for he had come up to Jesus and kneeled before him. That was sufficiently startling in itself, for he had very definitely not been of the kind to kneel to anybody. The splendor of his clothes,

And a certain woman named Martha received him into her house. And she had a sister called Mary, which also sat at Jesus' feet, and heard his word. Luke 10, 38–39.

By Vermeer (1632–1675)

XX. CHRIST IN THE HOUSE
OF MARTHA AND MARY

And a certain woman named Martha received him into her house. And she had a sister called Mary, which also sat at Jesus' feet, and heard his word. Luke 10, 38–39.

By Vermeer (1632–1675)

Photo Hislop and Day

the well-trimmed beard, the immaculate hands had shown him to be of a different order from the work-stained peasantry. Salome herself had instinctively acknowledged him as superior, probably a son of a wealthy sheikh. Even the respectful attitude toward him of the people around had shown him to be a person of note. But there he had been, in the dust, kneeling before the Master, even calling him by that title.

"Good Master," he had said, "what shall I do that I may inherit eternal life?" There had fallen a dead silence all around as Jesus looked kindly upon him.

"Why do you call me good? Only God is good. And surely you know the Commandments; do not kill, do not commit adultery, do not steal, do not bear false witness, do not defraud, honor thy father and mother."

The young man had said, "All these things have I observed from my youth."

It had seemed a perfect answer; but it had not been good enough for Jesus. For he had become grave, as though seeing through the easy emotion that was moving the other to the realities beyond. For to follow him was not easy, it never had been and it never would be. It involved sacrifice. The only way into the Kingdom was the hard way. But it had been clear he had felt drawn to the handsome, eager youth, for it had been with sadness that he had gone on to say, "Go, sell whatsoever thou hast and give to the poor, and thou shalt have treasure in heaven; and come, follow me."

For a long moment the young man had looked down, kneeling as he still was in the dust at the Master's feet. Then he had stood up, bowed briefly, and walked away. Jesus had looked after him sorrowfully. And then, turning to the rest of them, with that characteristic gesture of his, hands outstretched, "How hardly shall they that have riches enter into the Kingdom of God!" It was a strange thing to say. And Jesus had smiled, as he often did, when he saw they were puzzled. "Children," he had said, using the endearing term they so loved to hear, "how hard is it for them that trust in riches to enter into the Kingdom of God!" Then had followed the familiar easy proverb which made it all simpler for them. "It is easier for a camel to go through a needle's eye, than for a rich man to enter into the Kingdom of God."

But it was certainly baffling to hear that not even the rich could get into the Kingdom. After all, if they couldn't, who could? Some of the men had immediately come out with the question that was on everybody's mind. "Lord, who can be saved, then?"

"With men it is impossible," the answer had been. "But not with God: for all things are possible with God."

But of course that hadn't been enough for Peter; Peter the impetuous, the enthusiastic, who had immediately burst in with—"Well, we have left all, and have followed thee."

Jesus had been stern with his next words:

"Verily I say unto you"—he always put it like that when he wanted to emphasize something—"there is no man that has left house, or brethren, or sisters, or mother, or father, or children, or lands, for my sake, and for the Gospel's sake, but he shall receive a hundredfold now in this time, houses, and brethren, and sisters, and mothers, and children, and lands, with persecutions"—that had been the strange phrase, "with persecutions"—"and in the world to come eternal life." He had walked on a little, then paused and added, "But many that are first shall be last; and the last first."

B.M.G.—M

Yes, it was all puzzling. Maybe the men understood it better than she did, Salome thought; but at least there had been that promise of the Kingdom, and that was what was uppermost in her mind.

She looked up, sensing some change in the order of march. Jesus had moved in to the side of the road and was climbing down the little bank there that led to the stream that came, diamond clear, from the heights above, making its cheerful, singing way to the Jordan below. When she reached the bank above him, the others still some distance behind, she could see that he had made his way to where a miniature waterfall threw a crystal jet into a brown pool beneath. It was a green private place. Here was her chance, her last chance. She took it instantly, going down the bank after him, and, like the rich young man of the day before, kneeling at his feet.

The wetness from the soggy grass beneath the little waterfall struck cold into her knees. She did not even dare to look up; but just knelt there, waiting, as he drank, brown hands cupped, as she could see out of the corner of her eye, under the arc of water. She burned for him to speak before the others further down the road caught them up. Then she heard the voice above her.

"What wouldst thou?"

It all came bursting out of her, the hidden ambition for her two sons. They, at any rate, had borne the heat and burden of the day. They, if any, had given up all to follow the Master. They were fine men too. Surely if kinship meant anything she had a right to ask for something special for them. Was she not sister to Mary, the Master's own mother?

"Command," she said breathlessly, "that these my two sons may sit, one on thy right hand, and one on thy left hand, in thy Kingdom."

She saw it all clearly. The Master would be king; and next after him, in influence and power, would be her own boys. She asked nothing for herself; it would be enough to gain this for them.

There was a long silence, in which she became conscious of two shadows cast from the bank above down the slope to where she was kneeling. She looked up and saw that James and John were standing there. And from them her gaze moved upward to the face of Jesus. It had changed startlingly, as though for a moment the set calm of recent days had left him, leaving an expression of infinite sadness. His voice was low when he spoke. "Ye know not what ye ask." Then, looking up the bank to the two figures outlined there against the sun, he added in a louder tone, "Are ye able to drink the cup that I am about to drink?"

They looked at each other. But almost together they were ready with their reply, for Salome could guess that they had understood what she was about.

"We are able," they said. As always, they were eager and brave enough. And their dream of the Kingdom was the same as hers.

Before speaking again, Jesus raised Salome to her feet and beckoned the other two to come down the bank. When they were in a little group around him he spoke.

"You shall drink of my cup," he said. It was not in Salome's power, mercifully, to know what that cup was to mean. But the weight of knowing what was to be lay with mortal heaviness upon Jesus at that time. For the cup for him was to be bitter indeed, and to the dregs he was to drink it, and within a few days, too. Over the Jordan death awaited, that death which was to be so mysteriously the fulfilment of

XXI. THE RAISING OF LAZARUS

He cried with a loud voice, Lazarus, come forth. And he that was dead came forth, bound hand and foot with graveclothes. John 11, 43–44.

By Nicolas Froment (1420?–1482)

Photo Alinari

his earthly mission. But he could see beyond that too, beyond this little group, beyond the moment of this sunny pause, by the stream on the road winding down to Jordan. And as he looked down into the brave young face of James the agony of this foreknowledge moved him deeply. For James himself was to die, years hence. Not for him were there to be any of the joys of that earthly kingdom of which he was dreaming and in which his artless mother so much desired for him pride of place. A martyr's death was to be his, and the sword of the executioner of Herod Agrippa. Jesus added: "I cannot say who is to sit at the right hand or my left; such a choice as that belongs to God my Father."

He turned, took another drink from the little waterfall, then moved rapidly up the bank to regain the road and resume his march downhill.

Then happened what Salome had feared. Seeing that John and James and herself had come obviously from a private talk with the Master, the other disciples, who had now caught them up, demanded to know what it was about. When they were told they were extremely indignant, Peter especially.

"To ask for a thing like that!" he stormed. "You'd no right at all. Why should John and James, or anybody else for that matter, think they are going to get in ahead of anyone else? We've all served the Master equally, isn't that so?"

He was appealing to them all, and the little group stopped in the middle of the road. The love and fellowship which usually bound them so closely together in an instant disappeared. Voices were raised, hands waved in the air. They were in that posture when Jesus walked back to them and with a quick glance took it all in.

"Listen to me," he said.

They fell silent.

"You know how it is among the Gentiles," he went on. "The big men there have all kinds of respect given to them. But it is quite different in my Kingdom. For there, and that means among you, the man who wants to be really great must learn to be humble, and to act willingly as a servant rather than be filled with ambition to be a master." That was what it seemed to Salome he meant. But she remembered accurately, and often in after times recalled, the last phrase he used. It was this: "Even as the Son of Man came not to be ministered unto, but to minister, and to give his life a ransom for many."

They were quiet by that time, even shamefaced. There was no word among them as they followed Jesus down the road.

Thereafter the day went quickly. The final curve in the steep path they were following brought them in sight of the Jordan itself. Ahead and below across an expanse of caked mud left by the floods of earlier in the year, lay the ford itself. The river water, as they waded through it, was warm as a bath. It was a relief at last to see, after so many hours walking, the city of Jericho.

To those coming in from a long journey it was a luxurious place. The green of its palms and orchards contrasted with the white marble of the palace. There was an amphitheatre, which the Romans had made, and a citadel. Beyond lay the stark Judean hills through which led the climbing road to Jerusalem. And beyond again lay the rocky wilderness in which once Jesus was tempted of the devil.

Even when they were still some distance from the place, Salome could see the immense crowd of pilgrims that were already encamped. She had guessed rightly when she had thought from this point onward there would be little chance of a private word with the Master. The brown tents, the tethered animals, the constant restlessness of a great crowd of people, rather like the mob in a fair-ground, showed that already the pilgrims coming in from the north were staging here on the way up to the Feast of the Passover. And not only from the north either, for Jericho was a junction point of many routes. Here were Jews from all over the world, from Persia and beyond, from Syria, from Idumaea. It was indeed a vast, almost frightening mass. The sound of their voices even at a distance beat upon the air like surf. Thousands every year went up to Jerusalem, and here were some of the thousands already, although it was still a week to the Passover, for it was customary to come thus early in order to seek purification from the priests before the Feast itself began.

Things began to happen with dramatic suddenness as Jesus neared the place. He himself walked steadily forward, but the very first group they passed, a gathering of Galileans at a tent door, instantly recognized him. And thereafter the news of his coming spread like flame among brushwood. Those who knew him ran to tell those many who had heard of him. The characteristic intense excitement of a pilgrim crowd—that collective passion which made the Passover gathering every year a security problem for the Roman authorities—was instantly touched off. It was the Prophet who was coming, people said, many running forward to spread the news. It was the great Rabbi, the wonder-worker they had been hearing of for a year or more past. It was the man who was going to bring in by his own power the Kingdom of God at last.

Within minutes Salome found it hard to keep close, for a shouting, tumultuous mob had already tacked themselves on to the twelve. Even Jesus after a while had to slacken his pace. By the time they reached the city itself it was difficult to get along at all.

And then a strange thing happened. Salome, holding on to the sleeve of James, and entirely surrounded by a press of men, could not see what it was that was happening ahead. But a check in the crowd's progress, and a sudden roar of laughter, told her there was something. And then, when she managed to peep ahead, she saw the extraordinary sight of a little fat man up a tree. It was a fantastic vision; there he was, a tubby overdressed little figure with a greasy, sweating face agog with curiosity.

"Come down out of it, Zacchaeus," someone was shouting. "No taxes today!"

There was another roar of laughter.

The man they were jeering at had climbed one of the many fig-mulberry trees lining the road, and was holding himself up on one of its wide branches. He beamed in an oily, ingratiating manner, like one who was used to having insulting things said to him and who was equally practised in shrugging them off.

James asked a man in the crowd who this was. For answer the man spat in the dust.

"Zacchaeus is the name. Runs a big racket in taxes around here. You know, calls himself a chief inspector—just buys up the tax rights in this locality from the Romans and then sells them again. We've not much time for him or his kind, I can tell you! I reckon he's climbed that tree because he has heard this Jesus of yours is a bit of a friend of tax-gatherers. That's the novelty, no doubt. He's inquisitive as a monkey. Here, what's this?"

Everybody was looking now, because Jesus had paused under the tree and, head thrown back, was looking up, "Zacchaeus," he was saying, "make shift, and come down; for today I must abide at thy house."

He could not have said anything more utterly surprising. Salome could sense the shock of it pass through the whole crowd. And then a murmur began, growing, passing like an angry wave.

"He's asking to stay with Zacchaeus, with the publican!"

But Jesus was taking no notice of anyone but the man in the tree, upon whom his gaze stayed unwaveringly. And, strangely, the little man himself seemed to change. His whole expression altered, as though someone had said a wonderful, beautiful thing to him for the first time in his life.

All at once he stopped being ridiculous and contemptible, ceased to be a figure of fun and, as he clambered down from the tree, became invested with a curious kind of dignity. No one was speaking at all now, so that the next words of Zacchaeus were clearly heard:

"Behold, Lord, the half of my goods I give to the poor."

That was instantly recognizable, and the shock of it was enormous. Salome herself recognized that this which the publican was saying meant that he was making restitution for robbery as laid down in the book Exodus. Yes, he was really making restitution, right there in front of all his fellow citizens of Jericho, people whom no doubt he had many a time and oft squeezed hard. He was adding something else now too, his face working with emotion. "If I have wrongfully exacted aught of any man, I restore fourfold."

Salome saw the quick, delightful smile light up the Master's face. Laying his hands upon the little man's shoulders and towering above him, he said in a ringing voice, "Today is salvation come to this house." He turned to the speechless crowd and added, "He also is a son of Abraham. For the Son of Man came to seek and to save that which was lost."

Thereafter things seemed to move at a wildly accelerating pace. At the porch of the house of Zaccheaus, before a now truly enormous crowd, Jesus paused to tell his last story of the day. In after times Salome came to see that the reason for the telling of this tale was to remind them all of the special nature of his Kingdom, that Kingdom which too many of them were still thinking of in earthly terms, satisfying to the nationalists and hot heads. There were thousands there before him in the evening light ready to flame within themselves, as the bloody sun was flaming in the western heavens over toward Jerusalem, at the word of a leader who would take them forward against the hated Roman oppressors.

"A certain nobleman," he began, "went into a far country to receive for himself a kingdom, and to return." Here was a topical reference straight away, and the crowd knew it. During the lifetime of most of them, there had lived in Jericho a certain Prince Archelaus, elder son to Herod the Great. This Archelaus had in fact travelled to Rome to ask that he might be appointed King. Because he was brutal and despotic the Jews had in their turn sent representatives to Rome to beg that he should not be appointed over them. Nonetheless it had been done. But so harsh had been his rule that he had in the end been banished, and was at the time at which Jesus was speaking actually living in exile far away.

This lord, Jesus continued, before he went away, summoned some of his servants before him and gave them ten pounds each, commanding that they should trade with this money until he came back again. On his return, he called them before him again and asked them how they had done. The first said he had managed to make his original ten pounds yield a further ten and the lord said to him, "Well done, thou good servant; because thou wast found faithful in a very little have thou authority over ten cities." Then the second, being brought before him, reported that his gain had been five pounds. To him the lord said, "Very well, be thou over five cities."

But the third of the servants to whom the nobleman had given money had been timid and could say only that he had kept his original pound hidden away, so that all he had to show was the original sum with which he had started. The lord was very angry and said to the other servants standing near, "Take the pound away from him and give it to the man who has ten pounds." So this was done, and the lord visited his anger upon the servant who had not boldly done his best with the opportunities of service which had been given to him.

Like all the stories of the Master, this set the hearers speculating among themselves. For Salome, as for others, it was only in the light of after events that they began to understand; Jesus, as they came to see, had been teaching many things. The Kingdom would not come straight away, as so many of them were thinking. It would be necessary for him, like the nobleman in the story, to go away for a while; but when he returned he would indeed judge those who had been left in the world to carry on his work by the spirit and enterprise with which they had made the attempt. And then, too, he had been saying that they were not to be like the Jews who jealously kept their faith to themselves, but that true workers for the Kingdom had to be concerned with spreading the Gospel far and wide beyond the confines of their own race and world. And finally, surely, he had been saying that in the eyes of God the very refusal to work for him was in itself a thing worthy of hard judgment.

That night Jesus stayed in the house of Zacchaeus. The next morning began the journey up to Jerusalem itself. The whole pilgrim crowd was with the Master and his disciples by this time, children, women, pack animals, the whole moving in a crowd of dust and excited conversation.

Now just beyond the gates of Jericho sat a blind man. Salome took no particular notice of him at first, for it was a familiar sight in a land where blindness was so common. His eyes were hideously gummed and rheumy as he squatted on his haunches holding out the begging bowl before him. He had a thin pointed beard glistening with his saliva. He was a little isolated point of suffering in the bright splendor of the day. Suddenly he began to shout.

"Who is it?" he cried, "Who's there?"

Someone told him it was Jesus of Nazareth. Immediately, although some of those round about tried to stop him, he let out a piercing yell:

"Thou Son of David, have mercy on me!"

Jesus heard him, and halted.

"Bring him to me," he said briefly.

Two of the disciples took the man under his arm-pits and dragged him to where Jesus was. He hung there in their grip, dirty and disheveled.

Quietly, Jesus asked:

XXII. THE ENTRY INTO JERUSALEM

Behold, thy King cometh unto thee, meek, and sitting upon an ass, and a colt the foal of an ass. Matthew 21, 5 (cf. Zechariah 9, 9).

Ascribed to Fra Angelico (1387–1455)

Photo Alinari

"What wilt thou that I should do unto thee?" The blind man—and Salome had discovered that his name was Bartimaeus, a well-known local character—stammered out:

"Lord, that I may receive my sight."

Jesus made no move, only said, "Receive thy sight; thy faith hath made thee whole."

There followed a moment in which the man hung where he was. Then, convulsively, he jerked himself from the hold of those who supported him, sprang forward, and clapped his hands to his eyes. When he uncovered them they were open, wild, staring, and, miraculously, seeing. A shout went up from the crowd. It was a miracle, they cried, a great miracle! But already Jesus was pressing onward. Behind him, incoherently praising God, the once blind Bartimaeus followed.

Only then did some of those around grasp the significance of the title which Bartimaeus had used in calling upon Jesus. "Son of David," he had called him, as though at the prompting of some mysterious instinct. "Son of David." It was the title given only to him who was Messiah.

All that sunny morning they climbed steeply uphill. Now the way led toward the Mount of Olives, and beyond that across the valley of the Kidron into Jerusalem itself. And all the time the pilgrim crowd increased in numbers and enthusiasm, singing as it went the traditional Songs of Ascent:

> "I was glad when they said unto me,
> Let us go into the house of the Lord.
> Our feet shall stand within thy gates
> O Jerusalem."

But if wild enthusiasm carried along the multitude it was different, Salome noticed, with the disciples by now. They already had sensed the tenseness in Jesus. Noting the way he walked apart, they followed close behind him in a silent group. For he walked as a man alone, his face set toward that which they did not understand, but which they felt was large with menace.

But onward he had to go, for that was his destiny, however keenly the High Priest and the Sanhedrin up there in the city were debating how they might take him and put him to death. This was his hour; this, although it did not look like it, was the beginning of the end, in earthly terms, of his earthly ministry. Yet first he had to proclaim himself as indeed Messiah; and to do that he adopted a memorable, symbolic expedient.

They were within sight of the village of Bethany by early afternoon, a little place on the eastern side of the Mount of Olives. Jerusalem was but three-quarters of a mile away. Here Jesus paused. Summoning up two of the disciples he told them, pointing as he did so, "Go your way into the village over against you."

It was not Bethany he was pointing to, but a tiny little place called Bethphage a little further up the mountain-side.

"As ye enter," he continued, "ye shall find a colt tied, whereon no man ever yet sat: loose him, and bring him. And if anyone ask you, why do ye loose him? Thus shall ye say, 'The Lord hath need of him.' "

It was a mysterious command, but there was that in his manner just then which sent them off without a word. What happened to them Salome learnt afterward. They went into the drowsy little place, and there, in the single street, exactly as Jesus had said there would be, they found an ass tethered with a colt suckling her as she stood in the shade. By the quick way she raised her head as they drew near they knew she was unbroken, in other words, an animal upon whom no one had yet ridden. She backed away as they untied her head rope and the movement brought from the house a man who looked at them suspiciously.

"What are you doing with that colt?" he asked, and some of those in the doorways nearby muttered among themselves.

Yet when the disciples, doing as they were bidden, gave the reply, "The Lord has need of him," the owner made no further comment, only folded his arms and in silence watched as they led the animal away, the colt running after.

A number of pilgrims encamped on the Mount of Olives had by that time joined with the multitude who had come up with Jesus and the disciples from Jericho. So the crowd was bigger than ever when they returned to it with the ass. The significance of the whole act became plain when, at the sight of the Master mounting upon the animal, a great cry went up. For those people, deeply versed in the tradition of their Scriptures, recognized at once the symbolism of the action. For was it not written in the ninth chapter of Zechariah, "Behold, thy King cometh unto thee: he is just and having salvation; lowly, riding upon an Ass, upon a colt, even upon a colt the foal of an Ass"? Yes, indeed they recognized it. It was because of that recognition that a little later in the journey, as he was entering the city itself, they responded by strewing their garments before him for the little feet of the colt bearing him to trot over, thus making a sign of royal homage, as it is recorded in the second Book of the Kings that "They hasted, and took every man his garment, and blew the trumpet saying, Jehu is King".

The crowd was mad now. "Blessed is the King!" "Blessed is the King that cometh in the name of the Lord!" they were roaring. Some Pharisees, distinguished by their severe and disapproving mien, pressed near to Jesus to ask him to keep the people in order. But he knew then that nothing could stop this torrent of passionate enthusiasm. "I tell you that," he said, "if these shall hold their peace, the very stones will cry out."

And yet, strangely, as it seemed to Salome, he was not far from tears himself. Indeed, as they rounded the bend in the road and came in sight of the full splendor of the Holy City with its Temple and palaces, he stopped. Even while those around him were shouting "Hosanna!" "Hosanna!" he burst into tears. "If thou hadst known in this day, even thou, the things which belong unto peace! But now they are hid from thine eyes. For the day shall come upon thee when thy enemies shall cast up a bank about thee, and compass thee round, and keep thee in on every side, and shall dash thee to the ground, and thy children within thee; and they shall not leave in thee one stone upon another; because thou knewest not the time of thy visitation."

Again the terrible power of God to see into the future of the human story lay heavily upon him. Forty years hence that very city of Jerusalem, with all its glory, was to be visited with the full horrors of total warfare and sacked by the Emperor Titus.

But the vision of the Son of Man was longer, much longer, than that. The ruins of many a proud city lie sprawled across the pages of time. And maybe the ruins of more will yet be so until, in the fulness of time, men learn through suffering what it really is which "belongs unto their peace", until they learn that there is in fact no continuing future to their lives of getting and spending, of hatred and animosities, of national prides and ambitions, of wars and rumors of wars. So then it was not only Jerusalem that Jesus was weeping over, but all the cities of men in any age and in any place where there is wealth, and sin, folly and unrest, and a fatal blindness to the things which really matter.

Thus Jesus rode down from the Mount of Olives, across the valley of the Kidron, and into the city, while the crowd ecstatically waved palm branches along his way. He was fully committed now. And as though to make utterly plain his complete resolution to see all through to the end, he rode into the very precincts of the Temple itself, and then out again and back for the night into Bethany where he rested awhile in the household of Martha and Mary.

The sun set with great pomp among the hills that evening. After the quick twilight the flickering pinpoints of hundreds of pilgrim fires could be seen all around. And the stars came out, and streams chuckled among the hills.

Salome, listening to the murmuring conversation of the disciples, wondered much what the future held. It seemed an age since she had asked the Master to give the chief places in his Kingdom to her two sons.

The Anger of the King

Based on El Greco's

**CHRIST DRIVING THE TRADERS
FROM THE TEMPLE**

ON the morning after the day on which he had entered Jerusalem in triumph, acclaimed by the multitudes as the Messiah of Israel, Jesus went up to the city again from Bethany, where he, with his disciples, had passed the night. The ancient city, shining in the sun and throbbing with excited preparation for the Feast of the Passover but a few days hence, was the fit setting for the drama which was to follow.

Pontius Pilate, Procurator of Judea, had already come up from his coastal residence to Caesarea so as to be on hand during the difficult period of the Passover, when the crowded condition of the city and the high emotional flashpoint of the pilgrims thronging to it usually made it necessary to have a strong hand at the helm. It was not easy to be responsible for law and order in such a place at such a time. So Pilate in the Praetorium was having a grim morning listening to reports from the officers of his garrison. It was also very warm, and he felt himself sweating under his clothes in a way distasteful to so fastidious a gentleman. That, apart from the press of business, was his main preoccupation; he was uncomfortable, worried, and exasperated. He loathed the country, he loathed the city, and in particular he loathed this annual anxiety of Passover time.

However, he was there to serve the Empire, and serve it he would. But some time, some day, he promised himself privately, as the harassed hours passed, he would forget all this in the peaceful retirement of his Italian home; forget the dust, and the heat, and the uproar. Herod Antipas, the puppet local ruler, had also arrived for the Passover, for it was fitting that, however much he disliked the exertion it necessitated, he should be 'on hand also. So he had gone to his palace, and with his luxurious retinue was settling down to make the days pass as pleasantly as possible under the circumstances.

And somewhere among the crowds out in the city was a big-muscled, dark-skinned pilgrim from Cyrenaica in North Africa, wandering that sunny morning looking at the sights, utterly ignorant that, within a few days, he was to carry a Cross and be for all time remembered because of it. And there was Joseph of Arimethea, a member of the Sanhedrin, a grave and reverent man, and Nicodemus, a colleague of his, both of whom would have been beyond words astonished that Monday morning to be told that, before the week was out, they would be engaged in burying the most precious body in the world in its tomb.

Only one man among the thousands upon that immortal stage knew fully what his part was to be, and that was Jesus.

He walked purposefully, as a man consciously dedicated to a great purpose the perils of which he could see clearly. There was nothing distinguished about his dress. The robe he wore, woven in some cottage up in Galilee, was the customary dress of the peasantry. From the sandals on his feet to the staff in his hand he was the typical countryman up in town for the feast. There were hundreds in the crowds that morning similarly clad. Yet wherever Jesus went rumour moved before him and a crowd followed behind. Those who saw his face never forgot it. The prominent nose, the jet hair, the piercing eyes, tall forehead, all spoke of the extraordinary.

Jesus entered the Temple through one of the arched portals of the great enclosure and passed into the Court of the Gentiles. This Temple, rebuilt by Herod on the site of Solomon's ancient creation, was in essence the same as Jesus had known it throughout his life. It was a most wonderful place. As Jesus stood in the Court of the Gentiles looking northward over the crowds, the colonnades of Solomon's Porch were on his right, the stone partitions, three cubits high, which enclosed the sanctuary were at some distance ahead, beyond that lay the Court of the Women and beyond that again the Court of the Men, then a porchway leading on to the Holy Place itself. Here was the spiritual centre of Jewry.

Eighteen years before, when Jesus had been a boy of twelve, he had come with his parents for the Passover to this very place. And though, as a devout Jew, he had come many times since in the annual cycle of feasts, the memory of that first childhood visit, when he had stayed behind to talk with the learned Doctors, was with him still. Maybe it was something which had impressed itself upon his mind those eighteen years ago which controlled the course of action which he took now.

For then, as now, the money-changers were busy.

It was big business in the atmosphere of an oriental bazaar. In the course of years big financial interests had grown up around the opportunities for gain offered by the needs of the thousands of pilgrims flocking into the place.

What Jesus saw, therefore, as he took his stand, arms folded, and his friends around him, on the inner side of the porchway to the Court of the Gentiles, was the large rectangular space alive with activity. There were booths everywhere, temporary affairs on trestles under awnings to keep out the downbeating sun. There the money-changers, under licence from the Temple authorities, made a large income out of the trading. And also there were the stands of those who sold living creatures for sacrifice, from the bleating sheep and goats which only the richer could afford to the doves in their wickerwork cages. So the Court of the Gentiles was really a market-place, in spite of the fact that it stood upon sacred ground.

Something which Jesus saw within minutes of entering the place vividly pinpointed the scandal of it all. A grey-bearded man, who from his travel-stained clothes and sunburned face had come far on pilgrimage, came through the Porch and looked around him in simple wonder at the traditional scenes. At his girdle hung the leathern purse containing his savings. Heaven alone knew from what distant part of the ancient world he had come. But one thing was certain; he was at the culminating point of a lifetime's ambition, enabled at long last to keep the Feast within the very Temple itself.

But money-changers, keen men of business, anxious to make the most of this busy week, had sharp eyes for newcomers. Three from nearby booths almost simultaneously,

Jesus noticed, had seen the pilgrim and immediately set up their customary outcry; that he must pay the Temple tax and that he would have to change his money first in order to do so.

The newcomer, moving over to a booth near where Jesus was standing, carefully undid the leather lace which secured his purse. Then, he emptied, with great care, into the rough palm of his left hand a number of Greek drachmae. This was pure chance of course; they could have been coins from any city in the world, depending whence the pilgrim had come. Yet whatever the currency the requirement was the same: it had to be changed into shekels. For the coins of foreign states, often bearing upon them emblems such as the heads of emperors which could be regarded as idolatrous, were regarded as unfit for use within the Temple area. The dishonesty of the transaction lay in the very high rate of exchange which the money-changers charged.

When the pilgrim handed over his drachmae the money-changer, with the practised movement of his kind, threw the handful immediately into one of the scales which were on his table before him. When he pressed the lever the scale dipped against the drachmae. "Underweight," the money-changer sang out as one voicing a familiar formula, "you have to pay the difference." He then named the sum which made the eyes of the man before him open wide. It was quite extortionate, just as it was quite usual. Here was the second of the ways in which these money-changers made a profit out of hiring space in the Court of the Gentiles for their booths at festival times; it was necessary only, as this man had done, to assert that money offered was underweight, worn, or clipped at the edges, for them to do well out of the compensation claim. Now, with a worried look, he again drew out his purse. Contemptuously, hurriedly, for now there were other customers waiting, the money-changer handed him the shekels.

It remained now for the pilgrim, the main purpose of whose journey was to make sacrifice, to purchase the creatures wherewith to do so. He threaded his way up between the booths, until he came, as Jesus had known he would, to the place where there was one who sold doves. These, the cheapest form of sacrifice, were sold at extortionate prices. A dove bought within the Temple precincts, certified as without blemish, fetched a price as much as six times in excess of its actual value.

But this time the pilgrim reacted more violently. When the trader in doves named his figure, the man stepped back with an oath.

So in that corner there began one of the familiar uproars which commonly disgraced the sacred precincts. The pilgrim cursed, the merchant cursed in return, while the throng passed by with laughter or indifference, and the doves beat upon the bars of their cages and money-changers further down the line, well used to this kind of occurrence, continued to ply their trade. They could count on every protection.

The very booths were known as the booths of the Sons of Annas. This Annas was father-in-law of Caiaphas the High Priest himself. All the trading of the temple was in the hands of this family combine. A very great deal of money was made by Annas and by the subsidiary agents who traded under his protection. The whole thing was a dark scandal at the very heart of Judaism.

It was at this moment, the pilgrim and the trader in doves arguing, the people thronging by, that Jesus acted. It was not a sudden act; but a long premeditated plan put into action. He was about to challenge the priestly powers in a way they could not possibly overlook or forget or leave unavenged.

He stepped forward, put strong hands under the front edge of the table of the man who sold doves, and with a heave sent the whole lot over upon the floor. The further edge caught the trader as he stood there, and he went down with a shout under the ruins of his booth and its awning. The doves in their scattered cages fluttered wildly; sheep in a neighboring pen plunged and scattered, running out among the crowds; three Temple guards in bright breastplates began to push through the crowds towards the disturbance.

But Jesus had not finished yet. Striding down toward the nearest money-changer's table he treated this also in the same way, pitching it over, scattering the coins. And when this was done, he gathered up some strands of twine that had fallen upon the tessellated pavement and, rapidly, twisting some of this together, made of them a whip. With this, holding it above his head, he herded some of the sheep which had escaped from their pen through the crowds toward the further portal, not stopping until he had driven them through into the street beyond. Then he wheeled round, strode back into the center of the Court, and in a loud voice proclaimed the challenging words:

"It is written, My House shall be a House of Prayer: but ye have made it a den of robbers."

All who heard knew indeed where it was written. "Mine House shall be called an house of prayer for all peoples," had said the Prophet Isaiah. And, "Is this House, which is called by my name, become a den of robbers in your eyes?" had asked the Prophet Jeremiah.

No way more challenging than this quoting of the Scriptures could have been found to hurl the accusation of their own corruption into the teeth of the priests. Those who heard, and there was a multitude which did, knew instantly that this was no common happening, no isolated outburst of indignation by an individual; but a premeditated, extremely brave act of defiance which could not but be perilous in the extreme to the author of it. It made Jesus, already a marked man in the eyes of Annas and Caiaphas, one whom they now would have to destroy or face the alternative of being destroyed themselves.

In the Court of the Gentiles it was as though a trumpet call had sounded, calling all men of good will to action. The crowds, pushing hither and thither among the booths, gathered round Jesus in an exultant mass. Truly he was great whom they had welcomed with palms and hosannahs the day before. Truly he was a leader! So they cheered, and cheered again.

When night fell, Jesus and his friends did not return to the house of Martha and Mary in Bethany, for to do so would certainly have meant the Master's arrest after the events in the Temple. So they lay out under the stars, concealed among the shrubs and undergrowth clothing the sides of the Mount of Olives. There, uneasy and tense, they took it in turns to keep watch, fighting the temptation to sleep. Yet always as the disciples thus in their turn kept watch they saw at a little distance, ethereal in the light of the wakening Passover moon, the figure of the Master. Jesus was praying, silently communing with his Father.

But in the city, and far into the night, the priests took council among themselves how they might take him and put him to death.

On Tuesday morning, Jesus was back in the Temple at the scene of his triumph on the previous day. The money-changers' booths he had overthrown were in place again, the Court of the Gentiles was as busy as ever. Yet the atmosphere of the place was changed. The news of what Jesus had done had spread far and wide, so that wherever he moved he was followed by an expectant crowd. The same question was now in every mind: how would the priests deal with this challenge to their authority?

The answer soon became clear. Seeing plainly by this time that the popularity of Jesus with the people would make it physically dangerous for them to take him by force, and would certainly lead to a popular rising, they had resolved, by a variety of subtle questions, to make him lay himself open to arrest either on a charge of blasphemy or of insubordination to the Roman occupying power.

It was also clear on that Tuesday morning that their fear of Jesus had led three groups generally hostile to each other, for once to combine together in a common attack. Traditionally the Pharisees, forming a good proportion of the priestly aristocracy, disliked the extreme orthodoxy of the Sadducees. These, holding to the beliefs of Moses, and remaining in severe isolation from the mass of the people, represented a petrifaction of doctrine deeply suspicious of any liberality of thought. Perhaps the only emotion in which Pharisees and Sadducees were united was in contempt of the Herodians, the party pledged to subservient support of the Roman power.

That morning, when Jesus had entered the Temple, it was not long before he was approached by the first of the deputations sent to question him. Those who were about him listening to his teaching gave way silently before those who approached. This deputation came from the Sanhedrin itself. Its leader, after a mocking bow, looked Jesus up and down with hard eyes.

"Tell us," he began, in a high clear voice, "by what authority doest thou these things? Who is he that gave thee this authority?"

It was a fair question, and referred not only to the fact that Jesus at that very moment was teaching within the Temple, or to his action against the money-changers of the day before, but also to the many reports of his mighty works which had come in with ever-increasing volume for quite a year past.

The answer which Jesus gave matched the legalistic cunning of his questioner. He said that he would ask them a question first. It related to the baptism of John the Baptist whom they themselves had rejected but who was revered by the people.

"The baptism of John," Jesus said, returning the keen look of his adversary, "was it from heaven, or from men?"

They were placed in a dilemma. There were two possible answers, "From heaven", or "from men". Yet the first would lay them open to the charge of having rejected one who, by their present admission, they were saying had acted by divine sanction. The second answer would have exposed them to the wrath of the listening crowd among whom the memory of John was respected as that of a Prophet.

There was nothing that they could say, a fact quickly recognized by the astute leader of the deputation. With an expressive gesture of his hands he turned away. One of his companions, very conscious of the dangers of the crowd, muttered, as he followed: "We do not know whence was the baptism of John; we cannot say."

But Jesus called them back before they had retreated very far. The crowd, seeing his wish, by closing in prevented their further retreat. With the group from the Sanhedrin thus held before him Jesus told them a story which pierced their very hearts.

Once upon a time, he said, there was a man who planted a vineyard. Leaving it in charge of an agent he went away on other business. When the time came for him to claim his share of the fruits of the vineyard, he sent a servant to carry out this errand for him. The listeners, versed in the Scriptures as they were, saw at once the reference to the Book of Leviticus, where, in the nineteenth chapter, it is laid down that in the fifth year after the planting fruit may be claimed. However, Jesus continued, the agent beat the servant when he arrived and sent him away with nothing. Next, the owner of the vineyard sent a second servant, but he was treated in the same way. The owner then decided to send his son, feeling confident that the agent whom he had placed in charge of the vineyard would, at least, treat him with respect. But nothing of the sort happened. Indeed, the treatment given the son was worst of all, for they killed him.

The application of the story was only too plain. The vineyard was Israel itself; even the crowd grasped that, accustomed as they were to hearing their nation referred to as the Lord's vineyard. And those left in charge of the vineyard, like the agent in the story, were the Scribes and Chief Priests who should have been faithful custodians of the nation's soul. Who, then, were the servants who, in the story they had just heard, were so cruelly treated? They were the Prophets who, all through history, had suffered at the hands of the rulers of Israel. And finally, and most important of all, who was the son?

All eyes were turned upon Jesus. And as all thus gazed at him he uttered a telling quotation from the one-hundred-and-eighteenth psalm:

"The stone which the builders rejected,
The same was made the head of the corner."

So the Pharisees retreated discomfited while Jesus continued with his speaking to the people.

Yet before long a group of Herodians approached.

"Master," one of them began, "we know that thou sayest and teachest rightly, and acceptest not the person of any, but of a truth teacheth the way of God." This was the preliminary compliment characteristic of those used to groveling before authority. The speaker continued: "Is it lawful for us to give tribute unto Ceasar, or not?"

The question was, of course, a cunning one. Here again there appeared to be two possible answers. Jesus could either say that it was lawful, in which case he would alienate his hearers, to whom the paying of Roman taxes was an abomination; or he could say that the paying of tribute was not lawful, in which case he could be reported to the Roman authorities for spreading revolutionary doctrine.

His answer was to ask to be shown a Roman coin. There was a certain amount of fumbling in pockets before one could be produced, for these hated things were not commonly carried by the Jews. Eventually, one was handed up from among the crowd. It was a silver denarius.

Holding the coin between finger and thumb Jesus showed it to those who stood before him. People in the front ranks could clearly see the imperial image upon it.

"Whose image and superscription hath it?" he asked.

There was a slight pause before anyone answered. Then one of the Herodians spoke:

"Caesar's."

Jesus tossed the coin back to the man who had produced it.

"Render unto Caesar the things that are Caesar's," he said; "and unto God the things that are God's."

So once again his questioners were baffled. Turning away, they passed between the crowd, which parted before them.

It was afternoon when the third of the day's deputations came to Jesus. This time it was a group of Sadducees. Distinguished in their long white robes, they posed a question characteristic of their peculiar manners of thought. These people were no believers in the resurrection; indeed, their denial of the possibility of life after death was one of the main points of difference between their teaching and that of the Pharisees. This fact lay at the heart of the question which they now asked.

"Master," one of them began, stroking his long, scholarly beard, "Moses wrote unto us, that if a man's brother die, having a wife, and he be childless, his brother should take the wife and raise up seed unto his brother."

Thus far the speaker had stated no more than what was the common practice of devout Jews. But, he went on to ask, what would be the position if this happened seven times over, and the original widow had in her lifetime seven different husbands? Whose wife would she be at the resurrection?

The reply which Jesus gave made it plain that the life to come, being essentially spiritual, was not governed by material considerations. Those who attain to the spiritual life, he told them, would have passed beyond the stage where earthly circumstances and ties had any importance. They would be equal unto the angels and sons of God. What is more, he drove at the heart of his questioners' denial of the resurrection by citing a proof of it from the very scripture which the Sadducees revered. "That the dead are raised, even Moses showed in the place concerning the Bush," he said, "when he calleth the Lord the God of Abraham, and the God of Isaac and the God of Jacob." So the Sadducees in their turn were silenced, and they too moved away, watched by all, as Jesus warned his listeners of such as they.

"Beware of the Scribes, which desire to walk in long robes, and love salutations in the market-place, and chief seats in the synagogues, and chief places at feasts; which devour widows' houses, and for a pretence make long prayers; these shall receive greater condemnation."

They were strong words, and they were marked.

A little later that day Jesus saw another happening in the Temple which drew a memorable comment from him. He had moved by that time into the Court of the Women, where, along the wall, were set alms-boxes shaped, rather oddly, like wide-mouthed trumpets, into which it was the practice of the faithful to place a thank-offering. At so busy a season there was a continual procession of people passing by these receptacles. There would come some pilgrim from afar and throw in his offering, then a peasant to make his. As Jesus watched, a rich man, expensively dressed, paused impressively to make a large donation. The coins clattered loudly as they went down the trumpet-shaped orifice. Almost immediately afterwards a little

XXIII. CHRIST DRIVING THE TRADERS FROM THE TEMPLE

And Jesus went into the temple of God, and cast out all them that sold and bought in the temple, and overthrew the tables of the moneychangers, and the seats of them that sold doves, And said unto them, It is written, My house shall be called the house of prayer; but ye have made it a den of thieves. Matthew 21, 12-13.

By Domenikos Theotokopoulos, known as El Greco (1541-1614).

Photo Studio Fifty-one

woman, in shabby widow's weeds, halted by the same vessel, and modestly dropped in two lepta, as they were called. Now the lepton was the smallest copper coin, worth less than half a cent.

Jesus was immediately struck with the difference in the two offerings, and even more so by the different manner in which they had been given. True, the rich man had given more, but it had cost him less in proportion to his resources than the tiny gift of the widow had cost her.

"Of a truth I say unto you," Jesus said, "this poor widow cast in more than them all: for all these did of their superfluity cast in unto the gifts: but she of her want did cast in all the living that she had."

Now about this time there befell an incident of great significance. Some Greeks came asking to see Jesus. There were numbers of such people up in Jerusalem for the Feast, but they were not Jews by blood. Dwelling in lands far away they had been converted from their pagan faiths to Judaism with its teaching of the one true God. That such men should some and enquire after Jesus represented a momentous extension of his message far beyond the little bounds of Galilee and Judea in which the whole of his earthly ministry had been carried on. But now the wider world was asking of him, and the wider world was represented and symbolized by this humble group who came, not without shyness, to ask if they might see him.

It was Philip whom they sought out first, perhaps because he bore a Greek name. Yet Philip was not so sure what to do with them, for, like all the disciples, he was by this time anxious for the safety of the Master. So Philip whispered to his colleague Andrew and the two of them, when they found the opportunity, went to tell Jesus. Then, as Jesus looked upon the group of strangers, he had a sudden vision of the truth that, though he should be despised and rejected of men of his own race, yet in times and places distant by far from these last days in Jerusalem many others would come by means of the Cross which he was to suffer for them all, to honour and glorify his name.

The necessity and the glory of the Cross, the truth that out of his death would come splendor, as a flower springs from a seed, was expressed in the words which he then uttered: "Verily, verily, I say unto you, except a grain of wheat fall into the earth and die, it abideth by itself alone. But if it die, it beareth much fruit. He that loveth his life loseth it; and he that hateth his life in this world shall keep it unto life eternal."

Then he added something which awed as well as puzzled the disciples. "Now is my soul troubled; and what shall I say? Father, save me from this hour." But that was not to be. And he added simply: "For this cause came I unto this hour. Father, glorify Thy name."

Strangely, the brightness of the day seemed to have become overcast. The heat continued, but there were lowering clouds looming over the Temple and the city. It was the kind of weather in which people looked up instinctively into the sky for the first warm drops presaging a downpour. And in the hush of the moment, those around—and there were many besides the disciples and the waiting Greeks—heard a voice speaking, it seemed from nowhere, "I have both glorified it, and will glorify it again."

Some said the looked-for thunder was beginning. But there were others who, casting

B.M.G.—O

uneasy glances at each other, said it was an angel which had spoken. Jesus heard their mutterings and answered, looking the while upon them with a drawn and anguished face: "This voice hath not come for my sake, but for your sakes." And he added in a loud thrilling tone, "Now is the judgment of this world; now shall the price of this world be cast out, and I, if I be lifted up from the earth"—he meant on his cross—"will draw all men unto myself."

So the uneasy evening came, and with it the time for Jesus and his men to withdraw to their place of concealment on the Mount of Olives. Already the crowds about the Temple were thinning as the pilgrims made off toward their encampments. They would face the night hours in comfort, but the Son of Man, as once he had prophesied, would have nowhere to lay his head. Out, then, from the city, and down into the Kidron valley went the little band. As they reached the foot of the incline the westering sun, emerging briefly after the overcast, touched the ramparts of the city and the Temple behind them with departing splendor. The light showed up the massive buildings of the Temple in all their majesty. The vast place spoke in every outline of solidity and permanence.

"How great a place it is," one of the disciples remarked as they all stood awhile facing westward. But Jesus said that the time was coming when that enormous place, seemingly destined to last for ever, would be utterly destroyed, with not one of its huge stones left upon another. When they asked him when such a frightful thing would happen he signed to them to sit down awhile in the evening gloom while he spoke of terrible things to be.

There would come a time, he warned them gravely, when it would seem as though the end of all things were at hand. The disciples, especially Peter and James and John and Andrew, pressed him further. Would it be the end of the world? Would it be the sign of the final coming of the Son of Man in glory?

In asking these things they were but reflecting what was the common expectation of Jews of their time. The Master replied that there would be many signs. There would be false Christs who would arise to deceive the people; there would be civil commotions, wars and rebellions; there would be upheavals of nature and, further, to add to the terrors of those times there would be persecutions of the faithful, such as themselves, who would be called upon through physical suffering to testify to their faith. Also there would come a day when Jerusalem itelf, that great city now towering above them, would be encompassed by enemies and destroyed.

It all came to pass, as Jesus had already foreseen when he had wept over the city. The events which followed the investing of Jerusalem in the year 70 by Titus the Roman who had been sent to put down the Jewish rising, were every bit as terrible as Jesus foretold in this apocalyptic discourse.

The campaign was ferocious to the last degree, its terrors being added to by merciless civil war, when, within the besieged city, contending parties fought one another. To the terrors of the time was added also the horror of famine. Thousands starved to death, while an even worse fate awaited those who tried to escape. These, falling into the hands of the Romans encamped around, were crucified outside the walls in sight of the howling defenders.

The struggle continued for a hundred days. At last even the Temple itself, which had held out to the last, was set on fire, and in the flames its glory departed for ever.

To the group listening to Jesus down in the valley of the Kidron that evening, these prophecies were breathtaking. Yet the Master pressed on with his warnings. They were to be ready: he admonished them to be ready at all times, spiritually prepared for the time when the Son of Man should come for his last judgment, for it would happen suddenly in a time no man could foresee. To press home the lesson of readiness he told them two parables.

The first was the story of the wise and foolish virgins. It was a Jewish custom—a custom which his hearers would many times have seen in operation back in the life of their villages—on the night of a wedding for a procession to be sent to look for the bridegroom and to bring him to his bride. It would be dark, and they would need lamps. How lost, therefore, would be those who, because they had forgotten in their carelessness to put oil in their lamps, would not be ready to go forth joyfully to welcome the bridegroom when the cry arose that he was approaching. "Give us of your oil, for our lamps are going out," they would cry to those who had been more prudent. But it would be too late, and they would find the door shut against them. "Watch therefore," Jesus said, turning from his story to its application to his hearers, "for ye know not the day nor the hour."

The second parable was a story, rather like that of the pounds which he had told before, of a man who, going away for a while, called together his servants and gave to one five talents, to another two, and to another one, in order that each could use these gifts according to his individual ability. He who had received five talents used them to the full extent, and by his enterprise and industry made another five talents. Similarly, the man who had received two did well, and increased his capital by the same number. But the third, being timorous, hid the money away. When his master returned he had nothing to show beyond the original gift. So the master rewarded those who had done their best with the resources at their disposal. But the third he punished for his lack of industry and courage. The moral was clear. Those who work for the Kingdom of God, against the time when, at the Last Judgment, the Son of Man shall return, must make full use of all the opportunities which God has given them. And they will be judged, not according to the sum total of their achievement, but according to the results which they have obtained with their opportunities and abilities.

And now the prophetic vision of Jesus widened until he saw the whole world of men against the background of eternity. Upon the vast canvas of his imagination he drew a picture of the Last Judgment. This, the last and greatest of his prophetic utterances, ranged ahead into time to come far beyond the destruction of Jerusalem. This time he was looking to the end of the world itself.

The picture, at once splendid and sombre, was made up from familiar things which his hearers would many a time have noticed in their everyday lives. Often the shepherd on the hills herded sheep and goats together. It was only at the end of the day that he separated them, standing facing the incoming line of animals and, as they came up to him, directing with his staff the sheep one way and the goats the other. So shall it be at the end of the world at the judgment, Jesus said.

"When the Son of Man shall come in his glory, and all the angels with him, then shall he sit on the throne of his glory: and before him shall be gathered all the nations: and he shall separate them one from another, as the shepherd separatest the sheep from the goats: and he shall set the sheep on his right hand, but the goats on the left."

And after that, Jesus said that the righteous would be told why they had thus been placed on the right hand of God. "Then shall the King say unto them on his right hand, Come, ye blessed of my father, inherit the kingdom prepared for you from the foundation of the world: for I was an hungered and ye gave me meat: I was thirsty, and ye gave me drink: I was a stranger, and ye took me in: naked and ye clothed me: I was sick, and ye visited me: I was in prison and ye came unto me."

The righteous would be puzzled, because they would not be able to remember ever having seen Christ in that way. But when they expressed their bewilderment the King would say to them the memorable words: "Inasmuch as ye did it unto one of these my brethren, even these least, ye did it unto me." He would be saying that in every case of need, in the sick, the lonely, the poor, and the hungry in any place, in any age, there was a Christ to be served by those who sincerely desired to follow him.

But to the unrighteous, set on the left hand like the goats, he would say, "Depart from me, ye cursed, into the eternal fire which is prepared for the devil and his angels. For I was an hungered, and ye gave me no meat: I was thirsty and ye gave me no drink: I was a stranger, and ye took me not in: naked, and ye clothed me not: sick, and in prison, and ye visited me not."

And when the wicked were, in their turn, puzzled at the judgment, not being able to remember ever having, in the highways and byways of life, seen Christ, they would be reminded that he had in fact been there to be served in all the sufferings of mankind, but that they, being indifferent, had missed their opportunity. And so the righteous should enter into eternal life; but the unrighteous would go into a lasting punishment.

Only the barking of the dogs round some pilgrim fire at a distance broke the silence as Jesus finished speaking. Then he rose, and, followed by his little group of friends, moved toward the Mount of Olives and vanished into the night.

Do this in Remembrance of Me

Based on

THE LAST SUPPER

ascribed to Fra Angelico

WITH the coming of Wednesday morning, which dawned bright and clear, it was as though there were a pause in the doom-laden drama of the Passion. Jesus did not teach in the Temple that day but remained in and around Bethany. Thus it was as though for a moment the stage was empty.

But not for long. For soon there appeared, moving hurriedly and nervously up the road from Bethany, one of the disciples. Just one, alone. His name was Judas Iscariot, and there was no disguising his nervousness. When loitering pilgrims got in his way in the narrow streets, he brushed his way so brusquely through that there were many who looked after him muttering. But Judas did not hear them; his mind was on other things. So on his way he went, within the wall-encircled enclosure of the ancient city, making always for the southwestern corner where, overlooking the valley of Gehenna, stood, among a jumble of other buildings, the big house of Caiaphas the High Priest and of Annas his father-in-law.

That morning, as Judas thus made his way there, an important meeting was in session in the marble-floored Council Chamber. Its importance could be seen by the number of Temple guards on watch outside. The Chief Priests and the Scribes and the Elders of the people had come together for a specially convened gathering, summoned hurriedly the evening before as reports had come in from the deputations which had, with conspicuous lack of success, questioned Jesus in the Temple.

No one who looked on that scene in the Council Chamber could doubt for a moment what was the ultimate purpose of the gathering. It was reflected in the steely glitter of the eyes of Caiaphas himself; it was reflected in the troubled faces of some of those who listened to him. All knew that something had to be done: the city was in an uproar; tumult had to reach only a little further toward hysteria to invite intervention from the Roman garrison. That the cause of all this unrest was Jesus of Nazareth was not in doubt. He had to be stopped. "It is expedient," Caiaphas had already said, over-ruling the objections of some of the less ruthless, "that one man should die for the people."

The question was, how? There would be no difficulty in arresting Jesus; that could be done at almost any time. The whole problem lay in finding an opportunity to do it smoothly and secretly, before the crowds could hear of it. In that way the danger of civil commotion would be considerably lessened. How to take Jesus, then; that was the question. It was the problem they were all giving their minds to, there in the Council Chamber, when a whispering at the curtains draping the entrance to the room suggested a new development.

The whispering ceased. Caiaphas, from his chair at the opposite end of the Chamber, looked up keenly as one of his own servants came pattering across the marble toward him. The man bowed, then whispered something into the High Priest's ear. The whole expression of the face of Caiaphas altered as he listened. The message was electrifying. It was so exciting that he pushed the servant away before the man had finished his message.

"It is one of the followers of the Nazarene himself!" Caiaphas announced. "He is outside, even now, and he has sent to say he would speak with us."

He made a quick sign to his servant, who withdrew, to return again in a moment with Judas Iscariot. The whole roomful of men looked curiously at him. He had come to betray his master; that much was already certain from the reception which Caiaphas had given to the news of his arrival. Why was he doing it? The gathering in the Council Chamber that morning, seeing before them the broad brow, the intelligent face, the nervous gestures of Judas, had no idea.

Was it jealousy—jealousy of the comparatively obscure position which he had always seemed to hold among the other disciples? Was it disappointment at the discovery that the Kingdom of which Jesus so often spoke was not, after all, to be a kingdom of this world? Or was it just desire for money? It could hardly be that, for this Judas was, after all, one whom Jesus himself had chosen to be a disciple. Therefore, like the rest, he must have had qualities of a high order to recommend him to the Master. Or was it not that, he stood there before Caiaphas, merely an instrument of God's purposes, driven to do what he did in order that the Scriptures might be fulfilled and that the Son of Man might be delivered up to be crucified?

Judas spoke privately to the High Priest who, having heard what the other had to say, announced to the assembled company:

"He offers to deliver this Jesus up to us, and asks what we will give him to do so."

"Thirty pieces of silver," suggested one of the assembly in an ironic voice. A grim smile passed over the face of Caiaphas. The inference was not lost on him. Thirty pieces of silver was the price required as forfeit for the killing of a slave.

Thus it was agreed, and Judas, bowing low, withdrew from the room to consult outside with those of the guards who would be responsible for the arrest.

Meanwhile, in Bethany, Jesus was making his own private preparations for what was to follow. It was his desire to eat the Passover for the last time with his friends and to do that he needed a secluded room. So when the disciples asked him, "Where would thou that we make ready for thee to eat the Passover?" he said, "Go into the city to such a man, and say unto him, 'The Master saith, my time is at hand; I keep the Passover at thy house with my disciples'."

"To such a man——" This, it is thought, was a citizen of Jerusalem who had a wife called Mary and a son called John Marcus. They were tried and trusted friends. So to this family certain of the disciples went secretly to prepare the Upper Room for the Last Supper, taking with them, in baskets, the food and the wine which they would need. At the same time they made the arrangements that they would be led to the place at the appointed hour by the secret sign of a man—one of the servants of Mary's husband who would be sent for the purpose—carrying a water-pot. He would be easily noticeable because it was so unusual for a man, rather than a woman, to carry out the domestic task of carrying water.

So it was arranged, as the last Wednesday that Jesus was to know on earth drew toward evening.

Now there lived in Bethany a wealthy man called Simon, who also was a friend of the Master. This Simon gave a supper for Jesus. The gathering was marked by a disturbing incident. It was, of course, a party of men only, although Martha helped to serve the meal. Her own brother, Lazarus—he whom Jesus had raised from the dead—was present. As always, the guests reclined about the table, leaning on the left elbow while eating with the right hand, the while engaged in murmuring conversation.

Because of the peace and privacy it was all the more startling when a woman burst in upon the gathering. Her name was Mary, and it was clear she was in a state of great emotion. The roomful of men stared up in great astonishment, partly scandalized at this feminine incursion, partly alarmed at the wildness of her demeanour.

As her eyes went round the company it was seen that she carried in her hand a small alabaster jar of beautiful shape, its opening sealed.

Swiftly, she made for Jesus, and, kneeling beside him as he reclined, with a graceful movement, broke the narrow neck of the vessel. Tilting it, she gently poured the contents upon the dark hair of his head. Immediately a haunting, evocative scent filled the room, the scent of a substance used in the embalming of the dead. It was a kind of ointment called spikenard. It was expensive, being worth in that quantity about as much as a laborer would earn in three days.

Her action, clearly symbolic, and expressive of the tenderest reverence, spoke without words of her insight into the truth that Jesus was indeed close upon the moment of his death. The Romans themselves were in the habit of thus anointing their dead. Such was the inner significance of what she did. Yet it was the outer fact of what appeared to be an apparent waste of money which chiefly drew the comment of those who saw it done. Significantly, it was Judas who gave expression to this feeling. Speaking from his position among the guests he asked, "Why was not this ointment sold for three hundred pence and given to the poor?"

Down the length of the room, and looking straight into the eyes of the one who he knew was to betray him, Jesus said softly, "Allow her to keep it against the day of my burying. For the poor ye have always with thee, but me ye have not always."

The villagers who were looking in at the door, drawn thither in the first place by the desire to see Lazarus, marveled among themselves, not understanding the import of the Master's words. But those nearest to him, not only in physical presence but in understanding, fell silent as the woman who was called Mary, with a reverent salutation, gravely withdrew.

*   *   *   *

In the early afternoon of the following day, Thursday, two men were to be seen walking purposefully together through the Fountain Gate in the southeastern corner of the wall encircling the city of Jerusalem. One of the men, whose name was Peter, was large, shaggy, and bearded. His companion, whose name was John, was by comparison small and looked much younger, although in fact there was not a great deal of difference in their ages.

They had not gone far before they came upon an unusual sight near one of the public wells set in to the side of the roadway. It was a man, not a woman, bearing a pitcher of water high up on his shoulder. To the observant eye it was clear that he had been waiting for something, for as soon as he saw the two he ceased to loiter, as he had been doing, and set off decisively down the street. Without a word, or any sign of recognition having passed between them, the two followed him.

Each carried a basket of provisions, holding it with one hand while balancing the other edge of the container against his hip. Thus they came to a largish house upon the door of which the man carrying the pitcher discreetly tapped. It was opened by a slave girl. She admitted the three, the water-bearer and Peter and John, into the courtyard beyond. And now for the first time since they had entered the city one of the disciples spoke, the whiles bowing courteously to their host.

"The Master says," Peter began, exactly carrying out the directions Jesus had given him, " 'Where is the Guest Chamber, where I shall eat the Passover with my disciples?' "

The master of the house, silent as his servants, turned about and led them to the back of the courtyard, up the steps on the outside of the further wall and into a large upper room which was situated there.

Peter and John saw that, apart from the actual food, the room was already provided with all that would be necessary for the Passover meal. Ahead of them, as they looked through the door, couches had been set ready around the central space where the food would be served, leaving an open end—the end that now faced them—for the service of the meal. The place where the Master would sit at the head of the company was therefore facing them. In the right-hand corner of the room were set ready a basin, a jar of water, and a towel. On the table, before the place which Jesus would occupy, stood a large cup.

Seeing, then, that their host had gone as far with his preparations as he could, Peter and John bowed their gratitude to him and set about the task which they in turn had come to do.

Now the Passover, for which they had come to make ready, had, as the greatest of all the Jewish Feasts, its own especial and hallowed ritual—a ritual not to be understood unless seen against the background of the historical events which it commemorated. Once, in the far distant past, when the people of Israel had been slaves in Egypt, the Lord God, punishing the Egyptians for their cruelty to his chosen people, had afflicted their captors with a series of plagues. In the last and greatest the Angel of Death took off all the firstborn in the land. In order that the avenging angel, thus passing through by night, should avoid those houses in which were Israelites, God had commanded, through his servant Moses, that they should mark the lintels of the doors with the blood of a lamb which in each household had been previously sacrificed and eaten. So, when the Angel of Death passed through the land, the people of Israel were spared.

The Scriptures added this solemn command: "And this day shall be unto you for a memorial, and ye shall keep it in feast to the Lord; throughout your generations ye shall keep a feast by an ordinance for ever."

Throughout the years they had done so. It was natural, therefore, that Jesus should wish to keep this solemn occasion for the last time with his closest friends.

Toward dusk, and in the utmost secrecy, Jesus with his disciples set off from the

XXIV. THE LAST SUPPER

And as they were eating, Jesus took bread, and blessed it, and brake it, and gave it to the disciples, and said, Take, eat; this is my body. Matthew 26, 26.

Ascribed to Fra Angelico (1387–1455)

Photo Alinari

Mount of Olives on his final journey into the city. At the gate of the house where the supper had been prepared the same slave girl let them in. The same master of the house, this time attended by a servant bearing a torch, met them in the courtyard, where Peter and John were anxiously waiting. Then, still in silence, he led them to the steps leading to the upper room and at the foot, with another brief bow, left them. The disciples climbed the steps, entered the room, and secured the door behind them.

The chamber was lit by one hanging lamp; the food and the wine were on the table; all was ready.

Yet immediately two difficulties arose; difficulties arising out of the human pride and frailty of the disciples themselves. Strung up as they were, thrilled with love for the Master as they were, there yet burnt within them keen jealousies one of another. They looked at the table set ready. Obviously, Jesus would sit at the head; but who was to sit at his right hand and at his left in the places of honor? Who among them should take the lowest places down either side of the horseshoe-shaped board? After all, it was only a few days ago that John and James, through their mother Salome, had asked for the chief places in the Kingdom.

And then also there was the question—a question prompted by the ewer of water and the copper bowl and the towel standing ready on the right-hand side of the door—as to who was to wash the feet of the company. This was customary before a meal, like the washing of hands in the West. Generally, it was done by a slave or lower servant; but because this gathering was so secret there was no servant present.

The disciples looked furtively upon each other in the dead silence of the room. And then Jesus did a truly astonishing thing; so astonishing that the eyes of Peter especially widened as he saw what the Master was doing. For the Lord was taking off his outer garment and placing a towel about his waist. The meaning of it was startlingly clear. He was attiring himself as would a slave preparing to wash the feet of the company before dinner. When that was done, and still without a word, he poured some water from the ewer into the copper bowl, hung the towel over his left forearm, and, motioning to the company to be seated, began moving among them. He followed no particular order; just kneeling and washing the dust of the road from the feet of whomever was nearest, without any regard for who was the eldest or the youngest. He just took them as they came, and humbly washed their feet. They watched him in a burning quiet.

At last he came to Peter. But this was too much for the impetuous fisherman. "Lord," he burst out, "doest thou wash my feet? Thou shalt never wash my feet!" Jesus, having poured a little water and now using the towel, said only, "If I wash thee not, thou hast no part with me." He meant that, unless Peter could fully share with him this supreme act of humility, he could never be a true follower.

Peter understood this instantly, and, sensitive as always to any suggestion that he was not fully loyal, cried out, "Very well, then, Lord, wash not my feet only, but also my hands and my head."

Jesus looked up at him with a slow smile. "He that is bathed needeth not save to wash his feet," he said, "but is clean every whit: and ye are clean." He rose to his feet, looking around for the next disciple. It happened to be Judas. Jesus knelt to him, too, and, as he prepared to wash the betrayer's feet also, he added in a very low voice, "But ye are not all clean."

So they took their places around the table and Jesus, having returned the basin and the ewer and the towel to the corner of the room, placed himself at the head of them. Then he spoke:

"Know ye what I have done to thee? Ye called me Master, and Lord: and ye say well; for so I am. If I then, the Lord and the Master, have washed your feet, ye also ought to wash one another's feet. For I have given you an example, that ye also shall do as I have done to you. Verily, verily, I say unto you, a servant is not greater than his lord; neither one that is sent than he that sendeth." And before he began the meal with grace, he added, "If ye know these things, blessed are ye if ye do them."

Thus they turned to the repast set ready for them—the unleavened bread—unleavened in symbolic remembrance of the hurried flight of the people of Israel from Egypt, the bitter herbs evocative of the bitterness of their slavery, and the thin, brick-shaped biscuit made of a compost of fruit and nuts in remembrance of the bricks they had made as forced laborers in that alien land.

It was toward the end of the meal that they came to the supreme moment.

The disciples were still eating, the while talking among themselves in low tones. Then the conversation died away as it was seen that Jesus had taken a piece of the unleavened bread in his strong, brown hands. He broke it. In the abrupt quiet of the room, the snap of the fracture was clearly heard. When Jesus had thus blessed and broken the bread, he passed the fragments of it around the table, saying, "Take, eat; this is my body."

After that Jesus took up the cup which had been on the table when Peter and John had entered the room earlier in the day. Now it contained wine. This also Jesus blessed in the customary manner and gave to them.

They passed it around after he had said, "Drink ye all of it; for this is my Blood of the Covenant, which is shed for many unto remission of sins. Do this in remembrance of me."

So, simply and quietly, was instituted the greatest act of Christian worship and devotion. Whatever men have called it; the Communion, the Mass, the Lord's Supper; and however men have repeated the act, with splendor and ritual, or in stark simplicity; however even they have understood it, as the physical presence of Christ in the bread and wine or as an act commemorative of his love and of his promise to come again, they have found in it an unfailing source of strength and inspiration.

When Jesus had set down the cup the meal continued after a thoughtful pause. But now was coming the moment of the betrayal, and knowing of this Jesus became, as St John puts it, "Troubled in the spirit." The emotion showed clearly on his face. Seeing this, the disciples looked anxiously upon him. Then he said something which deeply disturbed them.

"Verily, verily I say unto you, that one of you shall betray me."

Now they looked not at him, but at each other, wondering of whom this terrible thing could be true. Once again it was Simon Peter who was the first to speak, gesturing in agitation and asking, "Tell us who it is of whom thou speakest." To this Jesus replied that it was the man to whom he would pass a piece of bread; just that. Then he took a piece from a loaf, dipped it into the dish before him and handed the

XXV. THE AGONY IN THE GARDEN

O my Father, if it be possible, let this cup pass from me: nevertheless not as I will, but as thou wilt. Matthew 26, 39.

By Andrea Mantegna (1431-1506)

Photo Studio Fifty-One

morsel to Judas seated on his left. "That thou doest," he murmured hurriedly, "do quickly."

Without a word, Judas rose. With no backward glance upon his erstwhile friends he made for the door, unbarred it, and passed out into the darkness. There was a momentary glimpse as he did so of stars like jewels against a velvet night. One who was present must have noticed the fact because St John adds the simple sentence, "And it was night."

It was indeed so, the dark night of the human soul.

In the Garden Secretly

Based on Mantegna's THE AGONY IN THE GARDEN
and on Giotto's THE KISS OF JUDAS

AFTER the supper was over, and when Judas had left them to go about his secret business of betrayal, the company lingered about the table, in intimate talk. This was a very special occasion, for it was, although the disciples did not know it, the farewell of Jesus to his friends. "Now is the Son of Man glorified," Jesus began when the door had shut behind Judas, "and God is glorified in him; and God shall glorify him in himself, and straightway shall he glorify him."

The words mystified. Jesus, seeing it, looked with a sad smile upon the company. "Little children," he said, "yet a little while I am with you. Ye shall seek me: and as I said unto the Jews, whither I go ye cannot come; so now I say unto you, a new Commandment I give unto you, that ye love one another; even as I have loved you." As if in emphasis he repeated, "By this shall all men know that ye are my disciples, if ye have love one to another."

Simon Peter, as always, trying desperately to understand, asked, "Lord, whither goest thou?"

Jesus replied, "Whither I go, thou canst not follow me now; but thou shalt follow me afterward."

"Why cannot I follow thee now?" Peter cried. "Why, I will lay down my life for thee!"

Then Jesus, looking upon his friend with affection mingled with compassion, said, "Wouldst thou lay down thy life for me? Verily, verily, I say unto thee, the cock shall not crow, till thou hast denied me thrice."

The words set the whole company murmuring in distress. "Let not your heart be troubled," the voice of Jesus cut across their protestations, "ye believe in God, believe also in me. In my father's house are many mansions. If it were not so, I would have told you; for I go to prepare a place for you."

They could follow that quite easily, for he meant that, as Peter and John had prepared the room for the Last Supper, so he himself would go ahead to prepare the great final Messianic banquet in the Kingdom of Heaven where there would be places for all who had been true followers of him.

Now it was the turn of Thomas to be puzzled. "Lord," he asked, "we know not whither thou goest, how know we the way?"

The reply of Jesus was memorable. "I am the Way, and the Truth, and the Life; no one cometh unto the Father, but by me."

They were all trying so hard to follow him, and now it was Philip's turn to join the questionings. He was frowning with concentration as he said, "Lord, show us the Father, and it sufficeth us."

116

Jesus, reclining as he was, turned to look at him. "Have I been so long time with you, and dost thou not know me, Philip? he that hath seen me hath seen the Father."

So the conversation went on. And it was now that he told them of how, when he was no longer in the flesh with them, there would be sent to them one whom he called the Comforter or Strengthener, even the Holy Spirit. The Father would send the Holy Spirit in His Name, Jesus explained. The Holy Spirit would teach them all things, and keep them in remembrance of all that their Master had said to them.

And he added a picture of himself as the vine and of they themselves, his friends, as the branches thereof. Just as the branches of the vine cannot bear fruit without keeping in constant touch with the tree of which they are a part, so a follower of Christ in any age will never be able to be fruitful in his life unless he similarly keeps in constant communication with Christ himself.

Once again he repeated, "This is my commandment, that ye love one another, even as I have loved you." But this time he added to it words torn out of his own inner, secret knowledge of what lay before him, in the form of a dreadful death. "Greater love hath no man than this, that a man lay down his life for his friends."

And then, his mind turning in great sorrow to those who were shortly to put him to death—the priests and the people of his own race—he said, "If I had not come and spoken unto them, they had not sinned; but now they have no excuse for their sins. He that hateth me hateth my Father also."

He went on to warn his disciples that harsh treatment lay in wait for them. "They shall put you out of the Synagogues, yea, the hour cometh, that whosoever killeth you shall think that he offereth service unto God. And these things will they do because they have not known the Father or me."

A saddened company reclined about the table looking anxiously upon him. And so he said to them, "Because I have spoken these things unto you, sorrow has filled your hearts. Nevertheless, I tell you the truth; it is expedient for you that I go away: for if I go not away, the Comforter will not come unto you; but if I go, I will send him unto you."

After he had spoken further of the powers of this mysterious Comforter, the Holy Spirit of God, who would guide them unto all truth, he said, "A little while, and ye behold me no more; and again a little while, and ye shall see me."

This mysterious saying, following upon so much else that they could not fully follow, hard as they were trying to do so, set the disciples to renewed questioning among themselves. Jesus, again seeing their bewilderment, sought to explain. His going, he said, and the sufferings of his followers thereafter until the time of his coming again, would be rather like what happens in childbirth, when a woman suffers pain which is amply compensated afterward by the joy of holding a newborn son in her arms. "Ye therefore," he said, "now have sorrow, but I will see you again, and your heart shall rejoice and your joy no one taketh away from you."

"I came out from the Father," he concluded, "and am come into the world again; I leave the world and go unto the Father."

Now at last they saw, or thought they saw, what he meant, so that round the table went a glad murmur of comprehension. "Lo, now speakest thou plainly," they said, "and speakest no proverb. Now know we that thou knowest all things and needeth not that any man should ask thee: by this we believe that thou camest forth from God."

"Do ye now believe?" Jesus asked them sadly. "Behold, the hour cometh, yea, is come, that ye shall be scattered, every man to his own, and shall leave me alone."

The time was indeed close; it was to happen within an hour or so. Yet he added resolutely, "In the world ye shall have tribulation: but be of good cheer, I have overcome the world."

And then it seemed to the disciples that in the spirit he passed beyond them into realms where they could not follow. It was as though in the long prayer, which he then went on to utter, that he was speaking not so much to those gathered about him in the room, but on their behalf, and on behalf of all men and women everywhere in all ages who have sought to follow him, to God himself.

He said that his hour had come, and he asked that in it he might be glorified, in order that God his Father might be glorified thereby. "The words which Thou gavest me," he said, looking up, "I have given unto them; and they receive them and knew of a truth that I came forth from Thee, and they believed that Thou didst send me. I pray for them; I pray not for the world, but for those whom Thou hast given me for they are Thine. . . . Holy Father, keep them in Thy name which Thou hast given me that they may be one, even as we are. Now I come to Thee," he went on, "and these things I speak in the world, that they might have my joy fulfilled in themselves. . . . I pray not that Thou should take them from the world but that Thou shouldst keep them from the evil one." He then prayed for the sanctification of his followers, who had been sent into the world even as he himself had been. It was for their sakes that he had sanctified himself. They, in their turn, should be sanctified in truth. Nor was it only for his closest followers that he prayed, but also for those that believed and were to believe, down the ages, through their words.

Jesus ended his prayer with the wonderful words: "Father, that which thou hast given me, I will that, where I am, they also may be with me: that they may behold my glory, which thou has given me: for thou hast loved me since the foundation of the world. O righteous Father, the world knew thee not, but I knew thee; and these knew that thou didst send me; and I made known unto them thy name, and will make it known; that the love wherewith thou lovest me may be in them, and I in them."

It was manifestly the end. The company rose, and Jesus rose with them. "Peace I leave with you," he said, "my peace I give to you."

When they had all put on their sandals again—the sandals which, after the feet-washing, had been set by the door—they put on their cloaks and went out. It was the night of the full Passover moon, in the lovely haze of which they passed down the steps from the Upper Room, into the courtyard of the house which had given them hospitality, and silently and carefully into the street beyond.

All was now quiet. It was high time for them to seek concealment on the Mount of Olives. Each night of this Passover week they had chosen a different hiding-place. The appointed spot for this Thursday was a dark wall-encircled olive grove called Gethsemane, a little spot where there was an oil-press used during the day but certain to be deserted at night. This, silent and lonely, was to be the place where Jesus was to pray in agony. But first it was necessary to get there and, since it was not permissible to pass through the Temple area by night, the only way thither, and the

XXVI. THE KISS OF JUDAS

Now he that betrayed him gave them a sign, saying,
Whomsoever I shall kiss, that same is he: hold him fast.
And forthwith he came to Jesus, and said, Hail, master;
and kissed him. Matthew 26, 48-49.

By Giotto (1270-1337)

Photo Giacomelli

wisest way, because the quietest, was around the southeastern corner of the city walls and thence down a steep slope to the left of the valley where ran the stream called Kidron.

It was eerie, walking so stealthily down there below the sleeping city, in and out among the trees which cast in the moonlight dense black shadows. When they had passed over a wall into the garden most of the disciples laid themselves down. But Peter and James and John, never willing to be separated from the Master, followed him further into the recesses of the place. He turned to them at last to say to them in a low voice, little more than a whisper, "Sit ye here while I go and pray yonder. My soul is exceeding sorrowful, even unto death: abide ye here, and watch with me."

He went a little further on from them, and in the moonlight they saw him fall upon his face. They waited, awestruck as the minutes went by. He did not move. As the time of waiting lengthened the heaviness of place and hour, coupled with the somnolent song of the stream at a little distance, weighed heavily upon them. The three disciples sat down, their backs against a tree. One by one their heads fell forward, for they were exhausted. Soon they were sleeping, and still Jesus had not moved.

Such was the scene then in that nocturnal garden: the moon, the shadowy trees, the three sleeping disciples, and, at a distance, the prostrate figure.

Meanwhile, Judas was busy about his sinister business. Events with him had moved swiftly since he had left the Upper Room. So hurried had been his pace, impelled as he was by the sense that, if he did not do swiftly that which he had been determined upon, he would never do it at all, that he was breathless when he had reached the summit of the slope leading out of the ravine. Thereafter, along the moonlit alleyways of Jerusalem he followed the route he had taken on the previous Wednesday—a route which led him, as then, to the house of the High Priest. He was immediately admitted, for they were waiting for him. Everything now had about it a sense of extreme urgency, because the beginning of the feast drew hourly nearer and it was essential to effect the trial and execution of Jesus before that hour struck.

The information which Judas brought with him was brief but to the point; he knew where Jesus the Nazarene was to be found that night. A party of Temple guards, who had been held in readiness, was alerted. They already had prepared their weapons and the ropes they intended to use for the binding of the wanted man. Out into the silvery street, therefore, moved this body of men with Judas at their head. They were accompanied by certain scribes as senior officials to see that all was done according to order.

Yet before they could hurry down into the valley of the Kidron there was another call to be made. Having, as Jews, no authority to make an arrest outside the immediate precincts of the Temple, it was necessary first to secure the co-operation of the Roman authority. What they needed, in fact, was a platoon of troops from the garrison to go with them, and that meant a call at Garrison Headquarters in the Antonine Fortress.

It was not a healthy place for any Jew to enter. The troops, mostly mercenaries under Roman officers, were a tough crowd, conditioned by long military usage to brutal exercise of their power. It was in the Antonine Tower that people were flogged and tortured.

So the party from the Palace of the High Priest approached the place with trepidation. The sentries at the door challenged them promptly, finally admitting only one spokesman—one of the Elders sent along by Caiaphas—to the guard-room beyond. Soon afterward harshly shouted commands within announced the turning out of the guard. A few moments later, with heavy tread and the clank of accoutrements, a detachment emerged from the arched entry of the fortress. They set off, surly at being disturbed at such an hour, along the streets, through the city gate on the southeastern side, and out and down into the moon-bathed, shadowy ravine beyond.

So large a body made a considerable noise in the silence of the night. The disciples whom Jesus had left by the entry of the garden of Gethsemane, when he had gone further in with Peter and James and John, were able, in consternation, to watch the procession of flaring torches coming down toward them, like the movement of some outsize, nightmare glow-worm.

The sight of the disciples brought shouts from some of the party whom Judas was leading. For they knew then that their quarry must be near. They fanned out among the trees and pressed forward into the garden.

Suddenly, there he was, the man they sought, a white-clad figure ghostly against a background of olive trees. They stood quite still. When they drew near and, as though suddenly abashed, stopped in their tracks, he asked calmly:

"Whom seek ye?"

He had but then and there emerged from an agony of lonely prayer. Rightly had he said that his soul was exceeding sorrowful, even unto death.

"Father, all things are possible unto Thee," he had cried; "remove this cup from me." Yet even then, as he experienced the full horror of foreknowledge of his crucifixion, he submitted himself to the will of God. "Albeit not what I will, but what Thou wilt." Three times during long intervals of intense prayer he had used the same words. And three times, likewise, he had gone over to his three sleeping friends. "Peter, Simon, sleepest thou?" he had said the first time. "Couldst thou not watch one hour? Watch and pray that ye enter not into temptation; the spirit indeed is willing, but the flesh is weak."

But so exhausted were they, that they slept again. When he went over to them the second time they could only stir and look at him. The third time they did not rouse, and he said only, "Sleep on now, and take your rest: it is enough; the hour is come; behold, the Son of Man is betrayed into the hands of sinners."

He had heard the sound of the approaching troops, and stepped forward into the clearing to face them. That was the moment, therefore, when the soldiers saw him standing in the moonlight and heard his question, "Whom seekest thou?"

What followed was brief and ruthless. "You will know the man you are looking for," Judas had told the guards, "because I will point him out to you by kissing him." So Judas did step forward, with that common salutation of the East, lightly touching with his lips the Master's brow. The guard thereupon sprang forward. But Jesus, drawing himself up, by something in his very presence caused them to hold back. There was a tense pause. Then he asked them the same question again. They replied that the man they sought was one Jesus of Nazareth. "I am he," Jesus told them. And then, gesturing round to the cowering disciples, he added, "If therefore ye seek me, let these go their way."

Peter, gathering up desperate courage, drew the knife which he carried at his girdle, and with a wild slash almost severed the right ear of one of the servants of the High Priest, a man called Malchus. As the blood flowed, and the man writhed on the ground, Jesus intervened sternly. "Put up thy sword into the sheath," he ordered; "the cup which the Father hath given me, shall I not drink it?"

It was as if the action had broken the spell. The guards closed around Jesus and in a moment had his wrists bound behind his back. At that the main body of the disciples fled wildly up into the garden, scattering among the dark trees. Only Peter and one other disciple halted at a little distance, watching what was to happen next and getting ready to follow when Jesus was led away.

They saw a strange occurrence. There was a certain young man who had hovered about Jesus and the disciples ever since they had left the Upper Room after the Last Supper and gone into the garden of Gethsemane. Because it was night they had not been able to see him clearly. But it could have been, and some think it certainly was, a young John Marcus, the son of the man in Jerusalem who had lent his upper room for the use of Jesus and his friends at the Last Supper.

This young man, stupefied by the rapid and violent things which had taken place, still lingered upon the scene. Seeing him, one of the guards made a grab for him. The hand caught in the boy's loin cloth. With a cry, he twisted himself free, leaving the linen cloth in the hand of his assailant. Thus naked, he fled upward into the darkness among the trees.

So they led Jesus away, and the flare of the torches and the voices of his captors climbed slowly up the steep way back into the city.

Trial

Based on Giotto's

JESUS MOCKED

THE first place to which Jesus was taken was the house of Annas, the father-in-law of Caiaphas the High Priest. So, as the commencement of his ordeal, Jesus was confronted by the very man who lay at the heart of all the plottings which were destined to take the Master to his death.

Annas was an exceedingly powerful person. He was old, wary and astute. He had also, a good many years before, been the High Priest himself. Since then he had wielded power through his relatives. Five of his sons, and now his son-in-law, had filled the office of High Priest. It was an astonishing record. This, moreover, was the same man who maintained the profitable abuses typified by the activities of the money-lenders in the Temple. It was therefore natural that Annas, the master-mind who had plotted the capture, should want to see Jesus first of all.

So see him he did: the old, cold, worldly Jew looking with keen interest and no little satisfaction upon the captured Nazarene. And while they thus looked upon each other messengers were already making their way to the nearby house of Caiaphas, a house which may have been separated from that of his father-in-law only by a courtyard.

Down below, having faithfully followed, Peter and John waited to see what the outcome of this preliminary confrontation would be. Yet all they saw was the Master, set-faced, being brought under escort from the house of Annas and taken under the moonlight over the cobbles to the Palace of the High Priest.

In that house there were already hurriedly gathering together the members of that select group drawn from members of the Sanhedrin who had already agreed together to send Jesus to his death. This group was the same which had met in the house of Caiaphas on the Wednesday before, and had been present when Judas had arrived with his promise of betrayal. The fulfilment of that promise was now at hand.

Still Peter and John followed to see what would happen. Now it was easier for John to get into the courtyard of the house of the High Priest than it was for Peter, because John knew the place.

As usual, it was a portress who kept the gate of the courtyard—a broad-hipped, black-eyed, strident harridan of a woman. With her, John, whom she recognized, had a whispered word about the friend of his waiting outside. So the portress let Peter in, peering closely at him as he passed by to join John with the group around the brazier that stood in the centre of the courtyard. The night was chill and the servants and the officers were warming themselves.

Meanwhile, in the audience chamber within the Palace, Jesus was facing the first

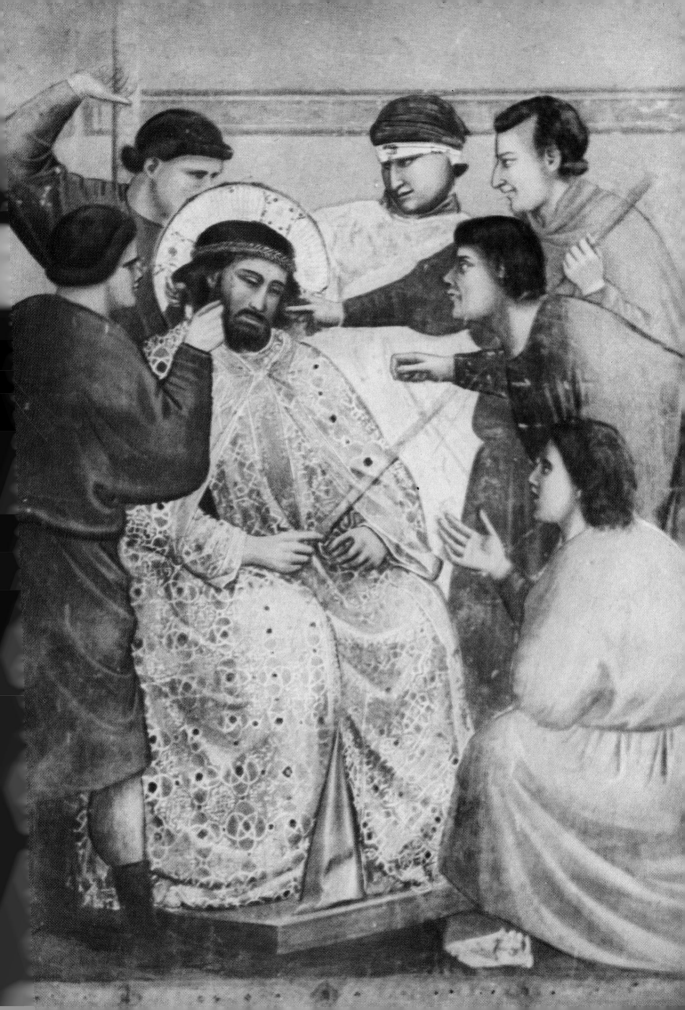

XXVII. JESUS MOCKED

And they bowed the knee before him, and mocked him. saying, Hail, King of the Jews! And they spit upon him, and took the reed and, smote him on the head. Matthew 27, 29-30.

By Giotto (1270-1337)

Photo Giacomelli

of his cross-examinations. It was hurried and hostile, for they were in haste to be done with him.

The first question which Caiaphas put to Jesus concerned his teaching. What had he taught? Why had he taught? The reply of Jesus indicated not only his own present fearlessness but also made plain the fact that he had never endeavored to conceal his activities in any way. "I have spoken openly to the world," he said; "I ever taught in Synagogues, or in the Temple, where all the Jews came together; and in secret spake I nothing." And he added, "Why asketh thou me? Ask them that have heard me, what I spake unto them: behold, these know the things which I said."

There was a guard standing at either side of Jesus, and one of these now struck him hard over the side of the head, saying, "Answereth thou the High Priest so?"

Jesus turned to him saying quietly:

"If I have spoken evil, bear witness of the evil: and if well, why smitest thou me?"

Still Peter with the others stood around the brazier in the courtyard. He was very nervous. Already the black-eyed portress had asked him once, when she had walked over to the fire at his first entering, whether he were not, as she had put it, one of the followers of the Nazarene. He had denied it. And then another woman in the company, who had been having whispered conversations with the portress, came close and looked at him in the flame flicker. She also asked if he were one of the disciples. Again he denied it, saying, "I am not."

And now an even more alarming thing happened, for one of the men, one of those who had been present at the arrest in the garden of Gethsemane, turned at the voice of Peter, recognizing something familiar in its typical Galilean accent. "Of a truth," he accused, "thou also art one of them; for thy speech betrayeth thee!"

The attention of the whole company was now attracted, so that all turned upon Peter. At the sight of their hostile faces his nerve completely went. With oaths and curses, speaking in the fast gabble of the terrified, he flatly denied any knowledge of Jesus whatever. Then, in the little silence which followed, from somewhere within the city, came the sound of a cock, crowing in the false dawn. It would be about three a.m.

Then the attention of all the group switched suddenly from Peter to a movement on the other side of the courtyard. It was Jesus, and they were bringing him out to put him for a while in one of the cells below the place, there to await his appearance before the full Sanhedrin. So Jesus with his tramping escort passed right by the brazier. As he thus passed by he looked straight into the eyes of Peter.

Immediately the horror of what he had done went like an arrow to the heart of the fisherman. He remembered the words which Jesus had said, "Before the cock crow, thou shalt deny me thrice." Anguished, he broke away from the group around the fire, staggered out into the moonlit street, and wept bitterly.

The period of waiting which followed was a bad time for Jesus. He was now in the hands of the Temple guards. They, meanly echoing the hostility of their masters, cruelly ill-used him; spitting on him, striking him over the face with swinging blows of their hands, the meanwhile mocking him and crying out, having first blindfolded him to make the fun more intense, "Prophesy unto us, thou Christ: who is he that struck thee?"

At the first flush of dawn, as it touched the tips of the mountains around the city, Jesus was taken under escort through the street and into the Temple. The whole

Sanhedrin was by this time assembled. It was an august body, representing the whole official authority of Israel. It had a full membership of some seventy, and included Scribes, Priests, Elders and Doctors of the Law. The justice which the Sanhedrin dispensed was usually of a high order, marked by decorum of procedure and care for the rights of the accused.

Yet in their treatment of Jesus, which was as hurried and perfunctory as the earlier proceedings in the Palace of Caiaphas, the Sanhedrin departed very far and very unusually from its customary standards. It may well have been that the result was pre-arranged. With the beginning of the Passover Feast so close, there was an urgent need to have the business done with.

Even so, at the outset it proved difficult to get sufficient agreed evidence to support a capital charge. At last two men stepped forward to testify that they had heard Jesus teaching in the Temple. They were prepared to swear they had heard him state that he was able to destroy the Temple of God and to build it in three days.

Jesus, of course, had once said something like that; but with an entirely different meaning from the crude suggestion of wonder-working powers contained in this testimony now made against him. The words he had actually used were, "Destroy this Temple, and in three days I will raise it up." The inference had been that, should the corruption of those in power lead to the eventual destruction of all that, for Jewry, was represented by the Temple, the spiritual power of the teaching of Jesus would be sufficient to replace it by a spiritual creation formed and founded upon the faith of his followers.

This present testimony, however, was sufficient to give Caiaphas the opening he was looking for. His urgent need and inflexible purpose being to fix a charge of blasphemy upon Jesus, he had but to pursue this accusation further, so it seemed to him, to achieve his end.

Dramatically he stood up in his place at the head of the assembly within the "Hall of Polished Stones", as it was called. Before him, quite alone and undefended, stood Jesus, still bound.

"Answereth thou nothing?" the High Priest demanded in a ringing voice. "What is it that these witness against thee?"

Jesus made no reply, only continued steadily to look into the flashing eyes of the powerful figure before him. Now Caiaphas played his trump card. "I adjure thee by the living God that thou tellest whether thou be the Christ, the Son of God."

A dead silence fell, and many of those present leaned tensely forward. For the words "I adjure thee" had put the prisoner on oath. He had to reply truthfully to this most terrible enquiry as to whether he had in fact said that he was God. There was no hesitation about his reply; all heard it.

"Thou hast said." A long sigh passed over the gallery—he had not denied it. And now Jesus was saying something else: "Nevertheless I say unto thee, henceforth ye shall see the Son of Man sitting at the right hand of power and coming on the clouds of heaven."

It was enough. With a ritual action the High Priest reached both hands to the throat of his long ceremonial robe and tore it down. It was the action required of a Rabbi at the hearing of blasphemy. Then he said, "He hath spoken blasphemy; what further need have we of witnesses? Behold, now ye have heard the blasphemy: what think ye?" There could be no other answer than that which was given, and the murmur of it, accompanied by much grave nodding of heads, came immediately: "He is worthy of death."

Strictly, according to the formal rules of the Sanhedrin, it was held necessary to wait until the following day after a trial before sentence of death was pronounced, thus giving time for the matter to be carefully weighed. But this time all rules were waived. Jesus was condemned. It remained now only to take him before the Roman Governor in order to get permission for the sentence to be carried out by the Romans themselves, it not being in the power of the Jews to apply the supreme penalty.

The Sanhedrin accordingly broke up. As its members mixed with the people then beginning to gather at the Temple for morning worship the news of their decision spread rapidly. Everywhere groups gathered, excitedly passing on the news. It was by such means that Judas heard the final result of his treachery.

He had passed through fearful hours since the arrest in the garden, not knowing where to go, not being able to find rest from the mounting torment of his soul, feeling friendless and lost and damned. And now in the clear light of early morning, within the precincts of the Temple he heard the news: Jesus was to die.

He stood a long time where he was, staring at the ground. Then, with a spasmodic movement, as of one who has come to an abrupt decision, he began to hurry, almost running, toward the Court of the Priests, where he thought he might find Caiaphas and those about him.

The man was clearly beside himself. The sweat was running down his face and his chest working as he gasped for breath. Then Caiaphas recognized him and arched his eyebrows in ironic enquiry. At last words came from Judas.

"I have sinned," he gasped, "I have betrayed innocent blood!"

The brows of Caiaphas arched even a little further. He shrugged his shoulders; the man was clearly mad, and in any event he had fulfilled his purpose. So he said coldly, "What is that to us? See thou to it."

For the last time Judas looked upon the faces of all of them, seeing there only contempt and indifference. Then he fumbled at his waist, pulling out the purse that was there and emptying its money into his hands. There were thirty pieces of silver. He threw them on the ground. They rolled and tinkled upon the pavement, coming to rest among the feet of those who stood there. With that, and with a final wild gesture, Judas rushed out the way he had come.

After an astonished pause, some of the priests began picking up the coins. But Caiaphas paused to warn them that, since the money was tainted, having been used to buy the blood of a man, it could not be returned into the Temple treasury from which it had come. So they disposed of the matter by arranging to use it for the purchase of a piece of ground as a cemetery for strangers on the southern outskirts of the city beyond the valley of Gehenna. It was called the "Potter's Field".

So was mysteriously fulfilled yet another prophecy of the Scriptures. As St Matthew puts it (although the quotation is in part from the prophet Zechariah), "Then was fulfilled that which was spoken by Jeremiah the Prophet, saying, and they took the thirty pieces of silver, the price of him that was priced, whom certain of the children of Israel did price; and they gave them for the Potters Field, as the Lord appointed me."

But Judas, driven beyond bearing by the demon of remorse that was tearing his very soul, went to a secret place—some say to the self-same burying ground, or Akeldama, which means "field of blood"—and there, taking a rope, hanged himself.

It was now about six a.m. Pontius Pilate, the Roman Governor, accustomed to begin the business of the day early, as was the Roman habit—especially in hot countries where the noonday hours were apt to become unbearable—was already present in his apartments. Word was brought to him by an aide, that an important deputation of Jews, led by the High Priest himself, urgently desired an audience of him.

The young officer who brought the message looked apprehensively upon his master's face as he spoke. The Governor was apt to be irritable so early in the day, especially at the beginning of so anxious a one as this was likely to be.

Pilate frowned heavily when he heard the news, as the aide had guessed he would. It was exasperating. He muttered something to himself. Then he stood and snapped his fingers. A slave stepped forward bearing his toga and his baton, a symbol of his magisterial authority. Thus officially attired, and with his secretary with tablets in attendance, Pilate went out from his quarters on to the balcony.

The morning sun, striking off the buildings around, at first dazzled him. But when he had focused his eyes he could see that the gathering below included, apart from the usual city crowd, which seemed capable of gathering together at any hour of the day, some members of the Sanhedrin itself and also Caiaphas the High Priest. In front of them all, closely attended by police, stood a tall, rather pale man with his hands bound behind his back. The face, as Pilate looked down upon it, was most unusual.

No one spoke, because it was not wise to speak first in front of Pilate. It was he who broke the silence by asking abruptly:

"What accusation bring you against this man?"

The High Priest stepped forward and the two men stared upon each other, the one looking up, the other looking down. Between them passed a sense of bitter mutual dislike. The Governor loathed and feared the High Priest, loathed him as a trouble-maker, feared him as a wily adversary. And the High Priest loathed the Governor because he represented a power greater than his.

So Caiaphas answered the Governor's question insolently: "If this man were not an evil-doer, we should not have delivered him unto thee."

Unwilling to be embroiled in the matter unless it were absolutely necessary, Pilate said curtly:

"Take him yourselves, and judge him according to your law."

But Caiaphas was ready for that. "It is not lawful," he said smoothly, "for us to put any man to death."

It was true, and was a clever stroke because it meant that Pilate would be bound by his authority to act. The members of the Sanhedrin who were with Caiaphas now brought forward their own accusations. They had found him perverting their nation, forbidding to give tribute to Caesar and saying that he himself was Christ, a King. These new charges were, of course, entirely different from those which had been brought against Jesus at the meeting of the Sanhedrin, for there the main accusation had been one of blasphemy. This fresh series of accusations represented a change of

XXVIII. THE JOURNEY TO CALVARY

And they took Jesus, and led him away. And he bearing his cross went forth into a place called the place of a skull. John 19, 16-17.

By Tintoretto (1518-1594)

Photo Giacomelli

front to suit a new situation. Pilate was more likely to be concerned with political than religious matters.

There was a moment's impasse, the Jews standing carefully outside the limits of the Roman residence, lest by entering it they should defile themselves before the Feast, and Pilate frowningly looking down. As he thus looked his eye was caught by the appearance of Jesus.

The man was certainly most unusual. A long experience of dispensing justice in Jewish territory had made Pilate accustomed to the usual types of offender. But this prisoner, with his fine, calm face and dignified demeanor, was obviously neither a common thief, nor some nationalistic rabble-rouser. By a gesture he commanded that the prisoner should be brought in while he himself stepped back and descended the stairs behind the balcony which led to the room within which it was his custom to try cases. This wide, cool chamber had within it his magistrate's seat on a semi-circular dais. Upon this chair Pilate now seated himself, adjusting his toga in digni-fied folds as through the further door Jesus was brought in to him. Immediately, Pilate went to the heart of the matter.

"Art thou King of the Jews?"

The reply was as puzzling as the way in which it was delivered, for without any hesitation and without his gaze wavering at all the prisoner replied:

"Sayest thou this of thyself or did others tell it thee concerning me?"

"Am I a Jew?" Pilate replied testily. "Thine own nation and the Chief Priests delivered thee unto me: what hast thou done?"

The prisoner's retort, in its mysterious content, was of a piece with his previous answer:

"My kingdom is not of this world: if my kingdom were of this world, then would my servants fight that I should not be delivered to the Jews; but now is my kingdom not from hence."

Pilate pressed his point.

"Art thou a king then?" He leant forward for emphasis, one hand on a knee, the other still holding his baton of office.

Again the prisoner answered calmly:

"To this end have I been born, and to this end am I come into the world, that I should bear witness unto the truth. Everyone that is of the truth heareth my voice."

Pilate leant back in his chair with a gesture of cynical hopelessness.

"What is truth?" he said to the room at large as though he knew, out of his know-ledge of the world of men, that there were no answer. Then, with a half smile upon his face, he went out again onto his balcony, and once more looked down upon the waiting High Priest and the crowd. Curtly he told them:

"I find no fault in this man."

There was an immediate, violent reaction, many indignant voices crying out, "He stirreth up the people, teaching throughout Judea, and beginning from Galilee even unto this place."

Pilate, who had closed his eyes against the grating of the many voices upon his nerves, now opened his eyes. He had caught the word "Galilean". If indeed this prisoner came from Galilee then he would come within the jurisdiction of the puppet ruler Herod. Here was another chance to get rid of this load of responsibility. He would send him to Herod, who would be flattered by the action. So Pilate ordered it thus, and Jesus was again taken under escort on yet another journey.

The city was now filling rapidly, for the morning was wearing on and the streets were thronged. The sight of a prisoner with an armed escort was sufficient to draw a considerable crowd which followed as Jesus was conducted through the heart of the city, to the palace of Herod in the northwestern corner of the walls.

So now it was the turn of Herod Antipas to play his brief and ignoble part in the drama of the Passion.

He was a man of evil life and weak character, the very image of a puppet ruler living in luxury at the price of his honor. He it was who, at a drunken banquet, had ordered the beheading of John the Baptist to satisfy the whim of a dancing girl. Like all his kind he was gullible, ignorant and superstitious. He was also vain to a remarkable degree. He was therefore highly gratified when the news was brought to him that Pilate had sent Jesus the Nazarene as a prisoner to him. He was also titillated by the knowledge that this wonder-worker of whom he had already heard so much would now be able to work some miracles for him. It would at least be something to help in whiling away the tiresome day.

As he waited, in childish excitement, in his audience hall, surrounded by his creatures and his women, Herod fully expected some strange-looking fanatic, rather like John the Baptist himself. Yet there was nothing of the sort at all about the prisoner who eventually arrived. On the contrary, he was calm, he was dignified, and, worst of all, he maintained absolute silence, the silence of contempt as the bulging-eyed Tetrarch eagerly questioned him. Herod could make nothing of him at all.

So at last he fell back upon mockery. If this man claimed to be a king, well then, they could at least dress him up as one. So they draped about him, with shouts of laughter, an old robe which had once belonged to Herod himself. They threw it on askew and were vastly diverted with the pathetic result. Then Herod, with his compliments, returned Jesus to the waiting crowd outside, and these in turn escorted him back to Pilate.

Now Pilate was still within his Hall of Justice, sitting slumped upon his magisterial chair. He had had a most disturbing experience, something quite without precedent. He had received a message from his wife Claudia, brought urgently by one of her own personal slaves. It appeared that she had had a dream from which, in her luxurious bed far within their quarters, she had just woken up. The message was that, because of what she had seen and learned in this dream, she had felt moved to warn him to have nothing to do with what she called "that righteous man".

Pilate had to confess to himself that he was deeply impressed, even shaken. Superstitious, though in a much more subtle way than Herod, he belonged to a race and culture which commonly gave much credence to the significance of dreams. After all, had not Caesar himself been warned in a dream of his own violent end?

Suddenly, Pilate heard in the distance the shouts of an approaching rabble. He straightened in his chair, and a creeping feeling of apprehension crept over him. They were bringing the man back again then. Disciplinary habit asserting itself, he stood, straightened himself firmly, and once again went out to his balcony.

They were all there as before, except that he noticed this time the prisoner was wearing a strange robe—the one Herod's people had put upon him—but still maintained his dignified, impassive attitude. But the crowd was now obviously more worked up than ever. There were cries of "Crucify him! Crucify him!" against a background of confused shouting. The situation was dangerous. Pilate's mouth set in a firm line. He signaled for silence.

"Ye brought unto me this man," he said in his high, clear, voice, "as one that perverteth the people; and behold, I, having examined him before you, find no fault in this man touching those things whereof ye accuse him: no, nor yet Herod: for he sent him back unto us; and behold, nothing worthy of death hath been done by him; I will therefore chastise him, and release him."

Yet again a howl of rage rose up, and again Pilate had to signal for silence. He had remembered, in a moment of quick thinking, that there was a local custom which allowed him at Passover time to pardon one prisoner and release him. Furthermore, he had in fact one such prisoner already under sentence, a certain Barabbas, whom some say had been a fomenter of rebellion and of whom others say that he was a common desperado. It occurred to Pilate that he could, perhaps, both satisfy the mob and save himself from the necessity of condemning Jesus if he were to offer them the choice of having the pardon given to Barabbas or to Jesus. It seemed inconceivable to him that, faced with such a choice, they could do anything other than choose the latter.

But to his astonishment and consternation the crowd cried out for Barabbas, chanting the name in unison over and over again.

For the first time in a long career of colonial governorship, Pilate felt himself nonplussed. It was becoming alarmingly clear that he would have to condemn this prisoner after all. Yet every fibre of his being revolted against the idea. He could at least delay the final and fateful decision. After all, he had ordered the man to be flogged, and it might well be that the infliction of such punishment would satisfy this priest-incited crowd. Pilate leant forward a little over his balcony and spoke to his own guard manning the entrance to the barracks below. He ordered them to take the prisoner and flog him.

Some half-dozen soldiers therefore stepped forward and led him within. With pity and concern, Pilate watched him go, well knowing what was in store.

His men were brutal mercenaries; well Pilate knew it. For that reason it was a fearful thing to fall into their hands. Obscene and horrible mistreatment went on in their barracks. But, in addition, a Roman flogging, such as he had ordered for Jesus, was a very terrible ordeal.

The Jews, when they used this form of correction at all, did so with moderation. When St Paul, at a later date, claimed that he had been several times beaten by the Jews with forty strokes save one, he was referring to the fact that in their law the maximum number of lashes allowable was forty. In practice thirty-nine were usually inflicted so as to exempt those responsible from the charge of having exceeded the statutory total. But the Romans recognized no such limitation. Indeed, it was by no means unusual for prisoners to die under the lash, cut to pieces. The weapon used was either a flagella, the heavy cords of which ended in knots or points, or alternatively a whip formed of a number of chains with weights on the end. So the soldiers took Jesus into the courtyard and tied him to a post. Then they stripped him, and the flogging began, It ended only when his tormentors felt that they had had enough.

B.M.G.—R

To Pilate, waiting within his own room, the sounds of the scourging, the sting and crack of the blows and the cries of the soldier-onlookers urging on the inflicter to greater efforts came clearly. Then there was a dragging of feet, a good deal of laughter, and a long pause. Pilate could not see what was happening but he could guess. His troops would have taken the prisoner into their own mess-room to amuse themselves with him. Pilate did not care to speculate upon the forms that that amusement would take. But again he could guess; they liked to guy their prisoners, and it would be against custom if he were to interfere.

Yet in spite of being used to this sort of happening Pilate was deeply shocked at what he saw when they brought Jesus before him again. He was bloody, torn, battered, and streaming with the sweat of agony. The face was gray, the great dark eyes staring. They had thrown on him again the crazy robe. But this time also they had rammed onto his head a circlet of sharp thorns. Trickles of ¦blood ran down where the spikes had entered into the scalp.

Pilate now took Jesus outside with him again, and instantly the howl rose up from a crowd which had by this time grown immense. "Crucify! Crucify!"

Pilate found himself too full of emotion to speak at first. And when at last he did manage it he uttered only three words: "Behold, the man!" And when they shrieked out again their demand that he crucify the prisoner Pilate said, in a sudden passion of disgust, "Take him yourselves and crucify him; for I find no crime in him."

One of the Priests below stepped forward, "We have a law, and by that law he ought to die, because he made himself the Son of God."

Pilate looked at the speaker, looked at the crowd, looked at Jesus. Then he took Jesus by the arm and moved him back a little to the privacy at the rear of the balcony out of sight of the mob. Pilate spoke hoarsely, feeling as he did so his heart hammering within him. "Whence art thou?" he whispered. The prisoner gave no answer. The Governor shook the arm he was holding. Under the robe it felt thin and hard. It was amazing that the man still stood and possessed himself. "Speakest thou not unto me?" Pilate said hurriedly. "Knowest thou not that I have power to release thee, and have power to crucify thee?"

As Pilate watched he could see Jesus struggling to speak. At last the words came out: "Thou wouldst have no power against me, except it were given thee from above: therefore he that delivered me unto thee hath greater sin."

It was terrible; Pilate felt he could not bear a moment of this torment longer. He rushed out to the front of the balcony again. But now the crowd was wild; they had pressed forward right beneath so that his own troops had formed a line and were standing grimly with interlocked spears at the ready. Civil commotion of the first order was not a hairsbreadth away. "If thou release this man," someone ¦yelled, "thou art not Caesar's friend: everyone that maketh himself a King is against Caesar."

That was the end of it for Pilate, for that was a dangerous truth. If he ignored such a warning as that he could be reported to Rome, and he knew he would be. So he drove Jesus forward, "Behold your King!" he cried in a loud voice.

Mad shouts came up in reply, "Away with him! away with him, crucify him!"

Now Pilate had to shout: "Shall I crucify your King?"

It was the High Priest himself who answered, "We have no King but Caesar!"

XXIX. THE CRUCIFIXION

And it was the third hour, and they crucified him . . . .And with him they crucify two thieves; the one on his right hand, and the other on his left. Mark 15, 25-27.

By Andrea Mantegna (1431-1506)

Photo Vizzavona

And the mob took up the end of the sentence, chanting it in crazed reiteration, "—king but Caesar! no king but Caesar! no king but Caesar!"

There was only one thing left to do now, and Pilate did it. Nothing could save this man of whom his wife had warned him in a dream; but at least he could signify his own personal disavowal of the injustice. He turned and spoke briefly to his secretary standing behind. This man went within, clapped his hands, summoning a slave. There was a little pause, while the crowd seethed and Jesus stood impassive. Then a white tuniced servant came out into the sunlight carrying a small pewter basin. Over his left forearm a little napkin was draped. He knelt before the Governor. Pilate dipped his hands in the bowl, went through the motions of washing them, then drew them out, wetness gleaming upon them. After that, with great deliberation, he wiped his hands on the towel, saying, "I am innocent of the blood of this righteous man: see ye to it."

It was an old ritual action which Pilate was performing. He was symbolically washing the stain of a sinful act from himself in a way well known and understood in the ancient world.

The crowd cried out when they saw Pilate thus ridding himself of guilt, "His blood be on us, and on our children." So Pilate released Barabbas, but Jesus was led away to be crucified.

Execution

Based on Tintoretto's THE JOURNEY TO CALVARY
and on Mantegna's THE CRUCIFIXION

AT about half-past eleven on that Friday morning a remarkable experience befell a certain North African Jew called Simon of Cyrene. Whether he was in Jerusalem for the Passover or whether he was temporarily resident there is not known. But it is known that he came from the capital city of Cyrenaica where there was a considerable Jewish colony. He had certainly been out of Jerusalem during the early part of the day, so was quite ignorant of the events that had gathered the crowds.

Yet the size and noise of the multitude around the Fortress of Anthony, when Simon got there, was sufficient to tell him that something very unusual was impending. A big man, and pacific, which is so often the way with big men, he yet felt sufficient curiosity to force his way to the front. He saw a balcony, empty, overhanging the steps which led up to the main entrance of the place. Across the entrance stood a guard.

And then, suddenly, as Simon watched he saw this guard move aside to make way for a procession just then emerging. The sight of the emerging column, greeted by a wild howl from the mob, caused Simon to catch his breath. He recognized it for what it was: an execution parade taking prisoners to their death. Living as he did in a Roman province Simon had seen its like before. First came the Centurion in command, a stern-faced Roman with his short sword drawn in his hand and a wary eye on the encroaching people. After him followed a platoon of troops in chainmail. Both the Centurion and the soldiers in red tunics and plumed helmets advanced heavily and resolutely. The crowd gave way before them. Following them, and escorted on either side by more troops, came the prisoners.

Each of them, moving slowly under the weight, carried the instrument of his execution, a wooden cross the tail of which bumped and slithered over the cobblestones. The cross piece was secured to the prisoners' shoulders by ropes, and they walked uncertainly beneath the grotesque encumbrance.

It was the leading prisoner who moved Simon to pity and horror. The other two were burly, villainous-looking men with the low forehead and coarse faces of habitual criminals. But the first was entirely different; fine drawn, almost aristocratic in the stamp of his haggard face, marked now by every symptom of grief and suffering. In addition, he seemed to have suffered more at the hands of his captors than either of the other two. Where the clumsy thing he was carrying had pulled aside the robe he was wearing, the deeply scored, bluey-red marks of flogging showed on his back. He also wore a circlet of thorns which had clearly been jammed hard down upon his brow. The other two sufferers managed to walk under their burdens; but this one tottered, veering at times across the narrow way so that the crowd lining it had to fall back while the soldier leading him by a rope round his neck had with oaths to pull hard on it to straighten him into the path again. Behind the three and their escort followed robed priests of the Temple. Behind them again, rapidly increasing as the news of the spectacle spread, a multitude characteristic of those who generally followed the popular spectacle of an execution, brought up the rear.

It was the forward movement of this press of people which carried Simon along with it and forced him to keep abreast of the leading prisoner. There was nothing orderly, or even particularly dignified, about the progress of the procession. For one thing the way was uneven and undulating. Where the route led down some steep street, the incline of which was marked by steps at intervals under the overhanging buildings on either side, the tail end of the crosses bumped and slithered more than ever. The crowd, too, was disorderly, obviously in a high state of excitement. Apart from a little group of men and women which followed at some distance, Simon could see little signs of sympathy. This surprised and moved him, for he thought in his heart that he had never seen a more pitiable sight.

It was a dolorous way the procession took, along narrow streets where brilliant sunshine vied with contrasting patches of black shadow.

Thus moving, it came at last to a gate in the northern walls of the city, a gate called in later ages the Sorrowful Gate. There, the leading prisoner fell. It happened quite abruptly; one moment he was staggering along under his cross, the next he had gone down with a clatter, and was lying face downward with the cross on top of him. People gathered round, pressing close, and the Centurion who was leading, turning and seeing what had happened, made his way back to the spot.

Simon could see the man was anxious, as well he may be, Simon thought, with all that crowd around and with only his comparatively small body of troops to rely upon.

The Centurion, tight-lipped, looked around, and his eye fell on Simon. The Cyrenaican felt a thrill of anticipation and dismay as he saw the level glance. Then the Centurion stood forward and took Simon by the arm, pulling him forward. "You carry that cross," he ordered. "You're big enough." They were lifting the apparatus off the collapsed prisoner by now. It took two soldiers to do it, and these, almost before Simon knew what was happening, were lowering it onto his own broad shoulders. It was immensely, astonishingly heavy. He felt the sharp edge of it bearing hard upon his collar-bone. The shadow it made fell forward on to the cobble-stones before him. Then he was being urged forward, and he heard the movement of the procession begin again behind him when the man who had fallen was now on his feet once more.

At that moment Simon heard him speaking. Turning slightly he was able to see that the words were addressed to a group of women, who, wailing and beating their breasts in sympathy, had pressed forward upon the sufferer.

"Daughters of Jerusalem," Simon heard him say, "weep not for me, but weep for yourselves and for your children. For behold the days are coming, in which they shall say, blessed are the barren and the wombs that never bear and the breasts that never gave suck. Then shall they begin to say to the mountains, fall on us; and to the hills, cover us. For if they do these things in the green tree, what shall be done in the dry?"

They were strange words, and Simon long remembered them.

He remembered, too, the woman who at that point bravely stepped forward and wiped with a towel the sweat streaming down the face of the prisoner. He remembered also how from the gate the way they took led steeply down and then up again.

Simon himself was drenched in sweat, for the morning was hot and becoming ominously overcast, when they reached a point in an embrasure of the walls where there was a bare space shaped like a skull and called for that reason Golgotha. This grim place, where the prisoners were to have their rendezvous with death, also bore signs of being used as a cemetery. It had an unmistakable air of mortality and gloom, and, adding to the impression, vultures floated in the rising currents of air further up the slopes of the hill.

On that comfortless eminence Simon was ordered to put down the cross he was carrying. He let it go and the thing clattered onto the hard earth. When he straightened up, and realized what was about to happen, the Cyrenaican felt a strong urge to get away from the place. Yet something held him. He felt that here things were about to take place which a man should steel himself to look upon. They were going to crucify these men.

In the case of the two criminals the prospect was horrible but not overwhelming. After all, it was a common enough occurrence. But the thought of it happening to the first of the prisoners, he who now stood bound and haggard, was quite shattering. Simon felt he could not leave the place, much as he wished to. He saw then that there was a placard nailed to the top of the cross which he had been carrying. It was the Titulus, or customary notice describing the crime of the men to be crucified. This one, written in Hebrew, Latin, and Greek, said only, "JESUS OF NAZARETH, KING OF THE JEWS."

Simon knew a lot about crucifixion. It was the most horrible form of execution imaginable, a torment reserved for slaves alone.

Characteristically, for the Romans were a cruel race, it was a speciality of theirs. Its chief horrors were threefold. It was degrading, representing naked exposure in torment to an extreme degree, since the suffering of the victim could be observed at leisure by passers-by. It was intensely agonizing, for the position of the body, pinned against the wood by excruciating wounds, was also so cramped that breathing soon became difficult, the whiles sun and thirst added to the torture, as did the pressure of the sharp piece of wood between the thighs which bore much of the weight of the hanging body. It was also prolonged. A man beheaded dies instantly, a man hanged by strangulation might last ten minutes. But a man crucified could survive many, many hours. Not for nothing, therefore, was the cross feared like a nightmare.

The details of the crucifixion which followed took place before the very eyes of Simon as, fascinated yet repelled, he watched. First they stripped Jesus, exposing the torn body, but leaving his loin cloth and the pitiable crown of thorns. Then they threw him down and spread his arms out along the cross beam.

At that point, while the nails were being prepared, some women, probably members of a charitable guild in Jerusalem which existed for this purpose, stepped forward to offer him a drink of the wine which, acting as some kind of anaesthetic, was commonly offered to sufferers at this juncture to ease the atrocious pain of the actual nailing. "Give heavy drink unto him that is ready to perish," had written the

XXX. THE DEAD CHRIST

And when Joseph had taken the body, he wrapped it in a clean linen cloth. And laid it in his own new tomb, which he had hewn out in the rock. Matthew 27, 59-60.

By Andrea Mantegna (1431-1506)

Photo Roberto Hoesh

Prophet Hosea, and this drug was what they now offered to Jesus. Yet, strangely enough, he refused it. Simon saw him shake his head when the cup was actually at his lips. So they passed on to the other two prisoners, while the soldiers busied themselves about Jesus. One forcibly held a hand open, a second bore down upon the arm, a third placed the nail upon the palm and raised his hammer.

"Father, forgive them, for they know not what they do," Jesus cried out.

Then the hammer descended, and Simon kept his eyes closed during the four heavy thuds which followed. The other hand they dealt with in the same manner. Then the cross was hoisted into position, with many creakings, in a slot in the ground.

Quite soon, all three crosses were up. The other two prisoners at first struggled, jerking their heads from side to side and shouting their curses. Jesus remained still, and, for the moment, silent.

It was now twelve noon, the hour when, symbolically enough, in the nearby city, lambs were being prepared for the Passover sacrifice. Around the crosses the crowd settled down to wait. The soldiers, although the stern-faced Centurion kept himself apart, occupied themselves, in the traditional manner, by squatting down at the foot of the crosses and throwing dice to settle the share-out of the clothes of the stripped prisoners which were their perquisites. Simon noticed there was some argument about the robe Jesus had been wearing, for it was in one piece, and to divide it up would have spoilt it as a garment. So it was left untouched and went as it was to one of the soldiers to whom it fell at the throw of a dice. Meanwhile, passers-by on the Jaffa road paused to look upon the victims, and to listen to the jibes of certain of the Priests who, by this time, had moved as close as they dared.

"Thou that destroyest the Temple and buildest it in three days," one of them called, "save thyself, and come down from the cross." Another added, turning round to the crowd, "He saved others, himself he cannot save. Let Christ the King of Israel descend now from the cross." Even the soldiers, busy with their dice, found time to look up and call out, "If thou be the King of the Jews, save thyself."

After that, there was silence for a time. Simon noticed, during that pause, that the sky was becoming appreciably darker; it was not one isolated cloud that had temporarily obscured the sun, but a greenish gloom which seemed to be over-spreading the whole of the heavens. The walls of the city behind were eerily outlined against it. The temperature had dropped also, and little puffs of uneasy wind scoured the ground, raising eddies of dust. The crowd had noticed it too, and were beginning to look questioningly upon one another.

But suddenly the attention of all was gripped by a shout which had come from one of the crosses. It was one of the thieves crying out. "Art thou not the Christ?" the voice croaked, while the speaker twisted his head to look at Jesus on the cross by him. "Save thyself and us." At that the robber on the further side answered him, "Dost thou not even fear God, seeing thou art in the same condemnation?" he demanded. "And we indeed justly; for we receive the due reward of our deeds; but this man hath done nothing amiss." And twisting his own head toward the central cross he said, "Jesus, remember me when thou comest in thy Kingdom."

Now Jesus spoke after his long silence: "Verily I say unto thee, today shalt thou be with me in paradise."

Simon saw now that four women who hitherto had kept themselves at a distance, moved forward until they were within speaking distance of the central cross. A young man supported what seemed to be the oldest of the women with an arm around her shoulders. She was, Simon gathered from the whispers around him, the mother of the crucified. The crucified also had seen her, for he bent his head to look down and said, "Woman, behold thy son!" And to the young man supporting her he said, "Behold thy mother!"

Now another very long period of waiting followed, while the skies grew darker about the earth, and the majority of the onlookers began to drift back into the city. Simon knew that the worst time for the crucified was now approaching, the time when the tortured flesh could take no more and when the soul would have to burst out of the tormented body.

At last Jesus spoke again, this time in a weaker voice, "I thirst," he murmured. At that, moved by a kind of rough pity, one of the soldiers took a sponge and dipped it in the jar of Posca, the wine they refreshed themselves with on these occasions, stuck the sponge on the end of his spear, and lifted it to the lips of Jesus. Fumblingly, Jesus managed to drink a little, then, as though temporarily strengthened, he called out strongly in Aramaic: "Eloi, Eloi, Lama Sabachthani." It meant, "My God, my God, why hast thou forsaken me?"

The words, as Simon well knew, were from the beginning of the 22nd Psalm which went on,

> "Our fathers trusted in thee;
> They trusted, and thou didst deliver them.
> They cried unto thee and were delivered:
> They trusted in thee, and were not ashamed."

His cry had riveted the attention of the remaining onlookers. One of them said, "This man calleth Elijah." Others said sardonically, "Let be; let us see whether Elijah cometh to save him."

Once more, and again in a startlingly strong voice, Jesus called out, "Father, into thy hands I commend my spirit." And last of all, in a resonant shout, he cried, "It is finished."

It was indeed finished. Unable to move, petrified with horror, Simon saw the Centurion move to the foot of the cross and look keenly and long up into the face of the dead man. There was a strange expression on his hard face as he stood there with the rising wind tossing the folds of his red tunic.

"Certainly this was a righteous man," Simon heard him say.

And with that a wailing arose of those about, and a tremor shook the earth. It was three o'clock. At that very hour, as Simon learnt later, within the Temple as the trumpets were sounding for the Feast, the veil of the Temple, enclosing the Holy of Holies, was torn from top to bottom.

XXXI. THE BLESSING OF CHRIST

And he led them out as far as to Bethany, and he lifted up his hands, and blessed them. Luke 24, 50.

By Giovanni Bellini (c.1430-1516)

Photo Vizzavona

Death

Based on Mantegna's

THE DEAD CHRIST

So Jesus was dead. There was no doubt about it whatever in the minds of the desolate group of disciples and the women, including his mother, who had so faithfully followed him. Fearfully, they crept nearer as the crowd dispersed and, looking up into that beloved face, saw only the countenance of death. The complexion was greyish white, the head, still surmounted by the crown of thorns, lay grotesquely to one side, and the sinews of the arms stood out like cord where they were drawn down by the sag of the inert body. There was nothing left for them to do but to lament, weeping and bewailing, and to drift back to what was left of their lives.

Meanwhile, there were three men who had a concern with what was to happen to the body. The first of these was Caiaphas, the High Priest. At six that evening the Sabbath would begin; and it was necessary, before that happened, that the bodies should be taken down and disposed of lest their horrid presence should desecrate the sacred day. There was thus no time to lose.

Caiaphas therefore once again sent to Pilate, with the request that the legs of the crucified should be broken so that their deaths, if necessary, could be hastened, and the bodies removed.

It was a routine request. The breaking of the legs of crucified persons was a well-known Roman practice. Even so, Pilate was short with the priests who came before him. Waving them from his presence—for the exhaustion of the events earlier in the day still lay heavily upon him and his mind was troubled—he gave an abrupt order which was transmitted to the barrack room. As a result a small platoon of soldiers, one of them carrying a heavy club or stave, shortly afterward arrived at the now almost deserted scene of the crucifixions.

They, too, being anxious to have done with the whole business, went about their business in a hurried way. First they moved to the cross of the thief who had been crucified on the right hand of Jesus. This victim, by his moanings, still giving some signs of life, the soldier who was carrying the club crashed it several times, with sideways swings, upon the man's legs until the bones were shattered. The man on the cross on the further side was then similarly treated.

When they reached the central cross, however, it was plain that the victim there was already dead. The soldier with the club shrugged and passed on. There was one of the company, nonetheless, who, perhaps to| make sure, or maybe merely as a gesture, reached up and drove his spear, with the characteristic Roman fighting thrust, into the side of Jesus. The head of the weapon sank deep, making a wide wound. Water and blood spewed forth when the spear was withdrawn. The soldier, lance in hand, stood awhile after his action looking up at the inert figure. There was no movement to be seen and his experience as a fighting man told him that the blood would not have trickled out in that way if in fact there had been life in the man on the cross. So he, too, shrugged and, shouldering his spear, moved off back toward the city with the rest of the troop.

Two men who had hitherto kept themselves carefully withdrawn from all these events, had been watching in deep anguish of heart. Both were members of the Sanhedrin; both consequently were men of honor and repute among the Jews; and both for that reason had been fearful of betraying the secret which they shared together. That secret was a profound reverence which they had come to have for this Jesus who now hung dead upon the cross. Joseph of Arimathaea was one of them. An honorable man, he had stood aside from the actions of his colleagues in the Sanhedrin when Jesus had been condemned; but he had not dared to speak, although his heart had been wrung. The other was Nicodemus, that Ruler of the Jews who had once gone to Jesus secretly by night, and, in a memorable interview beneath the stars, had asked him how a man may be born again.

He had never forgotten that conversation, nor the compelling power of Jesus, and he also had been tormented by what he had witnessed.

It thus befell that toward evening of that same Friday, Joseph of Arimathaea went, with every precaution of secrecy, lest his compatriots should hear what he was doing, to Pilate with a request. The Governor sighed deeply when the news was brought to him that yet another Jew wanted to see him. It had been a fearful day, and now he was keenly looking forward to a bath and a relaxed evening meal. Still, he knew Joseph of Arimathaea to be a man of sound repute. He had him in.

"Well?" he said briefly.

Courteously, the grave Jew before him asked permission to bury the body of Jesus. Pilate paused: could it be possible that the man was already dead? He summoned the man who had been in charge of the leg-breaking squad. Yes, he was assured, death had already taken place. Pilate sighed again, remembering the heroism and poise of the man whom he had, in the heat and glare of the morning, delivered over to the shouting crowds.

"So be it," he said, "you may have the body."

Elsewhere, and at the same time, in a little spice-seller's shop down in one of the alleys of the city, Nicodemus was buying myrrh and sweet-smelling wood of aloes used for embalming the dead. He purchased a surprising quantity, a hundred pounds weight, far more than was ordinarily required; enough, in fact, for the embalming of a king. It was, he felt, all he could do, to make this tribute to one whom he would infinitely have preferred to aid in life rather than in death.

So, at the foot of the cross, in the place of the Skull, outside the walls of the city in the evening time, a forlorn little group gathered. Joseph of Arimathaea was there, the richly dressed Nicodemus, with his lavish gift of myrrh and wood of aloes, was there; also there were some of the women who had faithfully followed, Mary Magdalene, and Mary the mother of James and John, and the mother of the sons of Zebedee.

To these fell the grim and heart-rending task of bringing down the body from the cross, the extracting of the long nails, the straightening of the stiffening corpse upon the ground, and the bearing of it away.

Now Joseph of Arimathaea owned a private tomb in a little garden. It had never been used, because he had intended it for himself, after the manner of rich men who commonly made this provision for the future. It was rare, indeed, it was against the law, for the bodies of executed criminals to be given a ceremonial burial. Their usual lot was to be thrown onto the fires in the public incinerator in the valley of Gehenna. It was an exceptional distinction which Joseph thus purposed for the body of Jesus in having it interred within his own private burial place.

To the tomb in the garden, moving slowly and awkwardly under the weight of the corpse, the group now made its way. Like the tomb of Lazarus—he whom Jesus had brought back from the dead—this one was hewn out of the solid rock. A great circular stone, now rolled back up an incline and held in place by a rock, sealed off the entrance. Within was an ante-chamber and, beyond that again, an inner cell containing a stone shelf for the body. On the shelf, according to custom, was a little heap of stones to support the head of the deceased.

In the ante-chamber of this tomb, amid dead silence except for the breathing of those about, and the evening twittering of birds among the trees outside, the body was prepared. They wound about it the linen shroud. Then the grave cloth was tenderly placed over the face upon which, as they thought, they were looking for the last time. The myrrh and sweet-smelling wood of aloes were placed about the body. There was not time for the lengthy process of embalming, for the Sabbath and the night were both approaching.

This done, the body of Jesus was reverently laid—and very long and imposing it looked—upon the stone shelf within the inner chamber of the tomb. There they left him. There they left him in the silence of death. Outside, the wedge was knocked away and the stone rumbled forward, vast and solid, into position.

*   *   *   *

The following morning, that is to say, the morning of the Sabbath, came bright and peaceful. To Pilate, relaxing in the privacy of his quarters in the Antonine Tower, the day was especially blessed in that it held the promise of a little peace after the tumults of the day before. Moreover, he had slept fairly well, his wife's disturbance over the dream which she had had during the Thursday night seemed to have left her. The immediate outlook seemed reasonably satisfactory. Consequently, he was deeply and seriously annoyed when his aide, apologetically entering the domestic apartment, whispered that still another deputation from the Jews required his immediate presence. They were led by Caiaphas the High Priest himself.

It was too much. Pilate felt anger rising within him, spoiling the calm pose with which he had begun the day. Would there never be an end to these Jewish wranglings? They were impossible! Heavens above! he thought to himself, I had enough of them yesterday. And now this formidable High Priest again. The Governor's rather fine face was flushed as he rose to his feet, excused himself to his wife, and strode from the room into his audience chamber.

With no salutation, Pilate took his seat on the magisterial chair.

"What is it you want this time?"

Caiaphas bowed low.

"Sir, we remember that that deceiver said while he was yet alive, 'After three days I rise again.' "

"The deceiver?" Pilate interrupted testily. "Who is this whom you speak of?"

Caiaphas explained that he referred to the man Jesus.

Pilate moved in his seat uneasily.

Caiaphas continued: "Command therefore, Your Excellency, that the sepulchre be made sure until the third day, lest haply his disciples come and steal him away, and say unto the people, 'he is risen from the dead'; and the last error would be worse than the first."

He paused: the whole deputation waited, looking closely upon the Governor. But now anger was overcoming uneasiness in Pilate. He was utterly sick and tired of the whole affair. He rose and it was clear the brief audience was at an end.

"You have a guard," he said, with a gesture of dismissal. "Go your way. Make this sepulchre as sure as you can."

It was enough. Caiaphas had the permission he had come to secure. Within an hour a Temple guard had been placed outside the tomb where the body of Jesus lay. The stone was sealed.

Life and Triumph

Based on Bellini's THE BLESSING OF CHRIST
and on Mantegna's THE ASCENSION

ALL that terrible Sabbath after the crucifixion the disciples had huddled together in Jerusalem. They were shattered men; their world had come crashing about them, their hopes become a mockery. Their Master was dead: their dreams of his triumph and of his Kingdom were alike seen as a gigantic illusion. He had left a void which they knew nothing could ever fill.

For the women things were perhaps a little better. True, they were equally desolate, but they had their household tasks to occupy them, and though the meals were served in silence and the men-folk were not to be spoken to, yet there was always the daily round and the common task to while the sad hours away. And also, as devout Jews, all of them had the duties of the Sabbath to perform.

But the women, and they included Mary Magdalene, Mary the mother of Jesus, Mary the mother of James, Salome and Joanna, were conscious also of another duty which lay upon them especially. The embalming of the body of the Lord had not been properly completed in the hurry of the burial in Joseph of Arimathaea's tomb on the Friday evening, and it was their resolve to return thither as soon as they possibly could in order to finish the task. By rights, they could have gone to the tomb when the Sabbath ended at sunset. But the way was dark and forbidding, even dangerous, for women alone. So they agreed among themselves to go at first light on the day following.

The little group of them, wrapped in their cloaks, crept into the street at dawn of that day. Whispering occasionally among themselves, they made their way out of the city, the domes and pinnacles of which the sun was just beginning to touch. Sometimes in their whispers they spoke of what was a common anxiety in their minds—however would they manage to roll away the vast stone which they knew sealed the entrance to the tomb?

Their hearts beat quicker as they reached the garden. It was an uncanny hour, and an uncanny task they were about. Dew glistened upon the trees which hung their branches immobile in the stillness of dawn. The very birds had scarcely begun to stir. So they came to the tomb.

A shattering sight immediately confronted them. The great stone had been rolled back! It had been rolled back, and the dark interior, like a gaping mouth into which the long rays of the rising sun were beginning to probe, was exposed. Clinging fearfully together, the women peeped in, first into the outer chamber, then into the cell beyond. *It was empty.* They swung round, for two shadows had come athwart the sun. They turned to see the figures of two men in the dazzling apparel of angels standing there. Because of the glory about them they could not see their faces; but they heard the voice of one of them:

"Why seek ye the living among the dead?" came a musical voice. "He is not here but is risen: remember how he spake unto you when he was yet in Galilee, saying that the Son of Man must be delivered up into the hands of sinful man, and be crucified, and the third day rise again."

Truly, the women did remember; but fear and awe moved them to panic action. With one accord they rushed from the place, their long garments flying about them. Breathless and terrified they returned to the city to burst into the room where the eleven disciples were together. Breathlessly they stammered out their astonishing tidings, corroborating each other as the story came out, imploring the men to listen. The tomb was empty; they had seen the angels! But they had not seen the Lord, for he was not there.

The disciples looked upon them dully. For the most part, they disbelieved the whole thing, regarding it as the outburst of hysterical women.

Yet there were two, Peter and John, who felt they could not go all the way with this. The eyes of Peter especially had gleamed for a moment at the tidings the women had brought. Could it be——? Could it possibly be——? He stood, and John stood with him. A sign passed between them. They ran from the house into the street, down the hill and out toward the garden. At a distance Mary Magdalene followed.

John easily outran the older and heavier Peter, so that he was the first at the tomb. True enough, *the stone was moved,* rolled back from the entrance and held by the wedge.

He stooped and looked in. Nothing. Beyond him he could see the smaller entrance to the inner cell, but something kept him from going further. Behind him now he could hear the hard breathing of Peter and he turned to him with a vague gesture of astonishment. Peter, knowing no hesitation, pushed by him and made straight for the inner chamber.

The light was poor in there; but he was able to make out two amazing facts. There was no body on the stone shelf, and the grave clothes were still there, neatly folded. The grave cloth which had covered the face was lying a little apart.

They had seen the incredible. Without a word, they turned and ran out to tell the others. At the entrance to the garden they passed Mary of Magdala. She saw their staring eyes and gaping mouths as they ran by, then she herself passed on in the opposite direction back toward the tomb.

She was glad to be alone, this woman to whom the Master had meant so much, for there burned within her the sorrowful need to know what had become of him. The tears which hitherto she had kept back flooded to her eyes as she stood just within the entrance of the tomb. Then, looking up, she saw two angels in white sitting, one at the head and one at the feet, where the body of Jesus had lain.

One of them spoke, very gently:

"Woman, why weepest thou?"

"Because," Mary sobbed, "they have taken away my Lord, and I know not where they have laid him."

Then she turned, stumbling brokenly from the place out into the sunlight. There was another figure there. Because of her tears, and because of the strong light behind and about him, she could not see, nor at the moment greatly cared, who it was; but she imagined it might be the gardener who looked after the place. This figure also asked her a question.

"Woman, why weepest thou? Whom seekest thou?"

Blindly, Mary Magdalene reached out imploring hands to him.

"Sir, if thou hast borne him hence tell me where thou hast laid him and I will take him away."

There was quite a long pause. Then, "Mary," a voice said very quietly, very evenly, most thrillingly. With that, she knew who it was, and the knowledge lanced her through.

She fell on her knees, reaching imploring arms upward. "Rabboni!" she breathed. The word meant "Master". It seemed to her then that this amazing, this new, this wonderful Jesus took a little step back, as she heard him say:

"Touch me not; for I am not yet ascended unto the Father: but go unto the brethren, and say to them, I ascend unto my Father and your Father and my God and your God."

That was why it was a Mary Magdalene shining-eyed, confident and joyous, who returned unto the city to tell the disciples what she, in her turn, had seen.

*   *   *   *

That afternoon, two disciples, one of whom was called Cleophas, set off from Jerusalem to walk home to the village of Emmaus where they lived. It was a fair step, perhaps sixty furlongs to the westward from Jerusalem, over the mountains and then along a valley and out into the country beyond. But the two friends had plenty to talk about. As they walked along, each with a staff in his hand, and stirring up the dust with their sandals, they talked eagerly together over what they had seen and heard so recently back in the city.

It was by a spring, where they had stopped to drink some little distance upon their journey, that a stranger joined them. He had been watching them and as they resumed their way he came up alongside. There was no-one else about.

"What is it that you two are talking about so much?"

The question surprised them. Surely, they thought, anyone who had been in the area of Jerusalem the last few days must have known of what had happened. The whole city had been talking of nothing else but the trial and crucifixion of the Nazarene. Cleophas, swinging into step with the long-striding stranger, said:

"Dost thou alone sojourn in Jerusalem and not know the things that are come to pass there in these days? The things concerning Jesus of Nazareth, which was a prophet mighty in deed and word before God and all the people: and how the Chief Priests and our Rulers delivered him up to be condemned to death, and crucified him. But we hoped that it was he which should redeem Israel: Yea, and beside all this it is now the third day since these things came to pass, moreover certain women of our company amazed us, having been early at the tomb; and when they found not his body, they came saying that they had also seen a vision of angels, which said that he was alive. And certain of them that were with us went to the tomb and found it even so as the women had said: but him they saw not."

The stranger, who had listened courteously with a half-smile on his face, now laid a hand on the shoulder of Cleophas as they walked along.

"O foolish men," he said, "and slow of heart to believe in all that the prophets have spoken! Behoved it not the Christ to suffer these things and to enter into his glory?"

And then he went on to explain from the Scriptures the reason why all these things had happened to Jesus, because they had been foretold and ordained by God.

His talk was so enthralling that they scarcely noticed the distance they were covering until Cleophas, looking up, saw that they were entering Emmaus. With the typical hospitality of the East, noticing that the sun was already well down, he invited the stranger to lodge awhile with him. In the humble house, removing their sandals, they reclined themselves down by the table. It was now dusk. The single lamp gave a flickering light. By that light they saw the stranger take into his hands a loaf of bread, say a blessing over it, and break it.

An electric thrill ran through the two of them; their eyes widened, they lay absolutely still. There was something evocative, something strangely memory-stirring in the manner in which he broke the bread. They had seen that done before; they had seen it done in exactly the same manner. And then, with a blessed certainty, *they knew*: the Lord himself had done just that at the Last Supper. They were speechless; they were immobile. And before they could move or speak he had gone. The space at the table where he had been reclining was empty. They scrambled to their feet, looking at each other with a wild surmise.

"Was not our heart burning within us, while he spake to us in the way, while he opened to us the Scriptures?" they asked themselves.

All thoughts of staying where they were, all thoughts even of supper, left them. There was only one thing to do; to return instantly the long way to Jerusalem and tell the other disciples what had happened to them.

It was very late when they reached the city again, and the door of the disciples' room was bolted and barred as usual. Cleophas and his friend waited impatiently as the wooden bar across it on the inside was removed. Yet when they entered they found all the company astir, the lamps lit and, in the light thereof, the faces turned to them aglow with excitement. Before they could even stammer out their own tidings they were told something equally amazing: the Lord had appeared to Simon Peter as well! They looked toward the fisherman. He, seated apart with a rapt expression on his face, said nothing as the talk rose and fell about him.

And then, suddenly—so suddenly that no-one present was ever able to recall how it happened—they were aware that Jesus was standing amongst them. The babble of talk was cut across as by a knife. He was there, tall and robed as they had been so used to seeing him, with the same expression of beneficent power and grace upon his unforgettable countenance.

Yet the door behind him, across which the bar had been replaced, still stood fast shut. A great fear came over the company.

Jesus spoke:

"Peace be unto you," he said softly with the customary greeting. "Why are ye troubled? and wherefore do reasonings arise in your hearts?"

XXXII. THE ASCENSION

And it came to pass, while he blessed them, he was parted from them, and carried up into heaven. Luke 24, 51.

By Andrea Mantegna (1431-1506)

Photo Alinari

He stretched out his hands, palms outward, so that they all saw the dark holes which the nails had made.

"See my hands and my feet," he said, "that it is I myself: handle me, and see; for a spirit hath not flesh and bones, as ye behold me having."

He held the hands forward toward them and after that lifted the hem of his robe a little to uncover his feet. Still they were motionless. Then he asked them:

"Have ye here anything to eat?"

With that, one of the disciples, gathering his wits about him, made haste to bring forward a piece of a broiled fish left over from their own supper. Before their very eyes, Jesus ate it, while the tingling silence remained as unbroken as before. At last he spoke again:

"These are my words which I spake unto you, while I was yet with you, how that all things must needs be fulfilled, which are written in the law of Moses, and the Prophets, and the Psalms, concerning me."

Quietly and evenly he went on to explain to them, as he had done to the disciples on the road to Emmaus, the truth concerning the fore-ordained nature of his crucifixion as it was set forth in the Scriptures. Finally, he added these words:

"Thus it is written, that the Christ should suffer, and rise again from the dead the third day; and that repentance and remission of sins should be preached in his Name unto all the nations, beginning from Jerusalem. Ye are witnesses of these things."

There was, however, an absentee from among the disciples upon that memorable evening. This was Thomas the twin. He came in later, when Jesus had withdrawn from them. Full of the excitement of what had happened the others burst upon him with the news:

"We have seen the Lord!"

For a moment Thomas stood stock still. Then he slowly shook his head:

"Except I shall see in his hands the print of the nails, and put my finger into the print of the nails, and put my hand into his side, I will not believe."

Eight days went by. Then, when evening came, and when the door was barred as before, Jesus appeared in the midst of them. Once again he gave them the greeting:

"Peace be unto you."

His gaze wandered round the room until it rested on Thomas. He beckoned the disciple. Trembling and pale, while the others remained fixed as they were, Thomas moved across the room until he stood before the Lord. Softly, Jesus said: "Reach hither thy fingers, and see my hands."

He held out the palms. Wonderingly, hesitatingly, Thomas with his forefinger touched in each of them the wounds of the nail. Next, moving aside his robe so that his breast was exposed, Jesus said:

"Reach hither thy hand, and put it into my side."

The disciple hesitated more than ever. In the side of the breast was clearly visible the great wound made by the spearhead.

"Be not faithless," Jesus said, "but believing."

Slowly and very gently Thomas ran his finger over the wound, then he sank to his knees.

"My Lord and my God," he breathed.

B.M.G.—T

Looking down upon his disciples with infinite compassion Jesus said:

"Because thou hast seen me, thou hast believed: blessed are they that have not seen, and yet have believed."

*   *   *   *

So the time passed until it became necessary for the disciples to return northward to Galilee. They went cheerfully, full of a boundless, inner joy; for now they knew the Lord was risen. And had he not said he would go before them into Galilee?

So Peter and his friends returned to the lakeside. They did not know, as they carried their nets down to their boat for the night's fishing, that a further wonder was in store for them.

Simon Peter, emerging at long last from the private day-dream which had seemed to hold him so long, announced one evening that he intended to go fishing. With him at the lakeside were Thomas the twin, Nathaniel, the sons of Zebedee, and two others. Welcoming the suggestion, glad to see their comrade his old familiar self again, they said they would go with him. They pushed off. The little boat glided into the nocturnal immensities of the lake.

It was a fine night, with the stars reflected in the shimmering surface of the waters. Even so, it turned out to be a bad one for fishing, for they took nothing. At last, at the first peep of day, they gave up, and stood for the shore.

The point for which they made was a little, pebbly bay giving on to a semi-circle of trees beyond. The boat glided in, Peter steering from the stern as the sail was run down.

None of them noticed the man standing on the little beach before them until he called out, his voice coming clear over the water:

"Children, have ye aught to eat?"

They were rather startled. It was an unusual occurrence to find a stranger at such a spot at such an hour. Nonetheless, they answered readily enough and in chorus: "No."

The voice hailed them again:

"Cast the net on the right side of the boat, and ye shall find."

They looked at each other, they looked at Peter. He nodded. So those in the bows who had been stowing the net let it go over the starboard side. The drag of it checked the way of the boat so that they drifted very slowly for a while, the man on the shore meanwhile watching.

Then one of the company, looking overside, saw in the clear water a mass of fish silvering the bulge of the net. He gave a shout, and began to haul inboard, joined rapidly by the others. But one of the disciples—it was probably John, because the Gospel says it was that disciple whom Jesus loved—looked up to Peter still by his steering oar in the stern, and with a quick flash of intuition said:

"It is the Lord!"

That was enough for Peter. Abandoning his steering oar, and pausing only to gird his coat about him, he jumped overboard into the shallow water and went splashing shoreward. More leisurely and calmly, the other disciples brought in the boat, although they did not wait to finish the task of dragging the net inboard but came ashore with it overside.

None of them spoke to the figure on the beach when they got there. Indeed, Simon Peter stood foolishly just looking at him, a wonderful joy upon his face.

Thus in silence they followed Jesus—for now they knew it was he—up to the edge of the trees beyond. There was a fire kindled there and fish and bread already prepared, after the customary manner, on flat stones among the embers. In their flurry they had forgotten the full net still alongside their own vessel.

"Bring of the fish which ye have now taken," Jesus said.

At that, Peter, starting out of his trance, wheeled about, went down to the boat and pulled the net ashore, finding it indeed full of big fish, quite enough in ordinary circumstances to have burst the net. Yet, strangely, this time the net was intact. Shouldering it, he went up to rejoin the group among the trees.

"Come and break your fast," Jesus told them.

Still none of them had the courage to ask him to his face who he was, although indeed they knew well enough.

So they sat together around the fire in the calm of the dawn in that lonely place while Jesus shared out the food. After asking a blessing upon it, he bade them fall to. Jesus broke the silence. "Simon, son of John, lovest thou me more than these?" he asked. Simon Peter looked up from where he was reclining on his elbow, boundless love and devotion on his honest face.

"Yea, Lord; thou knowest that I love thee."

Jesus nodded gravely.

"Feed my lambs," he said.

Then, after a little pause, he asked the second time:

"Simon, son of John, lovest thou me?"

"Yea, Lord," Peter said again. "Thou knowest that I love thee."

"Tend my sheep," said Jesus.

There was a further pause and then for the third time Jesus asked: "Simon, son of John, lovest thou me?"

This third repetition of the question stung Peter. He said: "Lord, thou knowest all things; thou knowest that I love thee."

"Feed my sheep," Jesus said and then, foretelling the time when Peter himself should suffer martyrdom, he added:

"Verily, verily, I say unto thee, when thou wast young, thou girdest thyself, and walkedst whither thou wouldst; but when thou shalt be old, thou shalt stretch forth thy hands and another shall gird thee, and carry thee whither thou wouldst not." With infinite solemnity he added: "Follow me."

"Follow thou me." These were the last words Jesus spoke to his greatest and staunchest follower.

*   *   *   *

Yet his friends were to see him once again in the glorious body of his resurrection. This time it was upon a mountain, in solitude, where the fresh winds blew and the clouds sailed by far above the traffic of the world. There was one final question they had to ask him:

"Lord, dost thou at this time restore the kingdom to Israel?"

His reply has rung down the ages.

"It is not for you to know times or seasons which the Father hath set within His own authority. But ye shall receive power, when the Holy Ghost is come upon you: and ye shall be my witnesses, both in Jerusalem and in all Judea and Samaria, and unto the uttermost parts of the earth."

He spoke no more. As they continued looking at him, a cloud passed over the mountain, its big shadow scudding across the hillside. When it had gone they saw that he was no longer there before them: the cloud had received him out of their sight.

The watchers became aware, as they stood looking steadfastly into the heavens, that two men in white apparel were beside them:

"Ye men of Galilee," one of them said, "why stand ye looking into heaven? This Jesus, which was received up from you into heaven, shall so come in like manner as ye behold him going into Heaven."

The promise remains, unto this present day.

Appendix

*

THE BIBLE IN ART

and

COMMENTARY ON THE COLOR PLATES

NOTE

This appendix has been especially contributed

The Bible in Art

THE great artists of Christian Europe, for century after century, have painted their version of particular events in the Bible, in the Old Testament and much more in the New Testament, as we would expect; and they have done this with the greatest reverence, for a very clear purpose.

The Catechism of the Church of England calls a sacrament—that is to say, the sacrament of Baptism and the sacrament of the Lord's Supper—"*an outward and visible sign of an inward and spiritual grace*". We may adapt these fine words to describe religious pictures of every kind, on walls, on wood, on canvas or in windows; whether paintings of the kind which are reproduced here or the stained glass which glows down into our churches, our chapels, our cathedrals, from the smallest country church to the National Cathedral in Washington. Each painting, each colored window is "an outward and visible sign" of something told to us or revealed to us in Holy Writ.

Bible pictures are not just illustrations. Compare them with writings or sermons about the Bible. We have, as well as the actual books of the Old Testament and the New Testament, our Bible commentaries. We have our commentators. Clergymen, we all know, instruct us upon the Bible, in the pulpit, in classes, in Sunday schools, and in books. They explain to us the texts of the Bible; and they often attempt to make more vivid, for example, the great events, the great mysteries, of the Life and Passion of Our Lord. They may enlarge upon the brief sentences and descriptions in the gospel narrative, saying more about the Birth of Christ, the Adoration of the Shepherds, the Adoration of the Wise Men, more about the Baptism of Christ by St John, about the Last Supper, the Agony in the Garden, the journey to Golgotha, the Crucifixion, Resurrection and Ascension. Their words explain, instruct, and fill out.

In the same way all the events just enumerated, and others as well, have been painted. The painters (themselves often instructed by the clergy in the particular purpose and the proper details of each picture) have also had the noble aim of making the Bible narrative and the Bible message as vivid as possible to our senses and our understanding. The painters have given, in other words, explanation and instruction, filling out the narrative, as they did so, through the eyes.

Again, that is not all. The clergyman in his sermon or in his book may, if he is eloquent or greatly skilled as a writer, speak or write in such a manner that the warmth of his words increases the warmth of our feelings toward God. More than two hundred years ago Thomas Burnet, Master of the Charterhouse in London, considered in such a way, in magnificent and tender words, the Second Coming of Christ.

"Only give me leave", he wrote, "to make a short reflection upon the wonderful history of our Saviour. . . . We now see him coming in the clouds, in glory and triumph surrounded with innumerable angels. *This is the same person, who, so many hundred years ago, entered Jerusalem, with another sort of equipage, mounted upon an ass's colt,*

150

while the little people and the multitude cried, Hosanna to the Son of David. Nay, this is that
same person, that, at his first coming into this world, was laid in a manger, instead of a cradle;
a naked babe dropt in a crib at Bethlehem (Luke 2, 12), his poor mother not having wherewithal
to get her a better lodging, when she was to be delivered of this sacred burthen. This helpless
infant, that often wanted a little milk to refresh it, and support its weakness; that hath often cried
for the breast with hunger and tears, now appears to be the Lord of Heaven and Earth."

In those moving words one of the masters of prose in our language tells of the naked
baby, of the helpless infant. Turn to Plate IX: what else does the great master
of Ghent, the great Hugo van der Goes (d. 1482), tell us and display to us in his
painting of the Adoration of the Shepherds, laying the helpless new-born child
who is God, there before us, stark and moving, in his foreground? Thomas Burnet
gives us in simple words his feeling about Christ entering Jerusalem on Palm Sunday.
Look at the painting of the scene, in Plate XXII, from the hand of an Italian artist in
the city of Florence five hundred years ago. Sometimes the painter will add many
details to the gospel narrative, sometimes only a few or none. Hugo van der Goes
added the ox and the ass, the delightful flowers and the telltale expression upon the
face of each shepherd, also taking the baby out of the manger, out of his swaddling
clothes, and laying him upon the ground. The painter of this Entry into Jerusalem
is content with much less addition. But he too has to invent the arrangement of the
figures and the whole of the scene. He too has to paint everything in his own colors
so that they sing their tune and work upon our feelings. Both artists intend, if they
can, to make our feelings stronger, purer and warmer. Neither one of them is content
just to illustrate or explain.

What we are enabled, then, to see, to gaze at, by painters, what they picture for us
in delightful pigments, can be as moving as anything given to us to read, as anything
said to us in the pulpit, as anything sung to us or played to us on the organ.

Of course every one of the arts has had, and still has, its religious application.
Architects, by their art, have placed beautiful cathedrals in valleys and on hills.
Music we have just mentioned, such as Handel poured out in *The Messiah* or Bach
in the *St Matthew Passion*. To the art of religious prose the poets have added the art of
religious poetry, a John Milton, a saintly George Herbert, a Donne, writing those
great religious poems we read over to ourselves—

> One short sleep past, we wake eternally,
> And death shall be no more; death, thou shalt die.

Or the poets, the song-writers—it may be Isaac Watts:

> His dying crimson, like a robe,
> Spreads o'er his body on the tree;
> Then am I dead to all the globe
> And all the globe is dead to me—

it may be John Bunyan:

> He that is down, needs fear no fall,
> He that is low, no pride:
> He that is humble ever shall
> Have God to be his guide—

it may be Charles Wesley or Cowper—have given us the words of the hymns and the carols which, two arts in one, are combined with music.

These other methods of praise by way of art we perhaps accept more readily than the great Christian paintings. Yet why? If we think—and look—we shall discover it no more surprising that men have used devotional painting than devotional words in prose and poetry and devotional notes in anthem and oratorio. Indeed, this art of painting from the earliest times to the time of Giotto (1270-1337), and from Giotto to the great masters of the fifteenth and sixteenth centuries, was developed in Europe precisely for the praise of God.

We must be clear what the painter does and how he goes to work. The painter has been called a "seeing and feeling creature". The writer feels and expresses his feeling in words, the composer finds and expresses that feeling in music, the painter feels and finds expression for his feeling in lines and shapes and colors, in light and shade, in things that we can see, taken from the familiar, visible world. All these are different "languages"; all three of them we know how to "read". The simplest form of that special visible language which painters employ is the green or red light which warns us on the road to stop or go. The light comes on: we do not need to translate it into words. We see a painting of Christ in the house of Martha and Mary or of Christ nailed upon the cross: that, too, we do not need to translate. That, too, acts upon us directly.

Using, then, his special language which we all of us can "read", the painter, first of all, *imagines*; that is, images of how things were, of what they mean and of how they move him—say, of Christ being mocked (Plate xxvii) or Christ being betrayed (Plate xxvi) or of Solomon meeting the Queen of Sheba (Plate vii)—rise up inside the painter, and are then, with the help of paints and brushes, put down in proper order in his special kind of language.

The painter was not there: Andrea Mantegna, living in Italy in the fifteenth century, was neither at Golgotha nor Gethsemane (Plates xxix and xxv). But then he was not a camera mindlessly recording waves of light on a sensitized film. He does not televise to us the exactness of an event in far off time in the Holy Land. Half a dozen painters paint for us—like Hugo van der Goes once more (Plate ix)—an Adoration of the Shepherds: even if they had been there in Bethlehem, each of the half-dozen would have seen the Adoration differently. Each one would have pictured the scene in the stable according to his personal way of seeing things and feeling them and recording them.

It is the same in ordinary life. Two journalists living at the same time, writing in the same language, will both witness and then report the same event—which they have both seen—in different words, picking out different points for emphasis.

When it comes to religious painting, many circumstances will account for differences in pictures of the same Biblical event or the same Biblical character. There will not only be these natural differences between the personality of painter and painter, but the differences of time, tradition, country. An artist from Northern Europe may think quite naturally of snowflakes falling around the stable in which Christ is born. Pieter Bruegel, in the Netherlands in the sixteenth century, painted such a snowy Nativity. By contrast the Italian painter Gentile de Fabriano was more accustomed to think of the winter sunshine of Southern Europe, so he painted Mary and the child Jesus and Joseph fleeing from Herod to Egypt through a landscape of roses.

Clothes and scene also may differ, according to the painter. Gerard David paints the Marriage in Cana (Plate xv) as though it were a banquet in the city of Bruges, where he had gone to live and follow his art in 1483. Piero della Francesca (1416?-1492), one of the supreme painters of mankind, imagines the Baptism of Christ in a Jordan and a landscape belonging not to Palestine, but precisely to the upper valley of the Tiber, where he had grown up. Neither of these two painters felt in the fifteenth century that the gospel events were so very distant in time or in place. They did not possess our sense of history or geography. So today a Japanese artist, belonging to a different culture and a difference race, would see and portray Christ with Japanese features, and not the features of Western race and Western tradition.

In Bible pictures, then, we are not to expect that the same person or the same place will look identical in every painting. Bible scenes have not all to be accurate transcriptions of Palestine. Bible characters of the New Testament are not compelled to wear clothes appropriate to the Jerusalem and the Bethlehem of the first century A.D. All that matters, once more, is how the painter uses his language of painting. How far, by the beauty of his colors, by the strength and warmth and profundity of his "story-showing" in paint, does he deepen men's wonder, men's reverence, men's faith and men's love? That is the point. Each of the good paintings from the Bible, therefore, is an act of Christian praise and devotion; it is not just a "pretty picture", it is a sure outward and visible sign of the inwardness of faith.

Full accounts have not come down to us of all the great masters of religious art. Some we do not know. Giotto (1270-1337), who painted scenes from the life of Christ around the Chapel of the Arena at Padua, including the awe and horror of the Kiss of Judas (Plate xxvi) and the infinite sorrow of the Mocking of Jesus (Plate xxvii), was described—and the truth of the description cannot be doubted if we look at his work—as a man of great goodness: "he rendered his soul to God, to the great grief of all his fellow citizens, and of all who had known him or even heard of his name, for he had produced so many beautiful works in his life, and was as good a Christian as he was an excellent painter". Indeed, to enter the small chapel at Padua which he surrounded with the paintings is to feel with a new intensity how solemn and how grand, how sad and how joyful were the events of the Passion.

Fra Angelico (1387-1455) was also among the more excellent of men. He certainly painted the great fresco of the Transfiguration reproduced in Plate xix and probably inspired or encouraged or supervised the Entry into Jerusalem (Plate xxii) and the Last Supper (Plate xxiv). Above all painters he has been famous for the humility, lovingness and sweetness of his life. "Some say", wrote Vasari, the historian of the Italian artists, "that he never took up his brush without first making a prayer. He never made a crucifix when the tears did not course down his cheeks." Vasari added that Fra Angelico avoided all intrigues, "living in purity and holiness, as benign to the poor as I believe heaven must now be to him. He was most gentle and temperate, and chaste in his life."

How deep, too, must have been the religious awe of Mantegna, who gave so rocky, pitiful and terrible an earnestness to his painting of the Crucifixion (Plate xxix). How grave and serene must have been the belief of Piero della Francesca, who so imagined the meeting of Solomon and Sheba (Plate vii) and that moment when St John baptized Christ in Jordan, after which the Spirit like a dove descended upon

Christ and the voice from heaven said, "Thou art my beloved Son, in whom I am well pleased." Piero's imagination, Piero's hand as he painted, it has been well remarked, must have been directed by his belief that God is always near to all of man's works and being. No artist, too, can have felt the pathos, sublimity and terror of the death of Christ more than Tintoretto (1518–1594), the Venetian painter of the Journey to Calvary in Plate XXVIII, and no artist can have been more alive to the grandeur of the creating God than Michelangelo (1475–1564) as he worked upon the sacred paintings of the Sistine Chapel.

Nothing indeed has more raised and increased the power of the Western artist in all the arts than faith, and the love of God. The most truly marvelous of the world's buildings are those mighty cathedrals raised stone by stone to the glory of God. The flames of religion burn in the greatest of our poetry, the greatest of our music; and it is Christian faith which has raised painting to its highest pitch of wonderment and performance. With God as the pivot of their being, the painters developed their new powers steadily from the fourteenth to the sixteenth century until unquestioned belief worked with an ability to express, by means of a simple paint-brush, the most powerful, the most penetrating and the most subtle thoughts of man about God. Men could both pray and give praise with the brush.

Yet there was a partial restriction upon their themes. As we should expect, and as we have already pointed out, the Christian artist was possessed most of all by the direct revelation of Christ in the New Testament. It was the life of Christ that moved him the most, was most constantly in his thoughts, and which gave him in consequence by far the greater number of his themes. That is one reason why in choosing paintings to insert in a Bible it is easier to match the New Testament than the Old. The other reason is that before translations of the Bible were made into the common tongues of Europe, the Old Testament was less read, and less familiar to the mass of Christians. Thus it offered fewer themes to the artist. At a later time paintings were made more frequently from a larger number of Old Testament subjects, but by then the art of painting had declined from its tall summits of the fourteenth, fifteenth and sixteenth centuries. The bulk of the later paintings arising from the Old Testament do not match the grandeur of the best of the earlier paintings arising from the Gospels.

Commentary on the Color Plates

I. THE FALL OF MAN

Detail from "Paradise" by Lukas Cranach the Elder (1472–1553)
Kunsthistorisches Museum, Vienna

In the one painting of the lovely garden eastward in Eden, the German master Lukas Cranach included the whole story of the second and third chapters of Genesis. Event follows event. The Lord God gives his commandments to the man, the noble beasts are there for him to name, Eve is created from him as he sleeps; and then comes the Fall.

The serpent, coiled around the tree of the knowledge of good and evil, which is so fairly laden with fruit, beguiles Eve; she takes of the fruit, and eats, and gives to Adam.

II. THE EXPULSION FROM THE GARDEN OF EDEN

Detail from "Paradise" by Lukas Cranach the Elder (1472–1553)
Kunsthistorisches Museum, Vienna

Here is the final scene from Lukas Cranach's painting of the garden of Eden (see above, Plate 1). *And the Lord God said, Behold, the man is become as one of us, to know good and evil: and now, lest he put forth his hand, and take also of the tree of life, and eat, and live for ever: Therefore the Lord God sent him forth from the garden of Eden, to till the ground from whence he was taken* (Genesis 3, 22–23).

III. THE SACRIFICE OF ISAAC

Painting by Michelangelo da Caravaggio (1569–1609)
Uffizi Gallery, Florence

Caravaggio in his day was what we think of as a "modern" artist. He startled and opened men's eyes. In painting events from the Old Testament and the New Testament he surprised everyone at first by painting in a new way so that the figures and the action were starkly, ruthlessly and dramatically "real", almost like stills from a color film. Everything is made more immediate by light and shade.

Thus the SACRIFICE OF ISAAC, painted about 1599, is no less direct, no less startling than the account in the Bible, and it follows it very closely:

And Abraham stretched forth his hand, and took the knife to slay his son. And the angel of the Lord called unto him out of heaven, and said, Abraham, Abraham: and he said, Here am I. And he said, Lay not thine hand upon the lad, neither do thou any thing unto him: for now I know that thou fearest God, seeing thou hast not withheld thy son, thine only son from me. And Abraham lifted up his eyes, and looked, and behold behind him a ram caught in a thicket by his horns: and Abraham went and took the ram, and offered him up for a burnt offering in the stead of his son (Genesis 22, 10–13).

IV. THE DEATH OF THE FIRSTBORN

Fresco by Bernardino Luini (c. 1480–1532)
Brera Gallery, Milan

And it came to pass, that at midnight the Lord smote all the firstborn in the land of Egypt, from the firstborn of Pharaoh that sat on his throne unto the firstborn of the captive that was in the dungeon; and all the firstborn of cattle (Exodus 12, 29).

Bernardino Luini was a gentle master of the Milanese school. His paintings are not at all strong or violent. The best of them, the series of frescoes from which this plate is taken, he painted early in the sixteenth century in what was already an older style. The frescoes were in the Villa Rabia at Pelucca near Monza, where they no doubt ornamented the chapel. The villa was destroyed, but luckily some of the frescoes were saved, and are now preserved on the walls of the Brera, Milan.

V. THE ADORATION OF THE GOLDEN CALF

Painting by Nicolas Poussin (1593 or 1594–1665)
National Gallery, London

This grave Frenchman painted many pictures from the Bible, making them monumental and austere, and often somewhat Roman, since by his time the ancient art and architecture of Rome had been rediscovered and were exceedingly admired. A Roman guise seemed right for scenes of the past, even Biblical scenes.

Yet in this famous picture Poussin is close to the description of the Golden Calf in Exodus 32. Here is Aaron displaying the graven image, here are the people rejecting God and Moses, and dancing.

All this was done while Moses was upon Sinai;

he descends, and Poussin places the wrathful Moses in the top left of the picture.

Poussin departs a little from the Bible by showing the people loosely clothed rather than naked as they had been made by Aaron (Exodus 32, 25).

VI. THE WATER FROM THE ROCK

Ceiling painting by Tintoretto (1518–1594)
Scuola di San Rocco, Venice

In the Scuola Grande di San Rocco, not far from the Grand Canal, in Venice, Tintoretto carried out in room after room decorations from the Bible which are among the sublime paintings of the world, and which come to their peak in a great Journey to Calvary (Plate XXVIII) and a greater Crucifixion. Many of the paintings are huge: this detail of Moses striking the water from the rock on the ceiling of the upper hall comes out of a painting measuring some fifteen by seventeen feet.

VII. SOLOMON RECEIVING THE QUEEN OF SHEBA

Detail from a fresco by Piero della Francesca (1416 ?–1492)
Choir of the church of St Francis, Arezzo, Tuscany

Solomon had asked for wisdom when God appeared to him in a dream and said, "Ask what I shall give thee." God acted according to the words of Solomon: "Lo, I have given thee a wise and an understanding heart." And since he had not asked for riches and honor, both were added to him (1 Kings 3, 5–13); and *king Solomon exceeded all the kings of the earth for riches and for wisdom* (1 Kings 10, 23).

All this was followed by the great Piero della Francesca. The Queen of Sheba came with gold, spices and precious stones, but her reason for coming was that she had "heard of the fame of Solomon concerning the name of the Lord". She desired "to prove him with hard questions". She came, and "communed with him of all that was in her heart" (1 Kings 10, 1–2). It is such a Solomon, bearded, grave and like a philosopher, yet also a king among kings, and such a queen, of dignity and earnestness, that Piero imagined and painted.

VIII. JEREMIAH LAMENTING THE DESTRUCTION OF JERUSALEM

Painting by Rembrandt van Rijn (1606–1669)
Rijksmuseum, Amsterdam

A prophet of the Old Testament is a man of passion, depth and grandeur, of a kind that Rembrandt, a secular prophet among painters, was well endowed to conceive and paint. Where earlier painters from the Bible so often worked by incident, detail and clear light, Rembrandt works by light among shadows, by attitude and by suggestion. In this painting Jeremiah's attitude suggests both strength and desolation, nobility and dejection. He laments over Jerusalem deserted and Judah carried away into captivity.

IX. THE ADORATION OF THE SHEPHERDS

Main part of the painting by Hugo van der Goes (*died in* 1482)
Uffizi Gallery, Florence

In this masterpiece of northern painting all is included, and a little more: the tiny burning babe is removed from the swaddling clothes and from the manger, and all surround the child in adoration, the delicate angels, the rough-handed shepherds, Mary, Joseph, the ox and the ass, the flowers and the fruits of the earth.

The ox and the ass adoring the child with benign faces are present in most paintings of the Adoration of the Shepherds or the Adoration of the Magi, and they are present in our thoughts of the Nativity. They are not mentioned by St Luke or St Matthew, and they find their way into tradition from the early medieval *Liber de Infantia* or Gospel of Pseudo-Matthew, one of the apocryphal gospels. Yet the ox and the ass stem from the Old Testament, from Isaiah's prophecy, *The ox knoweth his owner, and the ass his master's crib: but Israel doth not know, my people doth not consider* (Isaiah 1, 3).

In this and other paintings by Hugo van der Goes, of Ghent, in Belgium, attitudes and features reveal in a new way the emotions and thoughts which fill each of the *dramatis personæ*; which is wonderfully true of the three shepherds. The first-comer smiles in happy acceptance, the next to arrive, with his hands apart, has just gone from astonishment to meditative wonder and reverence, the latest comer, not yet kneeling, looks over their heads with no more—as yet—than a startled curiosity.

The reproduction cuts a little from the top of the painting.

X. THE JOURNEY OF THE MAGI

Painting by Stefano di Giovanni, known as Il Sassetta, (*c.* 1400–1450)
Metropolitan Museum, New York

St Matthew's Gospel says little about the wise men: *Behold, there came wise men from the east to Jerusalem, saying, Where is he that is born King of the Jews? for we have seen his star in the east, and are come to worship him.* From the presence of Herod they go to

Bethlehem, the star goes before them and stands over the place of the young child: they worship, they present gold, frankincense and myrrh, and depart into their own country. No more. Yet through the ages men have found their imagination profoundly and wonderfully moved by this element of the greater wonder of the Nativity; legends, nativity plays, splendid painting and splendid poetry have been the result: the wise men were thought of as kings from the mysterious East; honor, riches and wisdom, no less than the rough shepherds, adored the child.

All the wonder is expressed with an exquisite glow and with an exquisite simplicity and restraint by Sassetta, of the Sienese school, as the cavalcade from the east moves over the rocky hills toward Bethlehem, on a little panel nine by twelve inches. The star in the painting once stood over where the young child was; below, Sassetta painted another panel of the Adoration.

XI. JOSEPH THE CARPENTER AND THE CHILD JESUS

Painting by Georges de la Tour (1593–1652)
Louvre, Paris

Little is written in the Bible of Joseph as a carpenter. Only in St Matthew's Gospel is his profession revealed or mentioned. Jesus taught in the synagogue *insomuch that they were astonished, and said, Whence hath this man this wisdom, and these mighty works? Is not this the carpenter's son? is not his mother called Mary?* (Matthew 13, 54–5). Yet it was natural to think of the child Jesus helping Joseph in his carpenter's trade; and in St Mark's Gospel (6, 3) Jesus himself is called the carpenter. The thought of Joseph as a carpenter and of Christ following in his footsteps especially appealed to men in the sixteenth and seventeenth centuries, since it gave added dignity to the labors of ordinary folk.

Georges de la Tour, only recognized in our time as one of the great artists of the French school, paints the dignified Joseph bent over his work, with the child Jesus looking, and yet not looking, at him. The candle held by Jesus directs the full light of a moment's eternity only upon his own face, shining even through his fingers. He looks far beyond the business in hand. (See also Plate XVIII, by the same artist.)

XII. CHRIST AMONG THE DOCTORS

Painting by Jusepe Ribera (1589–1652)
Kunsthistorisches Museum, Vienna

The puzzled heads and hands of the doctors, turned this way and that, contrast with the clear illuminated face of the twelve-year-old Jesus, his raised hand and arm, the deliberateness and certainty of his attitude. Ribera, of the Spanish school, though he settled in Naples, was among those seventeenth-century painters who gave religious art new muscle and vigor.

XIII. TEMPTED OF THE DEVIL

Ceiling painting by Tintoretto (1518–1594)
Scuola di San Rocco, Venice

Tempting the Son of God, holding the stones up to him, the devil is made young in appearance; he is the fallen angel with the dark features of sensuality, the Machiavellian prince—the prince of the power of the air, the prince of this world, the ruler of the darkness of this world, as he is variously described in the New Testament; and his power of death will be destroyed by the death of Christ, which Tintoretto painted for the Brotherhood of St Roche as the climax of his great series.

XIV. SAINT MATTHEW

Upper part of a painting by Alvise Vivarini (c. 1446–1505)
Accademia Gallery, Venice

This conception of St Matthew, the man whom Jesus saw at the receipt of custom, to whom he said, Follow me, and who arose and followed him (Matthew 9, 9), was painted for a Venetian altarpiece. The panel now hangs separately in the Academy at Venice.

Most of Vivarini's painting is still in Venice, where he and his uncle Bartolommeo Vivarini before him were prominent as artists in the fifteenth century. Other Venetians of the time, Crivelli, for instance, and above all the great Giovanni Bellini (see Plate XXI), surpass Vivarini as a religious painter; yet Vivarini gave life and interest to the saintly features he imagined, he made face and pose expressive, and as a true Venetian he conceived his figures in captivating and delightful color which lifts them at once from the ordinary realm.

The reproduction shows the head and shoulders of St Matthew taken from a ong narrow panel.

XV. THE MARRIAGE IN CANA

Painting by Gerard David (1460?–1523)
Louvre, Paris

"This beginning of miracles" in Cana is painted by Gerard David in the guise of a banquet in the rich city of Bruges, where he had settled in 1483. Through the windows and the door appear the medieval buildings of Bruges. Yet despite the modern scene, the modern clothing, the tiled floor, the great earthenware pitchers of the time, all is stiff and strange. Everyone seems to have posed for an unmoving second—except for Christ, absorbed, with his hand raised in a blessing, and his mother with her head bent in the absorption of prayer. It is as if these two alone were yet conscious of the water into wine.

XVI. THE GOOD SAMARITAN AND THE MAN THAT FELL AMONG THIEVES
Painting by Jacopo Bassano (1510?–1592)
National Gallery, London

Jacopo Bassano delighted in painting Bible stories which could be set in the countryside he knew between the luxurious canals of Venice and his small native town of Bassano, to the north-west, underneath the mountains. He puts down each story honestly and directly, going to the heart of it. The good Samaritan lifts the man who has been stripped and wounded by the thieves, and left nearly dead; and will soon set him on the back of the waiting mule and lead him off through the landscape to the inn. How simple and complete! Yet Bassano gives this directness and solid simplicity a poetry of light and color.

XVII.   CHRIST AND THE WOMAN OF SAMARIA
Painting by Juan de Flandres (*fl.* 1496–1506)
Louvre, Paris

Christ, the woman, and the well of earthly water, in contrast to the water of life—how economically and effectively this little-known painter has given the essentials and enclosed them in luminous air! *There cometh a woman of Samaria to draw water: Jesus saith unto her, Give me to drink* (John 4, 7). The painter has chosen that precise moment: Jesus has risen from the well, where he sat wearied after his journey, the woman of Samaria has just drawn her pitcherful, and he asks for water.

The painter's name, John of Flanders, and his way of painting show that he came from Flanders. He worked in Spain, and this small panel is one of forty-seven paintings of the life of Christ and the Virgin which he made for Queen Isabella of Castille.

XVIII. MARY MAGDALENE
Painting by Georges de la Tour (1593–1652)
Louvre, Paris

Something is said of this grave and moving painter in the comment on Plate XI. Here he has depicted the penitent Magdalene, quiet, sad, contemplative, indifferent to the world, revealed in the darkness by the yellow flame of a night light.

Mary Magdalene was long identified with the penitent sinner who brought the alabaster box of ointment when Jesus sat at meat in the Pharisee's house.

Thus Mary Magdalene is often painted with the pyx or box of ointment, as here in de la Tour's picture.

XIX. THE TRANSFIGURATION
Fresco by Fra Angelico (1387–1455)
In the convent of St Mark, Florence

Fra Angelico, "Il Beato Angelico", angelic in his life and art, was the great fifteenth-century painter of the freshness of Christian joy. A preaching friar, he was properly called Fra Giovanni de Fiesole, from his birthplace. "He used frequently to say, that he who practised the art of painting had need of quiet, and should live without cares or anxious thoughts; adding, that he who would do the work of Christ should remain always with Christ."

The Transfiguration is painted on the wall of one of the cells of the convent of St Mark.

XX. CHRIST IN THE HOUSE OF MARTHA AND MARY
Painting by Vermeer (1632–1675)
National Gallery of Scotland, Edinburgh

Vermeer's picture is direct. Like so much of the Christian painting of the seventeenth century, with rich color, yet with simple means and familiar appearances, it gives at once the heart of the whole story.

This picture by the young Vermeer, painted in his twenties about 1654–55, skilfully manages figures near the size of life: the canvas is more than five feet high.

XXI. THE RAISING OF LAZARUS
Painting by Nicolas Froment (1420?–1482)
Uffizi Gallery, Florence

Jesus has just cried with a loud voice, "Lazarus, come forth." Lazarus has come again to life, still in his grave-clothes; and Jesus has given the command, "Loose him." Lazarus is a type of the resurrection: *I am the resurrection, and the life,* Jesus had just declared to Martha, the dead man's sister. *He that believeth in me, though he were dead, yet shall he live* (John 11, 25). Thus the drama of the Raising of Lazarus, tokening trust in God and the life to come, was much painted, especially by artists of the north. Nicolas Froment, a rare early master of the French school, was in fact a southern artist, who painted for King René at Aix-en-Provence, but he was akin to the medieval Flemish painters.

XXII. THE ENTRY INTO JERUSALEM

Painting ascribed commonly to Fra Angelico (1387–1455)
In the convent of St Mark, Florence

Again the painter is concerned to give in paint only those words in which the evangelist describes the meek and magnificent entry into Jerusalem. The disciples have fetched the ass and the colt, of which the Lord had need. They have set Jesus upon the ass.

The whole panel (not all of it is reproduced in the plate) is one of thirty-five scenes painted for the doors of a silver chest in the church of Santissima Annunziata. It hangs now in the convent of St Mark, in Florence, which is so much associated with Fra Angelico. Though long ascribed to Fra Angelico, and though it certainly has Angelico's simple and devout approach, the panel is in fact by another hand.

XXIII. CHRIST DRIVING THE TRADERS FROM THE TEMPLE

Painting by Domenikos Theokopoulos, known as El Greco (1541–1614)
National Gallery, London

El Greco (a Greek from the island of Crete who learned his art in Venice, and then settled in Spain) always emphasized in his great religious pictures the whole drama and movement and inner meaning of the subject, at the expense of those details which normally add up into a scene or a landscape. So in this famous painting Christ, with his arm raised to scourge those who defile the temple, is made all the more the central figure in thrilling majesty and isolation by the color of his robe, which is not repeated elsewhere in the picture, though men in yellow circle around him. And to Christ's countenance alone the painter gives the full intensity of feeling: it is Christ's eye alone in the picture which glitters with purpose.

XXIV. THE LAST SUPPER

Detail of a fresco ascribed to Fra Angelico (1387–1455)
In the convent of St Mark, Florence

This is a rare subject in painting. It is not only the Last Supper, which the artists depicted so often, but the moment of the Institution of the Eucharist.

Like the Transfiguration by Fra Angelico (Plate XIX, above) this Last Supper is painted on the wall of one of the small naked cells of the now disused convent of St Mark, in Florence.

This is my body which is given for you: this do in remembrance of me (Luke 22, 19)—so telling, and so immediate; yet the fresco was not painted by Fra Angelico himself, so it seems, but by one of the other, unknown, artists who worked with him on the scheme of paintings in the convent.

XXV. THE AGONY IN THE GARDEN

Painting by Andrea Mantegna (1431–1506)
National Gallery, London

All is made tense, strict and dramatic: *O my Father, if it be possible, let this cup pass from me: nevertheless not as I will, but as thou wilt* (Matthew 26, 39). Christ prays in a landscape fitting the circumstance. The rabbits, the conies of the rock, play unconcerned; the heedless plants grow up between the rocks. Peter, and John and James, the two sons of Zebedee, are asleep. In the sky before the praying Christ the painter has set five cherubs bearing the Instruments of the Passion, the column, the cross, the sponge and the spear. But across the picture the cormorant, the unclean bird of death, is perched on the withered branch of a tree.

Over to the right of the picture, in the distance, Judas enters from Jerusalem followed by the men with swords and staves.

XXVI. THE KISS OF JUDAS

Detail of a fresco by Giotto (1270–1337)
In the Chapel of the Arena, Padua

All the terror of a betrayal, above all of *this* betrayal, is concentrated by Giotto in the meeting of these two heads, in the contrast between these two profiles.

Here is the act, painted in the deep-set eye of Judas, who knows that Christ knows. Christ bends on Judas the gaze of knowledge but not of weakness or falsity. Judas thrusts out his lips for the kiss, and whereas the eye of Christ is stern and wide open, the eye of Judas peers from the dark triangle of his eye socket. All the hateful irony of using the gesture of love as the sign which will betray Christ, is involved in the painting.

Giotto gave the world in this fresco one of the greatest moments—and greatest shocks—to be found in all painting.

XXVII. JESUS MOCKED

Detail of a fresco by Giotto (1270–1337)
In the Chapel of the Arena, Padua

Again Giotto puts all that could be put by the art of man into the countenance of Christ, as events move to the crucifixion. The broad face, broader and fuller than in most representations of Christ, is at once noble and resigned, strong and terribly in pain which is both pain of body and pain of mind—pain that this thing can be done. Blood trickles down Christ's tilted face, his eyes are nearly shut, his mouth expresses tiredness as well as pain. All attention, as one stares up at this fresco, goes straight to this countenance between the mocking hands.

XXVIII. THE JOURNEY TO CALVARY

Painting by Tintoretto (1518–1594)
Scuola di San Rocco, Venice

For the walls of the last room of the Scuola di San Rocco in Venice Tintoretto painted the most sublime of his pictures—three of them, a huge Crucifixion, Christ before Pilate, and this profound drama of the Journey to Calvary (more than seventeen by thirteen feet).

XXIX. THE CRUCIFIXION

Painting by Andrea Mantegna (1431–1506)
Louvre, Paris

Golgotha, the place of a skull, is made also by the painter the place of dry, hard, stratified rock, in a landscape of rocks. The strict severity, allied with the richness of color, emphasizes the grimness and greatness of the event.

Wedges hold the crosses tight in the rock, which is pierced with more holes, showing that others have been crucified here. On the right of the picture is indifference, on the left the bitterness of sorrow and awareness. On the right the soldiers cast the lots and stand or move about indifferently: they are men used to suffering and execution. The man on horseback in the foreground stares idly up, not at Christ, nailed under the mocking superscription, but at one of the thieves. On the left St John the Evangelist wrings his hands, the mother of the crucified Christ stumbles and falls in grief and is held up by the women.

XXX. THE DEAD CHRIST

Painting by Andrea Mantegna (1431–1506)
Brera Gallery, Milan

The death of Christ is conveyed with stark science, strength and compassion by one of the greatest Italian painters of the fifteenth century and one of the greatest of the world. As in other pictures by Mantegna everything is in sharp and telling definition. St John and the Virgin Mary, her face lined with sorrow, contemplate the dead Christ. But all the emphasis is on Christ himself, lying on the cold stone with the frown and agony of death still on his countenance. The wounds of his crucifixion are visible to us (who are spectators allowed this revelation) on the wrinkled feet and the lax hands. But the body, taken down from the cross, has been washed and wrapped in linen and laid in the tomb by Joseph of Arimathaea.

XXXI. THE BLESSING OF CHRIST

Painting by Giovanni Bellini (*c.* 1430–1516)
Louvre, Paris

Depicted for us by one of the masters of Venetian painting, here is Christ whose face shows that he has endured all suffering, though it is filled as well with all of his tenderness and compassion for mankind. Bellini has painted Christ after the resurrection; by this Christ his disciples had at first been terrified and affrighted as if they had seen a spirit, and he had therefore shown them his hands and his feet.

XXXII. THE ASCENSION

Painting by Andrea Mantegna (1431–1506)
Uffizi Gallery, Florence

Andrea Mantegna this time paints Christ being carried up into heaven, from the top of that mountain (Matthew 28, 16) where he had called together his disciples for the last happening of the Gospels, his last moments in the flesh.

Again we see the rocky landscape that Mantegna knew how to paint so well, but this time the rock is less emphatic and less cruel. This time leaved instead of naked branches sprout from the rock; and Christ is carried up into a tall, serene cloud-flecked sky, surrounded and borne by an aura of cherubs, his hand still raised in the act of blessing, his face turned down to the upturned faces of his disciples and his mother.